COMPLEXITY
AND
CREATIVITY
IN
ORGANIZATIONS

COMPLEXITY
AND
CREATIVITY
IN
ORGANIZATIONS

RALPH D. STACEY

Berrett-Koehler Publishers
San Francisco

Berrett-Koehler Publishers, Inc.
155 Montgomery Street
San Francisco, CA 94104-4109
Tel: (415) 288-0260   Fax: (415) 362-2512

The two case studies in Chapter Eight—Enigma Chemicals and ETTC—are from
Ralph D. Stacey, *Strategic Management and Organizational Dynamics* (2nd ed.), 1996,
London: Pitman Publishing, and are used with permission of the publisher.

ORDERING INFORMATION

Individual sales. Berrett-Koehler publications are available through most bookstores.
They can also be ordered direct from Berrett-Koehler at the address above.

Quantity sales. Special discounts are available on quantity purchases by corporations,
associations, and others. For details, contact the "Special Sales Department" at the
Berrett-Koehler address above.

Orders for college textbook/course adoption use. Please contact Berrett-Koehler
Publishers at the address above.

Orders by U.S. trade bookstores and wholesalers. Please contact Publishers Group West,
4065 Hollis Street, Box 8843, Emeryville, CA 94662. Tel: (510) 658-3453; 1-800-788-3123.
Fax: (510) 658-1834.

Printed in the United States of America

Printed on acid-free and recycled paper that is composed of 85% recycled
fiber, including 15% postconsumer waste.

Library of Congress Cataloging-in-Publication Data

Stacey, Ralph D.
    Complexity and creativity in organizations / by Ralph D. Stacey. —
1st ed.
       p.   cm.
    Includes bibliographical references (p.   ) and index.
    ISBN 1–881052–89–3 (alk. paper)
    1. Organizational behavior.   2. Complex organizations.
3. Organizational change.   I. Title.
HD58.7.S73   1996
302.3'5—dc20   96–566
                                                                       CIP

First Edition

99 98   10 9 8 7 6 5 4 3

Book Production: Pleasant Run Publishing Services
Composition: Classic Typography

To the memory of my father,
Jack Stacey

Contents

Preface

On the day that I wrote the first draft of this preface, the newspaper's front pages were dominated by pictures of Nick Leeson, arrested after a flight from Malaysia. By the time you read this, his name may well be forgotten, but the story of how he brought down the Queen's banker, Barings, will probably be immortalized in business folklore: it so compellingly encapsulates a central conundrum faced by all who would understand and survive organizational life.

First, how is it possible that Barings survived for so long, well over two centuries, without changing all that much in fundamental, radical ways? Of course, it did change: it extended its occupation from a small Victorian building in London into large skyscrapers around the world, its clerks stopped using quill pens and turned to computers, and it added the trading of futures contracts on its own account to the management of other people's funds. However, in many truly fundamental respects it changed hardly at all: it remained under the control of the same family, it continued to rely on the talents of streetwise working-class traders in its operations even though its management came from the establishment, and its culture continued in a perfectly recognizable form. In other words, the Barings of some two centuries ago was still recognizable in the Barings that has just collapsed. The bank exhibited great stability, despite enormous changes in the relative political and economic power of Britain, a shift in the composition of economic activity and trade patterns, changes in society, and revolutions in financial markets. Clearly, the bank showed no sign of sensitivity to small changes—Barings was apparently a stable organization that was eminently fitted to its environment for a very long time, in other words, a stable equilibrium organization.

And yet a tiny change destroyed this stable institution. Having made his establishment bosses a fortune through his astute trading, an overconfident young man, brought up in a public sector housing project, embarked on an escalating pattern of vainly attempting to cover early losses in trades on the futures markets with bigger and bigger bets, until the bank was unable to meet the calls on its assets. What started as a small change that was, at least initially, undetected by the hierarchically most powerful led to the extinction of the organization, and from these ashes the bank is to be resurrected as a part of a Dutch bank. No one could have predicted this development a few months before and very few even dimly foresaw it a few weeks before it occurred.

The reaction to this affair followed a recognizable pattern as we all tried to make sense of what had happened: politicians, leaders of financial institutions, and all manner of other commentators called for increased controls and identification of those who were to blame. At first the events were reported as if they involve only the streetwise trader, but as the story unfolded it seemed that his establishment betters knew and perhaps even assisted him, possibly driven by greed or even caught up in something rather more complicated. As the story unfolded, we began to understand that behind the legitimate structures of Barings that we can all see lurked a shadow system within which much of what actually happened was shaped. What happened in that shadow system was disastrous, and this is what most of us would expect. But is it always so? Does the shadow system that all organizations possess have other, more positive functions?

This is the conundrum of stability versus instability. Organizations, and the social and economic systems they constitute, are quite remarkably stable when we think of just how complex they are. By and large, I can rely on being able to move from one part of the globe to another, more or less on time, and when I get there I will usually be able to dine on a McDonald's hamburger. The other side of this stability coin, however, is that when I join a team of consultants and design with them a program to change an organization in accordance with the wishes of its most powerful members who are our clients, the project almost always fails, and often this is a result of what happens in the organization's shadow system. Those who want to change organizations often experience major frustration as these organizations stubbornly stay the same no matter how sophisticated the culture change, Total Quality Management program, or Business Process Reengineering program. What we see in such organizations is a lack of sensitivity to any change and considerable predictability.

And yet, within short periods of time, events may escalate into trade wars that send avalanches of extinction through whole industries, or military wars that devastate whole countries, or product changes that wipe out whole organizations. Furthermore, these events, which are disasters for some, usually benefit others. Extinct industries, devastated countries, and failing organizations are creatively replaced by new ones. What we see demonstrated in these convulsions is great sensitivity to small changes and a complete inability to predict anything, sometimes with disastrous results, but often with creative, innovative results. In both cases, a key determinant is what goes on in the shadow system behind legitimate structures.

Faced with this intertwined stability and instability, this murky relationship between legitimate structures and shadow systems, we repeatedly experience the same difficulties in making sense of what is going on and, consequently, we continually adopt the same knee-jerk reactions as those displayed in relation to Barings. But despite the preaching and the exhortations to improve things, it all happens again, and current methods of explaining why it does, and why the preaching and exhortation do not work, are so inadequate that we continue to be puzzled. We need a new way of understanding life in organizations and that is what this book sets out to do, by looking for more useful ways of understanding the intertwined stability and instability, the dynamic between legitimate and shadow systems, that we repeatedly encounter in organizational life.

Acknowledgments

I thank the following people for their very helpful comments on an earlier draft of this book: Dan Bieger, Morten Flatau, José Fonseca, Jeffrey Goldstein, Brian Goodwin, Douglas Griffin, Robert Keidel, Ronnie Lessem, Mark Michaels, Eric Miller, Dorothea Noble, Patricia Shaw, Philip Streatfield, Paul Wright, and other members of the management doctoral program at Hertfordshire University. Although Lionel Stapely did not read the manuscript, I wish to acknowledge that my reading of his doctoral thesis had an important impact on my thinking, particularly his notion of "a good enough organizational holding environment." Working with Eric Miller and colleagues on group relations programs at the Business School has also had a profound impact on my thinking.

I am also grateful to Steven Piersanti, of Berrett-Koehler Publishers, for the interest and enthusiasm he has shown for this project. I acknowledge with thanks the part that my colleagues at the Business School of the University of Hertfordshire play in enabling me to write: they put up with my absences and my occasional obstructiveness, thereby helping to create space for thinking and writing. Of course, these comments apply with even greater force to those with whom I share my life. I believe they know just how much I appreciate their understanding and their contribution.

London, England   Ralph D. Stacey
February 1996

Introduction

In this book I invite you to explore with me how the newly emerging science of complexity might provide us with more useful frameworks for making sense of life in organizations than the approaches that currently dominate our thinking and therefore our acting.

Let me make it clear right at the start that I am not about to present you with a new recipe for organizational success, that is, the latest successor to Culture Change Programs, Total Quality Management, Business Process Reengineering, Future Visioning, Competitive Competencies, Investors in People, or the like. I have no aspirations to be a guru. Rather, I am interested in speculating about our reasons for so rapidly, and so desperately, jumping from one of these "savior" recipes, with its attendant gurus, to another, and then yet another. I am particularly interested in reflecting upon why each of these successive organizational saviors turns out to be so like its predecessor despite the initial, promising appearance of difference, in the end yielding much the same disappointing result. This kind of speculation and reflection does not lead to a new recipe that we can take away and apply in a step-by-step fashion and that yields foreseeable outcomes. Rather, it leads, I hope, to a whole new way of thinking about how organizations evolve and what part we all play in that evolution, a way of thinking that will inevitably alter the way we behave, with outcomes that, excitingly, we cannot now foretell.

My proposition, therefore, is at the same time more radical and more tentative than the application of a new recipe for success: it is an invitation for members of organizations to work at developing a whole new frame of reference for understanding organizational life. In other words, in this book I seek to present, not a finished product with known qualities, but views that I hope will assist in an ongoing process of organizational self-reflection, with unforeseeable outcomes. This tentativeness and focus on unique, specific experience is one of the principal strengths of an approach to explaining and understanding organizations that is derived from the science of complexity. It is an approach that stands in sharp contrast to the certainty and generality of the currently dominant received wisdom about managing and organizing.

But why should you expend the considerable effort that trying to understand the science of complexity will probably entail? What benefits will you reap from developing a whole new frame of reference? The answers to these questions, I suggest, have to do with escaping from the vicious circle that you may be caught in, before it crushes you.

My sense is that large numbers of people nowadays find themselves operating in an increasingly stressful environment to which they respond by withdrawing psychologically from the life of the organization in which they work. I believe that this is partly, at least, a consequence of the kind of vicious circle that I have depicted in Map A, a vicious circle that leads to ever-tighter controls that have a more and more alienating impact on individual commitment to work.

Map A. Today's Dominant Management Paradigm and the Vicious Circle It Leads To.

4
Our framework, however, defends us against that anxiety using the defense of denial. In other words, the framework insists that we must design organizations and intend outcomes, conditioning us to assume that there is no alternative—we simply must foresee and stay in control, for without this there can be no order, only anarchy.

3
This makes us anxious and fearful of failure.

5
So in our management research we seek the recipes and levers of change that produce successful outcomes and in our discourse about our management practice we insist that we must know the outcome before we act so that we stay "in control."

2
In today's environment, faster technology development/information flows + increasing interconnectedness + greater diversity, all make foresight and consensus more and more difficult, significantly reducing our ability to foresee and control.

HOW CAN WE DESIGN OUR ORGANIZATIONS SO THAT THEY WILL YIELD SUCCESSFUL OUTCOMES?

1
The dominant framework we use to answer this question requires us to
• *Analyze* external environments and internal capabilities, and then
• *Design* organizational structures, processes, and behaviors, so that they
• *Fit* the environments.

7
However, our framework conditions us to ignore the inconsistency so that when one recipe for success fails, we immediately jump to the next "savior recipe" and that fails too. The irony is that despite not being in control and not knowing the outcome, we still often produce order and innovation—the anarchy we expected usually does not occur.

And so the vicious circle continues.

8
Thus, the framework does not resonate with our experience, so that although the framework does defend us against anxiety in the short term, eventually anxiety levels rise and we become more hostile toward our organizations.

9
This makes it even more difficult to foresee and to stay in control.

6
But such foresight and control are completely inconsistent with what our analysis of the environment has revealed and so the recipes never work for long. We find that outcomes are a surprise and that it is impossible to be in control over distant time frames and geographic spaces.

The Vicious Circle

Whenever I consult to management teams, contribute to management development programs, or teach courses on management and
organizations, I am repeatedly faced with an insistent demand: even
before those concerned have time to absorb what I am trying to say,
they are pressing me to tell them how to apply what I am saying and
to explain what new behaviors I think they should adopt immediately. This kind of behavior is not restricted to one country or one
kind of organization: it is widespread and it must, therefore, reflect a
shared way in which managers are making sense of their world. The
starting point in this sense making is the question everyone seems
to share, shown in the center of the map: how can we design our
organizations so that they will yield successful outcomes? A widely
shared framework exists for answering this question; I have shown
this as step 1 on the map. The other steps in this circle follow.

Step 1

Together we construct in our minds the world we live in; the kind
of world we construct depends critically upon the ways of thinking
that we share with each other. We make sense of organizational
life using a shared frame of reference, a shared way of seeing, that
has been built up over the centuries from many sources, not the
least of which are the mechanistic models of Newtonian thinkers
and the models of organisms adapting to given environments
purely through random mutations that are drawn from Darwinian
and neo-Darwinian thinkers.

A few very basic assumptions derived from these fundamental sources underlie today's dominant way of making sense of life
in organizations. These assumptions are common to perspectives
of organizational life that seem to differ greatly, including the ideas
of Senge (1990) on systems thinking about learning organizations;
of Ansoff and McDonnell (1990), who hold that strategic choices

can be made in highly rational, analytic, and intentional ways; and of Mintzberg and Waters (1985), who point out that strategies come about in many complicated ways, some of them including an emergent component. What all of these perspectives share is an unquestioned assumption that successful organizations are systems tending to states of stable equilibrium adaptation to their market, societal, and political environments. A stable equilibrium system is one that behaves in a regular predictable manner that is adapted to its environment. The unquestioned assumption is that equilibrium systems are disturbed from equilibrium, or from a consistent journey to equilibrium, by disturbances in the environment. Success then flows from identifying these changes as soon as possible and aligning an organization to fit them.

In other words, success depends upon being "in control," or at least upon achieving control faster than one's rivals, by whatever means. As Hamel and Prahalad (1994) put it in their latest book, with the telling title, *Competing for the Future*, success depends upon getting to the future first, and to do this you must know at least a little more than your rivals about that future and be a little more in control of the competencies required to compete in it than they are.

So, at a very fundamental level, our dominant frame of reference is telling us that if we are competent enough and work hard enough, we will be able to know something useful about our organization's long-term future, and we will be able to secure at least some measure of control over movement toward it, if not by comprehensive plans, then at least by realizing visions, operating on leverage points, adopting logically incremental actions, and so on. Our dominant frame of reference tells us that we must be able to do all this, at least a little better than our rivals, or we will not survive as an organization. It tells us that if we are to have any order, we had better work out a blueprint for it in advance and put the order there; otherwise we will fall into disorder and anarchy.

The starting point of the vicious circle is thus a question, followed by a dominant framework for answering it that requires people to analyze rationally and design appropriate responses to analyzed and predicted changes. The framework encourages us to believe that we can know what will happen in advance and, since this is the case, those presenting ideas to managers should not beat about the bush but should get straight to telling people what the ideas mean in terms of immediate action.

Step 2

We are supposed to start off by analyzing the environment, but when we do we find that people are operating in organizational situations that are further and further from certainty, using methods upon which they are further and further from agreement with each other. Such situations arise for reasons with which we are well acquainted:

1.   Regional, national, and international linkages within and between organizations are proliferating more and more rapidly.

2.   Consequently, members of organizations have to cope with more and more diversity in the organization in ways of perceiving and evaluating situations and in ways of behaving and acting.

3.   As a result of these proliferating linkages, growing diversity, and more rapid technological development, members of organizations are having to cope with faster and larger flows of information.

In sum, uncertainty and disagreement about roles, purposes, tasks, and outcomes are rising to a critical level that significantly reduces our ability to foresee and therefore to stay in control. But these are the very things that our frame of reference is telling us we must do.

Step 3

The result is increasing anxiety and fears about individual security.

Step 4

However, the frame of reference does protect us from the anxiety that increasing uncertainty and disagreement arouse in us, at least in the short term. It does so because it actually denies the uncertainty and disagreement by encouraging us to believe that we can overcome it. And this leads us straight into steps 5 through 8.

Steps 5 Through 8

The belief that we must be able to foresee and be in control leads us to turn to the latest comprehensive recipe for organizational success. However, no matter how these recipes are packaged and labeled, they all end up being applied in much the same way, by increasing the pressure on fewer and fewer people to do more and to measure and justify more precisely what they are doing and what they are proposing to do. In other words, we respond to the fact that situations are uncertain and conflictual with a rigid injunction that people be more certain and more consensual, something they cannot do, of course, simply because it is all too uncertain and conflictual in the first place. So we find ourselves in a classic double bind: in situations far from certainty and agreement we vainly endeavor to behave in ways that are viable only close to certainty and agreement.

This denial of uncertainty itself allows us to sustain the fantasy of someone up there being in control and, perhaps, of things turning out for the best if we simply do what we are told, and so it protects us for a while from anxiety. However, because that defensive response involves dependency and a flight from reality, it hardly ever works. We end up paying lip service to the latest saving recipe, while we rush about doing something quite different under the pressure of events. This produces results that are frequently reasonably acceptable and every now and then excitingly creative. The difficulty, however, is that we do not quite understand what we are doing; we cannot believe that the mess we are engaged in, and the messy methods we are engaging it with, can be relied upon to produce order.

This disbelief is strongly reinforced by the very nature of the saving recipe that was supposed to get us away from the mess and put us in control. The fact that it has not may then be interpreted as a problem of implementation. In other words, it is our lack of skill and competence, our resistance to change, and sheer contrariness that are to blame. The first response must, therefore, be to identify the culprit and tighten the controls on performance. But this does not work and, as a result, confusion, frustration, insecurity, hostility, and fear increase as one recipe after another fails to do what we expect it to.

Our experience, however, is dramatically at odds with this belief. In fact, organizational life produces one surprise after another. The state of stable adaptation hardly ever seems to come in this life, and just when it does seem to have arrived, the whole system falls apart. When we look back we nostalgically see golden times that were stable and we devoutly hope for such times again, but in each sequential present, that stable state is quite clearly absent. And yet despite the fact that we are so frequently surprised and have been unable to grasp the kind of control we thought we should, the whole system works reasonably well, generating rapid technological advances and producing rising living standards for many. In a world in which all our best-laid plans go astray, an amazing amount of order is present. For a bunch of people who cannot implement the latest general scheme developed by the gurus, who resist change and frustrate our charismatic leaders, and whose blueprints continually disappoint, we produce an astonishing degree of stability.

When a frame of reference produces such dissonance with experience, it cannot perform what I think must be at least one of its primary roles, that of containing the anxiety of living. Frames of reference can contain anxiety, giving us the confidence to articulate what is happening to us and thus to design the next step we should take, only when those frames of reference resonate with our experience and with how we feel about it. Nowadays, however, we persistently believe that we ought to be able to foresee the outcomes of our actions and to be in control of our organization's future direction. Although we fear that anarchy and destruction will ensue if we lose control, we usually experience a lack of such control without the ensuing anarchy.

Step 9

Over the longer term, then, the attempts to apply today's dominant frame of reference end up provoking cynicism, disillusionment, anxiety, and hostility. Hostile, fearful, and anxious managers and other members of organizations do not cope well with situations that are far from certainty and agreement. In fact, fear and anxiety are two important parameters that push organizations even further away from certainty and agreement, reinforcing the factors listed in step 2.

In other words, the very steps we take to cope with increasing uncertainty and dissension themselves provoke more uncertainty and dissension, and this in turn makes us look even harder for the next saving recipe. The result is a continuing inability to make sense of our experience, thus driving us to even higher levels of hostility and psychological withdrawal from our organizations, and leading to yet another turn on the uncertainty screw.

The Science of Complexity

By now it is clear, I hope, why I believe that it is worth the effort of working to understand the science of complexity in the hope of developing a new frame of reference to get us out of the current double bind. But what is this science?

The science of complexity studies the fundamental properties of nonlinear-feedback networks and particularly of complex adaptive networks. Complex adaptive systems consist of a number of components, or agents, that interact with each other according to sets of rules that require them to examine and respond to each other's behavior in order to improve their behavior and thus the behavior of the system they comprise. In other words, such systems operate in a manner that constitutes learning. Because those learning systems operate in environments that consist mainly of other learning systems, it follows that together they form a coevolving suprasystem that, in a sense, creates and learns its way into the future.

Such network systems are ubiquitous in nature; not surprisingly, because we too are a part of nature, human interaction also sets up such systems. Each of us has a brain that is a complex adaptive system in which neurons are the agents. Each of us has a mind that is a complex adaptive system in which symbols and images are the agents. When we come together as a group we constitute a complex adaptive system in both a biological and a mental sense. It follows that all organizations are such systems. Organizations interact to form a national economic, societal, and political system, and national systems interact to form a global system, which interacts with natural systems to form an interconnected ecology, which now seems to be warming up. All are complex adaptive systems, each one fitting into another.

This way of looking at the world certainly resonates with my experience, but it would also resonate with that of an ant or any of nature's other species if, that is, they resonate, and I am told that they do. The science of complexity has so far focused primarily on the evolution of life and the behavior of chemical and physical systems. It has been developed by mathematicians and computer scientists, by physicists and chemists of great eminence like Murray Gell-Mann and Ilya Prigogine, the Nobel Prize laureates, and by other eminent scientists such as Stuart Kauffman, Christopher Langton, and John Holland at the Santa Fe Institute in New Mexico; researchers at the Center for Complex Studies at the University of Illinois; and Brian Goodwin, at the Open University in the United Kingdom. However, it is not only to natural systems that this science applies; as I will show in Chapter One, we too constitute such systems.

So, how does the science of complexity study these complex adaptive systems that we find everywhere and what does it have to say about them? The most important method of studying such systems is to simulate their evolution on a computer. We can quite plausibly think of members of an organization, or members of an ant colony, as agents whose behavior is driven by a set of rules for performing tasks, evaluating their performance, and changing the rules, as well as rules for copying themselves from one generation to the next. Some of those rules are conscious and explicit whereas others, at least in the case of humans, are implicit and unconscious. Nevertheless, we can, by observing a person, draw out the regularities in his or her behavior and then articulate a set of rules that produces such regularities—this is, after all, what psychologists and psychoanalysts do.

A computer program is a set of operating rules and instructions. It is perfectly possible to add a set of rules for evaluating those operations, changing the rules of operation and evaluation in light of their performance, and copying the program in some way. Such a program could quite realistically be regarded as an agent if some of its rules required it to examine the state of other computer programs and adjust its rules accordingly. In this way we could build up a population of computer programs that could interact with each other, breed, and thus evolve and learn. We would then have a complex adaptive system in our computer consisting of a collection of agents, each of which is a computer program.

Each computer program would be made up of a bit string, a series of 0s and 1s, because that is how computer programs are coded. The analogy with our rules of conduct is still very close; our rules of conduct are coded, not into 0s and 1s, but into symbols that take the form of words and images and, more fundamentally than that, the form of bursts of electrical activity in the brain. The analogy with our bodies is just as close: our physical code consists of genes that can be on or off, more or less. It is therefore quite legitimate to use such simulations to try to uncover the fundamental properties of complex adaptive systems everywhere. We will, of course, have to check to see whether human characteristics such as consciousness, whatever that is, and emotion alter the conclusions we reach, but as a first step, the simulations on a computer may, and I suggest do, yield some very important insights.

Those who have developed the study of complex adaptive systems have been most interested in this analogy between the digital code of computer program agents and the chemical code in the genes of living creatures. One of their principal questions has been this: if in its earliest days the earth consisted of a random soup of chemicals, how could life have come about? You can simulate this problem if you ask a system consisting of computer programs with random bit strings if it can evolve order out of such random chaos. The amazing answer to this question is that *such systems can indeed evolve order out of chaos* and, even more amazingly, this chaos, or mess, is essential to the process.

Now you can see the importance of this new science. Contrary to some of our most deep-seated beliefs, mess is the material from which life and creativity are built, and it turns out that they are built, not according to some prior design, but through a process of spontaneous self-organization that produces emergent outcomes. Any design consists of the basic design principles of the system itself. The system produces patterns in behavior; it consists of a network of agents driven by iterative nonlinear feedback to produce unknowable outcomes that have pattern. Complex adaptive systems have an inherent order that is simply waiting to be unfolded through the experience of the system, but no one can know what that order will be until, in fact, it does unfold in real time. In certain conditions, left to self-organize in what looks like a mess with no apparent order, agents interacting in a system can produce, not anarchy, but creative new outcomes that none of them ever dreamed of.

It is simply not true that if we cannot know the outcome and if no one can be in control, we are doomed to anarchy. On the contrary, these are the very conditions required for creativity, an exciting journey into open-ended evolutionary space with no fixed, predetermined destination. The whole universe, it seems, is lawful and yet it has freedom of choice. The price for this freedom is an inability to know the final destination or to be in control of the journey.

Insights About Life in Organizations

Let us consider now some of the key insights this new science provides us with about life in organizations.

Creativity Lies at the Edge of Disintegration

Physical, chemical, biological, and computer-simulated feedback networks are all creative—able to learn in complex ways—only when they operate right at the edge of system disintegration, in a kind of phase transition between a stable zone of operation and an unstable or disordered regime. In human terms this means that the old wives' tale about genius being close to madness may well have a scientific basis, one we share with the universe. We are creative when we manage to move away from the stability of neurotically defensive behavior but avoid the disintegration of psychotic episodes. Melanie Klein (1975a, 1975b, 1975c) called this place at the edge of mental disintegration the "depressive position," the place where we are able to hold the ambiguities and paradoxes of life and contain the anxiety they generate. She showed how this depressive position was the ground from which we make reparation for our destructiveness, the foundation of creative behavior. Donald Winnicott (1965) called this space a transitional one between the real world outside the mind and the inner fantasy world, and he located creative behavior there: the world of mythologizing and play that is the foundation of creativity.

In groups we mostly operate in a state in which we utilize structures and processes, covert politics and game playing, to block anxiety-provoking complex learning and stay in the group's stable zone. Alternatively we find ourselves tipped into shared psychotic fantasies, what Wilfred Bion (1961) called "the basic assumption behavior" of dependency, fight, flight, and so on—the unstable zone for a group. But at the edge of such disintegration we are able to contain the anxiety provoked by complex learning. Then we are able to question the fundamental assumptions we are making about our world and engage in true dialogue, beginning an exciting journey of discovery.

Paradox and Creative Destruction

The creative process that takes place at the edge of disintegration is inherently destructive, messy, and paradoxical. It involves a cross-fertilization that can take place with mental symbols as well as with genetic material or digital code. True dialogue between human beings results in just such cross-fertilization, and we all know that true dialogue is usually uncomfortable, which is why we so rarely practice it. The creative process involves competition, which, as we know only too well, takes place in the medium of ideas, power, products, and services as well as in genetic material and computer code. The creative process in human systems, therefore, is inevitably messy: it involves difference, conflict, fantasy, and emotion; it stirs up anger, envy, depression, and many other feelings. To remove the mess by inspiring us to follow some common vision, share the same culture, and pull together is to remove the mess that is the very raw material of creative activity.

Links Between Cause and Effect Disappear

Neither the messy creative processes nor their outcomes can be planned or intended, because long-term outcomes are truly unknowable at the edge of chaos. In fact, the links between our next actions and their long-term outcomes disappear, so that no one can be in control. This becomes far less anxiety-provoking once we accept it and understand that when a system is held at the edge of disintegration, the consequence is not necessarily randomness and anarchy, because the edge also has an inherent order brought about by redundancy and cooperation. That cooperation does not occur according to some blueprint, some prior intention of the most powerful. It is true empowerment, a bottom-up process in which agents follow their own best self-interest without waiting to be told that they may. Such spontaneous self-organization produces emergent strategies; that is, the interaction itself creates patterns that no agent individually intends or can foresee. Emergence means that it is not possible to foresee the global outcome of interaction between individuals or to reduce the global pattern to the behavior of the agents. This is not some kind of mysticism, but a hard, demonstrable property of interactive, nonlinear feedback.

When you insist on your vision, when you try to stick to your blueprint, when you cling with so much determination to control, are you destroying the capacity of your organization for complex learning? When you expel the surplus resource from your organization out into the community, have you become more efficient but also so brittle that you cannot survive turbulence? Is there time left for the play and the dialogue without which nothing truly new can happen?

A New Way of Understanding Life in Organizations

I hope that I have said enough to persuade you that the science of complexity holds out the possibility of revolutionizing the way we think about organizing and managing, and I now invite you to explore in more detail what that science is and how it applies to human systems. Now that I have been on this journey of exploration myself, I can do what I certainly could not have done when I started this book: I can draw a map of where my thinking has wandered as I wrote and invite you to retrace my steps with me before you go off on your own journey. With hindsight, I can see my starting point: it lies at the level of the fundamental question. This introduction started with Map A, which showed the fundamental starting question: how can we design our organizations so that they will yield successful outcomes? This question, however, leads us straight into a vicious circle; if we want to avoid it we must take a step back. My starting question, therefore, is: how can we make sense of our experience of life in organizations? It is with this question that Map B starts.

To answer this question effectively we need a new framework, one that will not get us caught up in the defense of denial and so set us off on a vicious circle. My suggestion is that this new framework is to be found in the science of complexity. In Part One of this book, we will identify the sense in which an organization is a complex adaptive system. Then, in Part Two, we will explore the science of complexity and draw out its principal insights.

Map B. A New Management Paradigm and Escape from the Vicious Circle.

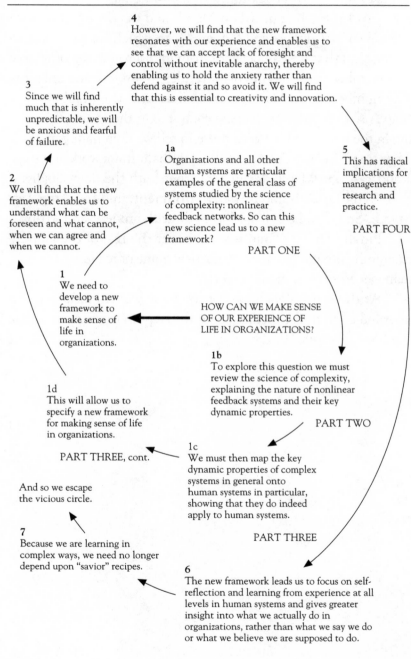

4
However, we will find that the new framework resonates with our experience and enables us to see that we can accept lack of foresight and control without inevitable anarchy, thereby enabling us to hold the anxiety rather than defend against it and so avoid it. We will find that this is essential to creativity and innovation.

3
Since we will find much that is inherently unpredictable, we will be anxious and fearful of failure.

1a
Organizations and all other human systems are particular examples of the general class of systems studied by the science of complexity: nonlinear feedback networks. So can this new science lead us to a new framework?

PART ONE

5
This has radical implications for management research and practice.

PART FOUR

2
We will find that the new framework enables us to understand what can be foreseen and what cannot, when we can agree and when we cannot.

1
We need to develop a new framework to make sense of life in organizations.

HOW CAN WE MAKE SENSE OF OUR EXPERIENCE OF LIFE IN ORGANIZATIONS?

1b
To explore this question we must review the science of complexity, explaining the nature of nonlinear feedback systems and their key dynamic properties.

PART TWO

1d
This will allow us to specify a new framework for making sense of life in organizations.

PART THREE, cont.

1c
We must then map the key dynamic properties of complex systems in general onto human systems in particular, showing that they do indeed apply to human systems.

PART THREE

And so we escape the vicious circle.

7
Because we are learning in complex ways, we need no longer depend upon "savior" recipes.

6
The new framework leads us to focus on self-reflection and learning from experience at all levels in human systems and gives greater insight into what we actually do in organizations, rather than what we say we do or what we believe we are supposed to do.

In Part Three, we will see how we might take the key in-sights of this science back to the world of human systems. These are steps 1a, 1b, 1c, and 1d on Map B and in covering them we will also move along steps 2, 3, and 4, in which we will come to understand that we can accept our inability to foresee or to stay in control without having to surrender to anxiety and anarchy. The numbering on Map B corresponds with the numbering of Map A so that you can compare each step in the chain of reason-ing in the new paradigm with those in today's dominant paradigm. Thus step 1 in Map A sets out the dominant framework and steps 1 and 1a–1d in Map B are all concerned with the new paradigm. Step 2 in Map A is about the environment, and so is step 2 in Map B. Step 3 in both maps has to do with anxiety, and so on.

Finally, in Part Four, we will cover the rest of the map by examining the implications of this new frame of reference for both management research and practice.

At the start of each part of the book we will return to the map and fill in further details about the steps in the argument that the book presents.

PART ONE

THE COMPLEX NATURE OF HUMAN NETWORKS

This book claims that the science of complexity offers a comprehensive new framework for drawing together a number of already existing insights about human systems into a coherent theory of organizational evolution that is dramatically different from the one currently dominating our thinking. The first step in sustaining this claim must, therefore, be to demonstrate that human systems are indeed the kind of system that the science of complexity deals with. That is the purpose of this part of the book. In Map C the central message of Part One is displayed as an expanded step 1a.

The introduction has already briefly defined the science of complexity. It is the study of systems consisting of large numbers of agents who interact with each other to produce adaptive survival strategies for themselves and hence for the system, or parts thereof, that they belong to. Their system in turn interacts with others, making up a larger suprasystem in which they are agents that coevolve together. The total system, therefore, has a holographic

Map C. Organizations Are Complex Adaptive Systems.

4
However, we will find that the new framework resonates with our experience and enables us to see that we can accept lack of foresight and control without inevitable anarchy, thereby enabling us to hold the anxiety rather than defend against it and so avoid it. We will find that this is essential to creativity and innovation.

3
Since we will find much that is inherently unpredictable, we will be anxious and fearful of failure.

1a
Organizations are networks consisting of large numbers of agents—people—who interact with each other according to a set of behavioral rules we can call a schema. A dominant part of this schema drives current survival strategies, the primary task carried out by an organization's legitimate system. But there is also a recessive part that drives playful and destructive behavior in a shadow system that may or may not support the legitimate (see Figure 1.1). Schemas change in organizations; that is, organizations are systems that learn in complex ways. We can describe groups, minds, and even brains in similar ways.

PART ONE

2
We will find that the new framework enables us to understand what can be foreseen and what cannot, when we can agree and when we cannot.

5
This has radical implications for management research and practice.

PART FOUR

1
We need to develop a new framework to make sense of life in organizations.

HOW CAN WE MAKE SENSE OF OUR EXPERIENCE OF LIFE IN ORGANIZATIONS?

1b
To explore this question we must review the science of complexity, explaining the nature of nonlinear feedback systems and their key dynamic properties.

PART TWO

1d
This will allow us to specify a new framework for making sense of life in organizations.

PART THREE, cont.

1c
We must then map the key dynamic properties of complex systems in general onto human systems in particular, showing that they do indeed apply to human systems.

PART THREE

And so we escape the vicious circle.

7
Because we are learning in complex ways, we need no longer depend upon "savior" recipes.

6
The new framework leads us to focus on self-reflection and learning from experience at all levels in human systems and gives greater insight into what we actually do in organizations, rather than what we say we do or what we believe we are supposed to do.

or fractal aspect in which the parts interact continually to re-create the whole and the whole affects how the parts interact. (A fractal is a pattern that is repeated in a self-similar way at many different levels. The pattern is self-similar in that it is always recognizable but never exactly the same. It is a pattern that is repeated in an irregular way.)

Throughout, the interaction between agents and systems is of a nonlinear form in which feedback on the consequences of behavior is used to construct models of the world from which rules of conduct, or schemas, are extracted. These schemas are then changed in the light of further behavior to produce more adaptive behavior. We are now talking about learning systems.

In the following chapters, we will consider the sense in which human systems are all nonlinear feedback networks and the sense in which they are fractal, or self-similar, in nature.

1

Organizations Are
Complex Adaptive Systems

Every human organization is a network of people, that is, individual agents who interact with each other and with agents in the other organizations that constitute its environment (Charan, 1991; Mueller, 1986; Nohria and Eccles, 1992). All organizations try to survive and to do this they have to make a living; that is, they have to perform the tasks required to get other organizations and people to interact with them. It is this that determines their purpose, their aims, and their primary tasks. Figure 1.1 is a network map of two organizations that depicts the circular interaction between agents within each organization and across the boundary to other organizations.

Nonlinearity in Human Networks

Two types of interactions, or links, between agents can be distinguished: the legitimate network and the shadow network. In Figure 1.1, the legitimate network is shown in solid lines and the

Figure 1.1. Human Networks.

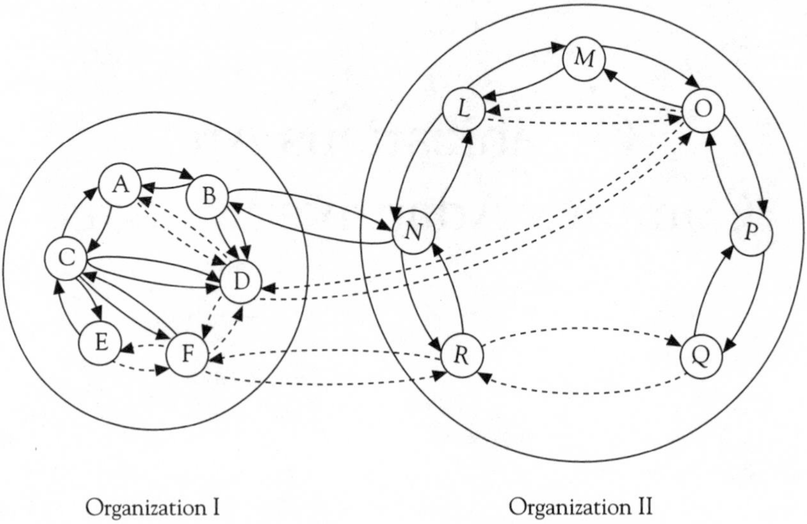

Organization I   Organization II

shadow network in dotted lines. As we will now see, both of these networks are driven by nonlinear feedback to evolve adaptive behavior and are, therefore, exactly the kind of system that the science of complexity deals with.

The Legitimate Network

The first type of network interaction, shown by the solid lines in Figure 1.1, consists of links that are either (1) formally and intentionally established by the most powerful members of an organization or (2) established by well-understood, implicit principles that are widely accepted by members of the organization—that is, a shared culture or accepted ideology. Such links exist well before action is taken and are normally designed, or evolved, to enable the performance of what is judged by the most powerful, or the majority, to be the organization's primary task—what the members of an organization need to do to sustain the support of others outside the organization at a given time.

The formality and the prior, shared intentionality of these network links are meant to secure surprise-free, regular, system-wide patterns of behavior compatible with an organization's primary task. These links, intended by the most powerful, establish the nature and direction of the authority and responsibility of each individual agent in relation to others and to the primary task; in doing so the links constitute a legitimate network system consisting of a hierarchy, a bureaucracy, and an approved ideology. The result is a table of formal and approved informal rules—schemas—that stipulate the nature of local interactions between agents in the system. These rules are external to the individual agents and are universally applicable to all of them: in a sense, agents determine what to do by consulting this external, shared table of rules. The set of rules governs how people in an organization jointly carry out the current primary tasks of their organization; in this sense it is the dominant schema. The interactions driven by this dominant schema are themselves flows of information, energy, and actions that are characterized by uniformity, conformity, and repetition.

Ideally, the links in the legitimate system are linear in the sense that:

- One and only one response is permitted for any given stimulus.
- Any outputs are proportional to inputs.
- The system is not more or less than the sum of its parts.

If these conditions are not satisfied, surprises could arise simply out of the addition of the parts or from the idiosyncratic behavior of the agents, and that would endanger the predictability that the legitimate system exists to secure. In practice, however, the shared rules are not always followed, opening up the possibility of many nonproportional responses to a given stimulus: in other words, nonlinearity. Ideally, the legitimate system is deterministic in the sense that all agents behave according to it rather than following their own unique schemas and the rules in the dominant schema remain constant for lengthy periods.

The boundary of this legitimate system is clear-cut: either particular agents are members of the system or they are not. Furthermore its purpose is clear and relatively easily understood: it is to perform the current primary tasks of the organization so that the organization survives.

The Shadow Network

The second category of links, shown by the dotted lines in Figure 1.1, is completely different. These links are spontaneously and informally established by individual agents among themselves during the course of interacting in the legitimate system. The result is another network, a kind of shadow of the legitimate system consisting of informal social and political links, in which agents develop their own local rules for interacting with each other in the course of that interaction. Some of those rules come to be shared in small groups, or even across the whole system: in other words, group and organizational cultures develop that are not part of the officially sanctioned culture or ideology. Other rules of conduct within this shadow system, however, remain specific to individual agents. In the shadow system, therefore, agents themselves determine what to do. Sometimes they do this by consulting an external cultural table of rules, either group-specific or system-wide, that is not officially sanctioned, but at other times they follow individual rules of conduct internal to themselves: in a sense, they consult their own table of rules. This set of partially shared and completely unshared rules of perceiving and behaving constitutes a recessive schema in that it is not, by definition, engaging the current primary tasks of the organization.

These shadow rules constitute a repertoire of thoughts, perceptions, and behaviors that are potentially available to an organization but are not currently being utilized for its main purpose. Instead, the shadow system serves a myriad of other diverse purposes that are often quite difficult to understand. These purposes range from individual politicking to unofficial efforts to support or sabotage the legitimate system (Trist and Branforth, 1951; Miller and Rice, 1967; Blauner, 1964; Festinger, Schachter, and Back, 1950).

The shadow system is quite clearly nonlinear. Many possible responses to any given stimulus are possible and those responses may be more or less proportional to the stimulus: agents may appeal to a number of sources for their rules of conduct, such as individual rules, group rules, or system-wide cultural rules, and which of these is appealed to will vary from one occasion to another, so that surprising, unexpected actions are likely to be produced. Furthermore, the phenomenon of group processes, which cannot be explained purely in terms of the individuals present, indicates that an informal social and political system is more than the sum of its parts. This too is a hallmark of nonlinearity.

In the shadow system, interactions take more diverse forms than is usual in the legitimate system: for example, added to flows of information, energy, and action are flows of emotion, friendship, trust, and other qualities. Shadow systems are characterized by varying degrees of uniformity and diversity, conformity and individuality.

The boundaries of the shadow system are fuzzy and normally do not coincide with the clear-cut boundaries of the legitimate system. The shadow system extends into and overlaps with the shadow systems of other organizations; indeed, shadow networks are probably the principal route for interaction between organizations simply because they have sufficiently porous boundaries. This lack of clear boundaries, however, leads some to question whether we can talk about the shadow as constituting a system at all (Kellert, 1993). The position taken in this book is that, despite fuzzy boundaries, the informal links between people in an organization do constitute a system, because they relate to, and in that sense belong to, the legitimate system. The informal system is the shadow of the legitimate one and the boundaries are therefore provided by the legitimate system. If boundaries had to be absolutely clear-cut before the concept of a system could be applied, few fields would exist in which it could be used.

An organization, then, is a network consisting of two subsystems, one ideally linear but in practice nonlinear to some extent and the other quite definitely nonlinear. Although these subsystems are conceptually distinguishable, they are operationally so intertwined that they must be understood as a whole; that whole is nonlinear because the shadow component is always nonlinear and the legitimate component sometimes is. We will now consider the nature of feedback in this nonlinear network system.

Feedback: How the Network System Operates

An organization develops over time through a feedback process in which individual agents within it:

1. *Discover*—that is, sense the state of those parts within their organization as well as those parts of its environment they are in contact with

2. *Choose* a response to those states from either universal or specific tables of rules or both

3. *Act*

These actions have consequences for each other and for agents in other organizations; they may either change the internal state of the organization, provoke a response from agents constituting its environment, or both. Each agent then discovers what the changes mean, perhaps changing the rules governing discovery and choice; chooses another act; and acts. In other words, individual agents, groups of agents, and therefore whole organizations move around an endless feedback loop of discovery, choice, and action as depicted in Figure 1.2. We will now consider what each of these steps involves.

Discovery

Discovery is an information-gathering and sense-making process that serves as the basis for making a choice. It can be thought of as a process in which each agent in a system examines the state of other related agents in the system, as well as the state of the other systems that constitute the environment of the agent's system, and then derives meaning from the information gained from

Figure 1.2. Feedback in Human Networks.

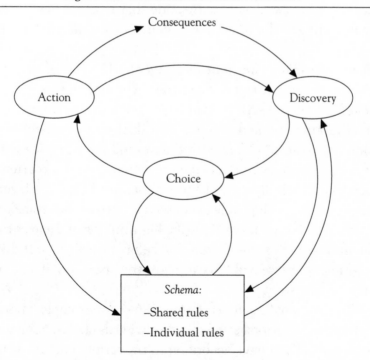

that examination. The important point is that agents select what to examine and in a sense select the meaning to be attached to the information gathered from their examination, in a manner determined by all the social and psychological aspects of their previous experience. What agents choose for examination is therefore the pivotal step in the functioning of a system.

Choice

Agents in an organization choose what to discover, how to make sense of what they discover, and what action to take in response to that meaning. To make all these choices, agents use schemas. Although I will now describe schemas in terms drawn from the literature of human behavior, you will see in Chapters Two and Three that this coincides with the way complexity scientists talk about schemas in complex systems in general. Schemas in organizations have two components, one that is specific to an individual agent and the other that is shared by a number of agents.

Schemas Specific to an Individual Agent.　The part of an agent's overall schema that is specific to the agent may be thought of as a set of behavioral scripts, evaluative rules, decision-making or operating rules, or mental models (Baddeley, 1990). Behavioral scripts are patterns of behavior that an individual typically follows. They have been developed from a lifetime's experience, much of which is driven by factors either just below the level of consciousness or completely unconscious. Even though some rules are unconscious, we are still justified in thinking of them as rules that an observer can infer from the behavior observed. If this is impossible, then we will have to leave the operation of a human system as a mystery.

　　Transactional Analysis (Berne, 1964), for example, presents a number of behavioral scripts that individuals choose from: some people typically behave according to the script "I'm OK; you're OK," whereas others follow the scripts "I'm OK; you're not OK,"

"I'm not OK; you're OK," or "I'm not OK; you're not OK." Other schools of psychology present different categorizations of behavioral scripts—Freudians talk about anal-retentive, anal-expulsive, and orally fixated scripts; Jungians talk about personal archetypes that are universally available, potential behaviors activated by specific experiences (Gordon, 1993). What is common to all of these approaches is the assumption that individual human behavior is driven by a finite number of possible behavioral scripts that can, however, be pursued in so many different combinations that individual behavior becomes infinitely variable. Indeed, if we take all the major schools of psychology and remove the overlaps in the behavioral scripts they propose, it would probably be difficult to come up with more than twenty to thirty distinct and frequently encountered scripts.

The scripts all imply sets of rules taking an if-then form. For example, suppose that I frequently use the script "I'm OK; you're not OK." Then, when I discover an undesirable state of affairs, my evaluation will be made according to the rule "If something goes wrong, then it is your fault" and my subsequent action will flow from the rule "If something goes wrong, then I will attack you and/or those associated with you."

From this we can see that behavioral scripts are expressed in the form of mental models or evaluative rules, that is, ways of making sense of the world, of interpreting and attaching meaning to events, of selecting and evaluating information. A person's mental models consist of the regularities that person has perceived in the complex world she or he has to operate in, and these models form the basis of the behavioral rules for operating in that world. Other terms used to describe essentially the same thing as a mental model are *paradigm* and *cognitive map* (Kuhn, 1970; Huff, 1990). Behavioral scripts are also expressed in the form of decision-making or operational rules, which turn the sense made of information into action. Such operational rules constitute an in-use theory (Argyris and Schön, 1978), or a theory of action. Both the

mental models, or evaluative rules, and the action theory, or operational rules, may be conscious or they may be well below the
level of awareness and therefore automatically employed, as in
either highly skilled or highly defended behavior.

Therefore, the first component of an agent's schema is a table
of if-then rules that he or she refers to in order to make a choice.
Agents may make two kinds of choices: evaluation—that is, the
selection and interpretation of information—and operation—that
is, acting upon the sense of that information. Schemas of agents
in organizations contain rules about discovering not only what
has happened but what might—in other words, the formation of
expectations and the making of forecasts.

Schemas Shared by Agents.   The second component of the schemas
that agents in organizations use to make choices consists of rules
that are shared with other agents. Some of these shared rules are
embodied in a bureaucracy and others are expressed as a shared
culture. Both can apply to a whole organization or to specific
groups within an organization.

Action

Choices governed by schemas lead to action, that is, strategies
that agents adopt to adapt themselves as beneficially as possible
to what those around them are doing. Each action an agent takes
has an effect upon other agents, leading them to respond and
causing effects that feed back again into the first agent's discovery stage.

Figure 1.3 illustrates this using an organization that consists
of three agents, x, y, and z, showing how they interact using
schemas and listing some of the key properties of those schemas.
In Chapters Two and Three, we will use this diagram to compare
the systemic nature of organizations with the nature of systems that
complexity scientists have been studying. Figure 1.3 also lists key
points on what might be called the internal structure of the human

Figure 1.3. An Organizational Network Consisting of Three Agents.

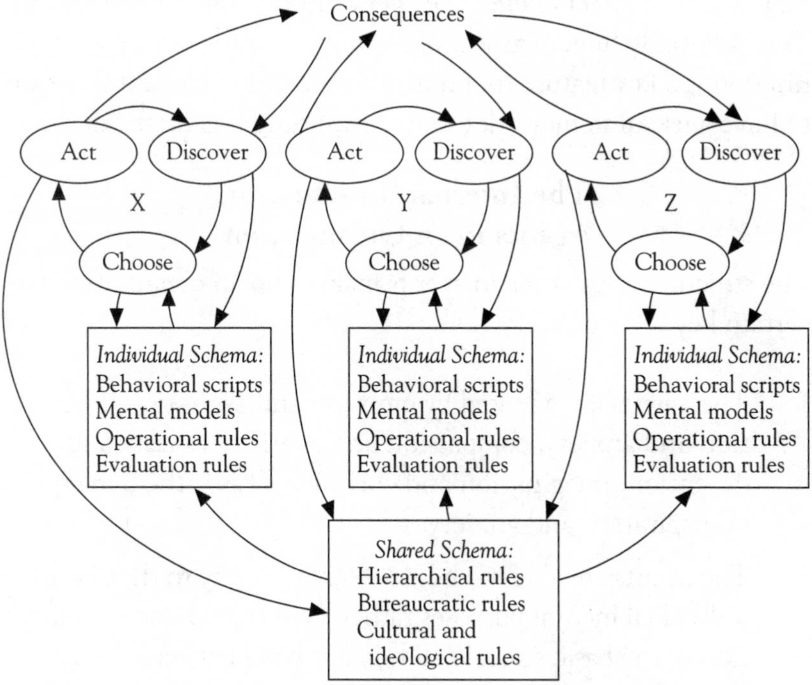

Consequences

Act Discover	Act Discover	Act Discover
X	Y	Z
Choose	Choose	Choose

Individual Schema:
Behavioral scripts
Mental models
Operational rules
Evaluation rules

Individual Schema:
Behavioral scripts
Mental models
Operational rules
Evaluation rules

Individual Schema:
Behavioral scripts
Mental models
Operational rules
Evaluation rules

Shared Schema:
Hierarchical rules
Bureaucratic rules
Cultural and
   ideological rules

Schemas: –Individual and shared
         –Reactive and anticipatory
         –Shared: evolves through interaction and dialogue
         –Individual: changes through learning

*Agent
Structure:* –Inspiration and anxiety
         –Conformity and individualism
         –Leadership and followership
         –Participating and observing

agents in organizations. By this I mean that each agent is also a system, with the system being the agent's individual human nature. The essentially human aspect of the agents who make up an organization is a key feature that must be taken into account if we are to have a useful framework for understanding organizations.

The Internal Structure of Agents in an Organization

The structure of the human agents making up an organization has certain key aspects:

1. The agents are affected by emotion and aspiration, inspiration and anxiety, compassion and avarice, honesty and deception, imagination and curiosity. This is the dynamic of inspiration and anxiety.

2. The agents are able to choose to give priority to their own individual mental purposes rather than shared ones, a reflection of the basic struggle all humans have between being themselves and conforming to group requirements sufficiently to belong. This aspect of human behavior can be summarized as the dynamic of conformity and individualism.

3. The agents are affected by power differentials among them, that is, the leadership-followership dynamic that reflects the basic human tendency to take on omnipotent, omniscient, dominant roles at some times and submissive, dependent roles at other times.

4. The agents are capable of systemic thinking, that is, of observing, reflecting upon, and altering behavior according to their perceptions of the operation of the whole system of which they are a part. This amounts to an ability to reflect upon themselves and take up the role of both participant and observer. It is the property of consciousness and self-awareness.

These key features, then, can be summarized as four important dynamics flowing from tensions between inspiration and anxiety and its containment, conformity and individualism, leadership and followership, and participant and observer roles.

Coevolution and Learning

As human agents and the systems they make up move around the behavioral loop of discovery, choice, and action, they are clearly engaging in a coevolutionary feedback process in which what one does affects the others and then returns to affect the first. This feedback process has a number of important characteristics.

First, the feedback may be negative or positive. Feedback is negative when agents or systems have some prior intention or target and then compare the outcomes of actual behavior against the target, feeding the information about deviations back into the discovery-choice-action loop in order to remove the deviation. Negative feedback is the process of intentional development and control in an organization that damps down change and secures stability. It is what agents and systems do when they plan and is the only form of feedback employed by an organization's legitimate system, which consists of a deterministic set of rules that ideally are linear but that often turn out to be nonlinear.

Feedback is positive when agents or systems feed back information into the discovery-choice-action loop in a way that amplifies and destabilizes it. Much of politics and most rumors are a form of positive feedback, but so is the spreading of revolutionary new ideas to change activities in beneficial ways. An organization's shadow system is frequently driven by positive feedback, but it may also be driven by negative feedback as, for example, when people unofficially cling to old ways of doing things that are no longer supported by the legitimate system. The shadow system is thus a nonlinear feedback network in which positive feedback is quite possible and indeed quite usual, with small events sometimes blowing up into large consequences.

Second, these two forms of feedback are linked to the ways in which agents and their organizations learn, and it is learning that drives the coevolutionary process. When schemas remain constant, then obviously behavior is driven by the same rules and only the behavior is adjusted in the light of its consequences. An agent acts, discovers how other agents respond, and, if the response is favorable to him or her, repeats the action. If the response is not favorable, the behavior is modified. In other words, the deviation between desired and actual consequences is dampened by taking corrective action. This application of negative feedback is simple, single-loop learning (Bateson, 1972; Piaget, 1953; Argyris and Schön, 1978). Anything more complex than this has already been done before action is undertaken and is embodied in the schema that is then being used. Planning is learning done prior to action.

Complex learning (Bateson, 1972; Piaget, 1953; Argyris and Schön, 1978) occurs when the schema driving behavior is altered in the light of the responses that the behavior provokes. Thus, it is the behavioral rules that are altered and, at more or less the same time, the behavior is altered too. This is learning in real time, reflection-in-action (Schön, 1987), and it clearly involves positive feedback in some way because behavioral consequences must be amplified to provoke changes in the schema. The schema is destabilized in that part of it is replaced.

Organizations move around the loop of discovery-choice-action, evolving through both positive and negative feedback, both simple single-loop and complex double-loop learning, co-creating and co-constructing their world, and acceptable organizational models must account for this. The feedback process described above produces a stream of actions, a stream that has some pattern and is undertaken to meet some purpose. At its most basic level, this purpose is the survival of the system, or parts thereof, in competition with other systems, or parts thereof.

As we will see in Part Two, the kind of network structures and learning processes identified for organizations so far are typical of the general class of systems that complexity science seeks to understand.

The Self-Similar Nature of Human Systems

Another key feature of the systems studied by complexity science is their holographic or fractal nature; clearly, this is also a property of human systems. Organizations are wholes that are parts of larger wholes, such as economies and societies, and they consist of parts that are themselves wholes, namely, human individuals. Throughout, the parts interact continuously to re-create the wholes, and the wholes in turn affect the interaction of the parts, all in eternal cycles of birth, death, and rebirth. In other words, life in organizations is continuously unfolding in irregular patterns of a self-similar nature at all levels and over all time frames, exactly the phenomenon that complexity science focuses on in biological evolution. Let us consider now how organizational life is essentially holographic, which is to say that the whole is in all the parts as well as all the parts being in the whole.

The Brain

Start with the brain of one member of a particular organization. That brain is a whole that takes the form of a network system consisting of an enormous number of parts or agents. The agents are neurons, which are connected to each other by means of synapses. The brain functions when some stimulus coming from inside or outside the brain causes the neurons to fire, that is, when chemically induced electricity is discharged across the synapses between neurons. In this way, neurons interact to create patterns of electrical activity across the brain that represent particular stimuli.

So when we smell cheese, say, a pattern of electrical activity passes across the olfactory bulb of the brain that is associated with, or symbolizes, the odor of cheese. The pattern, then, is modeling a particular regularity in the mass of stimuli confronting a brain at any one time; this model of a regularity in experience can be called a schema. Once the brain has laid down this schema, it can use it, in the future, as part of a complicated reconstruction process to determine whether or not a stimulus is cheese.

In other words, the operation of the brain establishes a symbol system that takes the form of a rule for determining the nature of a particular odor. Further experience may then operate to extend, modify, or change the rule and thus the symbols of which it is composed. This process of modeling is not a simple one in which a particular stimulus is faithfully represented by a particular pattern of neuronal activity. It is a complex feedback process in that only a small part of the brain activity associated with a stimulus comes directly from that stimulus; the greater part comes from the brain activity that internally reconstructs the external stimulus by drawing on previous experience (Damassio, 1994; Harth, 1993). Thus the neuronal pattern of the cheese odor is not some faithful electrical representation of a real odor but rather an electrical pattern that is re-created each time the stimulus is encountered, using not simply the stimulus itself but also neuronal firing patterns developed in previous experiences—that is, schemas. The patterns will therefore never be exactly the same even though the odor of the real cheese may be. It is this feedback loop that makes possible the creativity of complex learning, that is, the ability to change schemas. We are not physically locked into concrete representations; our brains are capable of endlessly re-creating those representations with different meanings.

All perception is governed by schemas in this manner; they are also employed to govern the sense that is made of perceptions and the behavior that is then chosen to deal with a particular stimulus. In this manner, behavior is adapted to the stimuli being presented to the brain, a form of single-loop learning. So the odor of cheese might lead to the adaptive, or learned, behavior of eating it, or perhaps avoiding it if the odor indicates that the cheese is too old. Thus schemas in brains are symbol systems in which each symbol is an electrical discharge. The schemas are made up of an interconnected set of symbols, a pattern of electrical activity, that enables the brain to respond to regularities in its environment. Furthermore, as the brain is exposed to new regularities, schemas change to reflect this. These changes may lead to alterations in behavior to secure closer adaptation to the environment, a form of double-loop learning.

Brain functioning in the form of schemas is thus continuously re-created by the interaction of neurons and only secondarily provoked by outside stimuli; this brain functioning, in the form of thinking, in turn affects the firing of neurons. At any one time, part of the pattern of neuronal firing, or schema, is dominant: it drives, or reflects, the current primary perceptions, thoughts, or actions of the individual. This may be thought of as the current primary task—the one the brain must carry out if it is to survive. However, the pattern of neuronal firing has more to it than is utilized in relation to current primary tasks; a recessive background of other activity waits its turn to be used.

The Mind

The brain, with its patterns of electrical activity interacting with the rest of the body, may be thought of as the foundation and source of the mind. An individual mind may be thought of as a whole system consisting of an enormous number of symbols, this time taking the form, not of electrical discharges, but of images and feelings of one kind or another. Perceiving, thinking, feeling, and acting involve manipulation of these symbols and the interaction between them that produces patterns representing regularities in experience. The symbol patterns take the form of the rules, mental models, behavioral scripts, and paradigms (Baddeley, 1990) already discussed. Together they form a schema that determines the behavior of the individual, and as the behavior is adapted to the environment, the individual performs single-loop learning. The behavior in turn may lead to changes in the schema and then further changes in behavior. The individual is rearranging the pattern of symbols in the mind in a process of complex learning. At any one time, part of the symbol system, or schema, is dominant in the sense that it is driving current mental preoccupations and thus performance of the current primary task, but a recessive symbol system, a part of the schema that is not currently being used, is available for use later on: the preconscious and the unconscious.

Thus the mind as a whole is continuously re-created by manipulations of its component symbols, which then affects the symbols and their interactions. Such manipulations reflect and provoke shifts in the patterns of electrical activity across the brain, that is, changes in the neuronal interaction patterns that continuously re-create whole-brain functioning.

The Group

Just as brains require minds and minds require brains if anything is to happen at all, so individual minds require other minds, or groups of people, if anything is to take place that is more complicated than one individual is capable of. More strongly, nothing can take place at an individual level without some interaction with others. A group of people is a whole taking the form of a system that consists of a number of members or agents. These agents interact with each other to produce patterns of group activity that take the form of shared perceptions and thoughts as well as joint action. The common patterns of thought and perception, made up of a huge number of mental symbols, come to be embodied in a shared schema, a shared set of rules of behavior that we call a culture, an ideology, or a bureaucracy. This shared schema can be thought of as the group's dominant schema, the set of rules driving its current primary task. However, a recessive schema also exists in the repertoire of individual, unshared rules of behavior not currently being utilized by the group.

Group processes are thoughts and behaviors that are driven by a group schema and that in turn affect individual thinking and behaving. Thus, manipulations of the symbols that make up the shared schema affect manipulations in the unique schemas of each individual, which then take the form of different patterns of neuronal firing. Whole patterns of group behavior are continuously re-created by interactions between group members, and these group wholes in turn affect the interactions between members. Thus, neuronal firing patterns re-create mental thought patterns, which re-create shared schema, which re-create patterns of group behavior, which affect shared schema, which alter individual schemas, which then affect patterns of neuronal firing.

The Organization

Just as brains require minds and minds require other minds if anything rather complicated is to happen, so groups of people require organizations if they are to undertake even more complicated joint actions. Organizations are wholes taking the form of networked systems that consist of either individual or group agents, and usually both. Agents in organizations interact with each other to produce patterns of thought and action at an organizational level. Regularities in those patterns come to be embodied in a shared schema—a culture, ideology, or bureaucracy at the organizational level—that then drives further behavior and thought. The shared schema can be thought of as the dominant one because it drives the performance of the current primary task, but a recessive schema, consisting of all the unshared perceptions, thoughts, and behaviors of the members of an organization, could become available to an organization later on.

The interaction of the agents creates and continually re-creates an organization as a whole, and that organization in turn influences the groups of which it is composed and the manner in which those groups are continuously re-created. This process of re-creation is what is meant by learning. Also, as we saw previously, groups affect individuals' minds, which affect brains, and so on back up to the organizational level.

The Society

If the behavior of people is to have even more complexity, then organizations must form societies and economies. A society or an economy is a whole taking the form of a networked system that consists of huge numbers of organizational, group, and individual agents. When these agents interact, they generate patterns of thought and behavior. Regularities in these patterns come to be embodied in a shared schema—a national culture, ideology, or bureaucracy. Once again a dominant schema and a recessive schema exist, the latter containing the repertoire of thoughts and behaviors that are not currently being used for the society's or the economy's primary tasks. Interaction between agents continuously re-creates the whole patterns that make up a society or an economy and those wholes in turn influence the organizations of which they are composed.

The International Community

An extra turn of the complexity screw is given by societies and economies that interact with each other to constitute international networked systems. Here, too, a whole is reflected in a shared schema, which affects the national societies and economies, with a ripple effect down to the organizations, the groups, the individuals, the minds, and the brains, and then back up again.

The Ecology

As we are now becoming increasingly aware, the societies and economies of the globe interact with the natural environment, affecting how it develops, and this in turn affects how the global economies and societies develop. The concern about global warming is an example of this growing awareness that the Gaia hypothesis— the view that the earth is one interconnected complex adaptive system of which we humans are only a part—offers something of practical importance (Lovelock, 1988).

A Complex, Self-Similar Whole

The result of the interactions described above is a complex system with self-similarity at every level. At each level the whole constitutes a networked feedback system of coevolving parts, or agents; this whole is in turn a component of, or agent in, a coevolving whole. Thus, an agent at one level is a system one level below. At each level the system is driven in the performance of its primary task by a dominant schema, and in the background is a recessive, or currently dormant, schema. The systems at all levels learn in both simple single loops and complex double loops.

Conclusion

The description of human systems that I have given above started with the behavior of an individual, seeing this person as the agent in an organization. At its most basic, this takes a behaviorist perspective in which the agents simply adapt their behavior to make that behavior more beneficial to themselves; this is simple condition, or single-loop, learning. The cognitive perspective is introduced when we take account of how humans perceive and make sense of a complex world through constructing schemas that they then change in a complex double-loop learning process. As soon as we take account of the self-similar nature of human systems— that is, of the manner in which one human system nests in others from the mind, to the group, to the organization, to the society, and so on—we inevitably move to a social constructionist view of the evolution of human systems. An individual human agent is in a sense the schema that drives his or her behavior, and that schema is what it is because of the interactions those individuals have had with each other. Individuals co-construct both their individual selves and the world of other selves, and they do so in interaction with each other. So in our understanding of human systems we move from the behaviorist, to the cognitive, to the social constructionist viewpoint. At one end of that social construction, however, there are the biological systems of embodied brains that nest in what is being socially constructed as a world, and at the other end there is the ecological system in which the socially constructed world nests.

Figure 1.4 summarizes the key features of human systems that this chapter has identified. From this it is clear that, in a general way, human systems are nonlinear feedback systems and that they are coevolving, interacting networks of agents and subsystems whose behavior is driven by schemas and who learn. I have demonstrated here that it is possible to describe the essential features of human systems in language that is immediately recognizable both to those who study human systems and those who study complex adaptive systems in nature. Human systems, therefore, fall within the class of systems for which the science of complexity logically identifies fundamental, dynamic properties; this can be seen by comparing Figure 1.4 with Figure 3.4, which summarizes the key features of complex adaptive systems. The new science of complexity must have something to tell us about human systems.

There is, of course, a difference between human systems and the general class of complex adaptive systems to which they belong. The difference is that agents in human systems have internal structure, whereas those in simulated complex adaptive systems do not. The internal structure of agents in human systems relates to peculiarly human aspects having to do with tension between inspiration and the containment of anxiety, conformity and individualism, leadership and followership, and participant and observer roles. In mapping the fundamental properties of complex adaptive systems onto human organizations it will, therefore, be necessary at each stage to ask whether these four dynamics alter any conclusions that straightforward mapping might lead to. Particular attention will be paid to this in Part Three.

But first, we must understand what the science of complexity is all about.

Figure 1.4. Key Features of a Human System.

A human system:
- Has a basic purpose of performing tasks and surviving
- Consists of networks of large numbers of interacting agents
- Interacts with an environment consisting primarily of other human systems and therefore coevolves
- Interacts in an iterative, nonlinear manner
- Discovers, that is, acquires information about the systems constituting its environment and information about the consequences of its own interaction with those systems by employing feedback
- Chooses, that is, exercises an element of free will to identify and select regularities in the feedback information it acquires and then condenses those regularities into a schema or model of its world, in effect selecting one of a number of competing models that might "explain" the regularities and yield effective rules of behavior for coping with that world
- Acts according to its schema rules in relation to the systems that are its environment
- Discovers the responses its action provokes, as well as the consequences of those responses
- Uses this information to adapt its behavior, that is, to perform simple or single-loop learning
- Revises its schema so as better to adapt, that is, to perform complex or double-loop learning

The key to the whole process lies in the schemas, as follows:
- Agents have unique individual schemas.
- Agent behavior is also conditioned by common culture, a schema shared with all or some other agents.
- Schemas consist of simple reaction rules, more complex rules requiring formation of expectations and taking anticipatory action, performance evaluation rules, rules for evaluating schema rules themselves.

Agent's internal structure is as follows:
- Agents and groups of agents get caught up in sequences of responses driven by emotion and aspiration, inspiration and anxiety, compassion and avarice, honesty and deception, imagination and curiosity.
- Agents share a common purpose but also develop their own individual mental purposes leading to tension between conformity and individualism.
- Some agents are, or become, more able and/or more powerful than others and apply force and persuasion, whereas others follow.
- Agents are conscious and self-aware, that is, they can adopt the role of observer and think systemically.

PART TWO

THE SCIENCE OF COMPLEXITY

Human systems, that is, individuals, groups, organizations, and societies, are all nonlinear feedback networks that nest within each other to form a highly complex whole. Each of these systems consists of what we might think of as two subsystems:

1. A legitimate subsystem in which behavior engages current reality and is driven by a dominant schema that all the agents in the system share, thus leading to conformity

2. A shadow subsystem in which behavior is driven, not by current reality, but by recessive schemas, most of which are unique to individual agents, thus leading to diversity

Human agents and systems all coevolve in interaction with each other, utilizing both single- and double-loop learning processes through which they develop strategies for interacting with each other and so surviving.

The majority of management researchers and practitioners currently employ a common way of making sense of these human networks that focuses attention on legitimate subsystems, where negative feedback processes are designed to secure centrally intended outcomes. In the extreme, this currently dominant way of understanding organizations amounts to the following proposition: if all the members of an organization follow the rules of the legitimate system, and if these rules are the correct ones in the sense that they are detailed enough to cover all current eventualities and produce behavior adapted to an environment that does not change, then their organization will stay in a state of stable equilibrium in which it is adapted to its environment and will, therefore, succeed. Taken to the logical limit, the way in which prescriptions for Total Quality Management and Business Process Reengineering are typically implemented amounts to setting deterministic rules that are implicitly supposed to produce success if they are rigidly adhered to and the environment does not change. The need for change in the rules is perceived to arise from changes in the environment.

The question then is this: is it true that a perfectly deterministic nonlinear feedback network will produce stable adapted behavior if the environment remains unchanged and the rules are followed rigidly? To answer the question we need to understand the dynamics of deterministic nonlinear feedback systems.

In fact, environments will change; therefore, the rules in an organization's shared schema will have to be adapted. Furthermore, individuals will sometimes behave according to their own unique schemas and will sometimes change them for purely internal reasons. What we really need to study, if we are to understand human systems, is not deterministic feedback networks, but adaptive ones.

Where are we to look for a deeper understanding of both deterministic and adaptive feedback networks? Most physical, chemical, and biological systems in nature display much the same

Map D. The Science of Complexity.

4
However, we will find that the new framework resonates with our experience and enables us to see that we can accept lack of foresight and control without inevitable anarchy, thereby enabling us to hold the anxiety rather than defend against it and so avoid it. We will find that this is essential to creativity and innovation.

3
Since we will find much that is inherently unpredictable, we will be anxious and fearful of failure.

1a
Organizations are networks consisting of large numbers of agents—people—who interact with each other according to a set of behavioral rules we can call a schema. A dominant part of this schema drives current survival strategies, the primary task carried out by an organization's legitimate system. But there is also a recessive part that drives playful and destructive behavior in a shadow system that may or may not support the legitimate (see Figure 1.1). Schemas change in organizations; that is, organizations are systems that learn in complex ways. We can describe groups, minds, and even brains in similar ways.

5
This has radical implications for management research and practice.

2
We will find that the new framework enables us to understand what can be foreseen and what cannot, when we can agree and when we cannot.

PART ONE

PART FOUR

1
We need to develop a new framework to make sense of life in organizations.

HOW CAN WE MAKE SENSE OF OUR EXPERIENCE OF LIFE IN ORGANIZATIONS?

1b
The science of complexity explores the nature of deterministic (see Figure 2.1) and adaptive (see Figures 3.1 and 3.2) networks. The latter—complex adaptive systems—are networks of large numbers of agents who interact according to schemas that contain both dominant and recessive parts. The key discovery complexity scientists have made about complex adaptive systems is that they are creative only when they operate in what might be called a space for novelty. This is a phase transition at the edge of chaos, that is, at the edge of system disintegration. The state is a paradoxical one that is both stable and unstable at the same time, driven by contradictory dynamics of both competition and cooperation, both amplification and constraint, both exposure to creative tension and protection from it. Such systems evolve dialectically with radically unpredictable outcomes. The coevolving process is that of self-organizing creative destruction and reconstruction in which a recessive schema undermines a dominant one to produce emergent outcomes (see Figures 2.3, 3.4, and 3.5). These are systems that learn in complex ways and they are ubiquitous in nature.

1d
This will allow us to specify a new framework for making sense of life in organizations.

PART THREE, cont.

PART TWO

And so we escape the vicious circle.

1c
We must then map the key dynamic properties of complex systems in general onto human systems in particular, showing that they do indeed apply to human systems.

PART THREE

7
Because we are learning in complex ways, we need no longer depend upon "savior" recipes.

6
The new framework leads us to focus on self-reflection and learning from experience at all levels in human systems and gives greater insight into what we actually do in organizations, rather than what we say we do or what we believe we are supposed to do.

complex network structure as the one shown in Chapter One to be characteristic of human systems, and they also coevolve, driven by learning processes to produce strategies for survival. Perhaps we should not be surprised by this, because humans are also part of nature. Furthermore, inanimate physical and chemical systems are deterministic feedback networks and living biological systems are adaptive nonlinear feedback networks. On the face of it, therefore, those who are trying to understand organizations may have something to learn from those who are studying deterministic and adaptive systems in nature. It is the purpose of the two chapters in this part to review recent developments in the natural sciences with the intention of identifying new insights and metaphors that might help us to reflect upon and understand the dynamics of organizations.

Chapter Two will focus on what is now known about the dynamics of deterministic feedback networks, and Chapter Three will be concerned with how scientists are coming to understand adaptive feedback networks. Map D shows where the material in this part of the book fits into the overall argument, with step 1b expanded to summarize the key points to be made in this part.

2

Deterministic Networks:
Chaos and Dissipative Structures

A deterministic nonlinear feedback system is a network of agents whose behaviors are determined by a common schema consisting of a few rules that are fixed over time, apply to all agents without exception, and do not have to do with achieving some purpose. It follows that agents do not adjust their behaviors in the light of their consequences for a particular purpose. In other words, there is no learning of any kind. Despite the fact that this kind of system is so far removed from human systems, it is worth our attention for reasons that will be presented later.

One example of a deterministic feedback system is a simple pendulum. A pendulum follows a pattern of movement over time in which its position at any one moment is determined by the force and friction applied to it at the previous moment and in which what is applied to it at this moment will be fed back into the laws of motion governing it to determine its position at the next moment. This system can be expressed as a mathematical

model of a network consisting of agents, where each agent is a
position of the pendulum.

Another example is provided by the weather. At any one
moment, each point in the atmosphere has a temperature, an air
pressure, a humidity level, and so on. The laws driving the weather
system are nonlinear feedback rules: the state of each point in the
atmosphere and its neighboring points at a given moment are fed
back into the rules to determine their state in the next. This system can also be expressed in terms of a mathematical model of a
network of agents, where each agent is a point in the atmosphere.

In yet another example, a population of organisms may be
thought of, at the macro level, as a deterministic feedback system.
The number of ants in a population at the present time is determined by the difference between the birth and death rates in the
last time period, and the number of ants in the next time period
will be determined the difference between the birth and death
rates at the present time. If a food constraint on growth is built
into this relationship, we have a model for population growth in
which the control parameter is the difference between birth and
death rates applied to a population level according to a particular
equation known as the logistic (May, 1976). Once again we have
a mathematical model of a network of agents, and this time the
agents are ants. Although the ants are alive, the whole population of ants is being treated in this model in a mechanistic manner: birth and death rates that the ants themselves cannot
influence determine the population size, given the food constraints that they also can do nothing about.

The above mathematical models are in effect models of networks with standard schemas that remain constant over time. These
schemas fully determine the behavior of the pendulum, the weather,
or the ants' population growth. This structure is depicted in Figure
2.1. By comparing it to Figure 1.3, you will be able to see what it
has in common with a human organization and how it differs. It is

obviously a gross simplification if we are looking for insights about human systems, because this system has no purpose, no unique individual schemas, and no possibility of schema change (complex learning) or even of adapting behavior according to its consequences (simple learning). It is, nevertheless, worth the effort to understand such deterministic networks because some theories of organization make implicit assumptions of determinism and because the study of deterministic systems provides us with concepts that will be useful in understanding the more complex adaptive systems to be examined in the next chapter.

What follows in this chapter is a rather brief summary of the key concepts relating to deterministic nonlinear feedback systems;

Figure 2.1. A Deterministic Feedback Network Consisting of Three Agents.

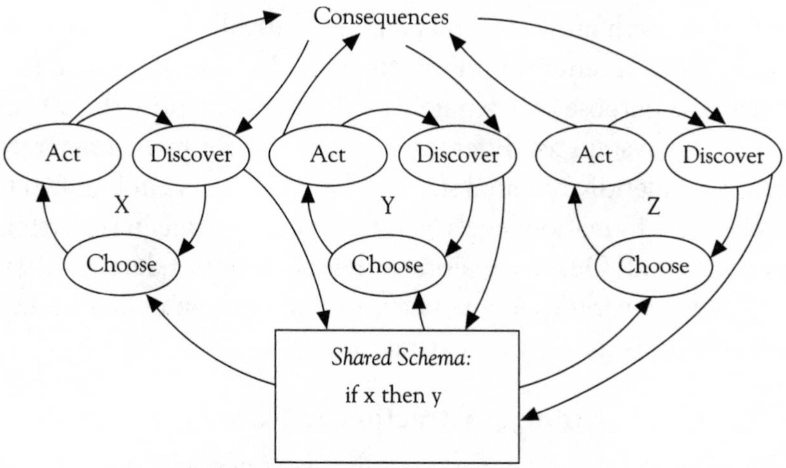

Schema: –Shared only
            –Deterministically reactive only
            –Fixed over time

Agent
Structure: –None

more detail on their general aspects is available in Gleick (1888), Briggs and Peat (1989), and Stewart (1989), and applications to the world of organizations can be found in a number of other books and papers (Baumol and Benhabib, 1989; Gemmell and Smith, 1985; Zimmerman, 1992; Stacey, 1991; Hsieh, 1989; Goldstein, 1994, 1994b; Peters, 1991; Schenkman and Le Baron, 1989; Wheatley, 1992; Richardson, 1991; Nonaka, 1988).

The dynamics of systems of the deterministic kind depicted in Figure 2.1 can be identified by mathematical analysis, by computer simulation of the mathematical models representing them, and by laboratory experiments with physical and chemical systems. This analysis, simulation, and experimentation seeks to show how the pattern of behavior of a particular system as a whole changes as its control parameters are altered. The pendulum's control parameters are force and friction, the weather's are factors such as air pressure and wind speed, and the ant population's are birth and death rates. Control parameters usually reflect levels and rates of flow in energy and information. In more technical language, the purpose of a dynamic analysis is to identify the attractors of the system for different states of the control parameters, that is, to identify the final states of behavior a system is drawn to as energy, information levels, and rates of flow through the system are increased. Our discussion of the dynamics of deterministic feedback networks therefore needs to start with an understanding of just what is meant by an attractor.

Strange Attractors and Chaos

In mathematical terms, an attractor is the set of points to which the trajectories followed by a system converge asymptotically over time. In other words, an attractor is a pattern of behavior into which a system ultimately settles in the absence of outside disturbances. Translating this into more philosophical terms, we might say that an attractor is a potential state of behavior, a disposition, or an archetype that is in the process of being realized or actualized through the specific experience of a system. This is much the same as Bohm's notion (1980) of an implicate order that is unfolded as a system operates and Aristotle's notion of the Ideal Forms, or Ideas, contained in rules of behavior (Tarnas, 1991). So two potential forms of behavior for a population of ants are a regular swing between expansion and contraction phases and wild gyrations in numbers that rise explosively and then fall catastrophically.

Note that I am not using the word *archetype* here as meaning some ancient pattern that a system is preordained to return to—the Ur-form of archetype. Nor am I using the terms *potential* and *disposition* to imply that the system is being drawn to an already existing future state or purpose—a telos. When I use the terms *archetype*, *potential*, or *disposition*, I am seeking to describe a possibility that is enfolded in a set of rules of interaction. Because such possibilities flow from the interaction itself, it follows that novel rules of interaction will generate novel kinds of possibility that have never existed before and that are not yet embodied in some known purpose or future state. In other words, I am holding open the possibility that feedback networks might be able to produce completely new archetypes by developing new rules that govern the interactive games they play with each other.

Having tried to clarify what an attractor might be, we now need to consider the different kinds of attractors that are open to a deterministic nonlinear feedback system. The point of a dynamic analysis is to identify which control parameter states produce a given kind of attractor. Two rather different types of attractors have been known for a long time: stable equilibrium attractors and unstable attractors.

Stable Equilibrium Attractors

In mathematical terms, stable equilibrium is an attractor in which all trajectories followed by a system are drawn to a single point or to some periodic cycle. In more philosophical terms, it is a potential or archetypal behavior that takes the form of perfectly regular, predictable patterns, as when the population of ants remains constant and the pendulum swings regularly back and forth.

Deterministic nonlinear feedback systems are attracted to stable equilibrium when their control parameters are low, that is, when information or energy is disseminated rather slowly through the system. The potential or archetype of stability is actualized through negative feedback processes that damp down any small disturbances to the system, thus compelling it to return to its stable equilibrium behavior. So when the difference between the birth and death rates in an ant population is small, the population will tend to change slowly at a constant rate. Such stable patterns may be very complicated, because as control parameters are increased, behavior repeatedly bifurcates: a single state is replaced by a two-period cycle, which in turn is replaced by a four-period cycle, and so on. In other words, as the control parameters are increased, the system has a choice between a number of equilibriums, and the ant population could grow according to very complicated but regular and predictable cycles.

Given enough time, the stable archetype is actualized in an exactly repeatable form by the experience of the system over time; it is the archetype of complete integration and rigid order.

Unstable Attractors

The control parameters in a deterministic nonlinear feedback system may be set at very high levels, with information or energy being pumped around the system at a very rapid rate. In these conditions the system is drawn to infinity, to an unstable state in the presence of any external constraint, or to some form of completely random behavior. Thus, when the control parameters are set at high levels, the attractors are unstable, and this potential or archetype of instability is actualized by positive feedback that exponentially amplifies small disturbances to the system without any kind of internal constraint. The unstable archetype is also actualized in its exact form, and the system speeds toward infinity until it is brought to an explosive halt by some external constraint. Ultimately, then, the unstable attractor might take the form of an inert system characterized by completely random behavior on the part of its agents—an archetype of disintegration. A birth rate that greatly exceeded the death rate in an ant population would lead to explosive growth, which would bump violently into food constraints and lead to a catastrophic population decline.

Stable and unstable attractors are not the only ones available to a deterministic nonlinear feedback system. Recently, chaos theorists have uncovered the presence of other attractors called strange attractors, and this discovery may well be the beginning of a major paradigm shift in science as a whole. What is a strange attractor and why is its discovery of such major significance?

Strange Attractors and Chaos Theory

As we have seen, when the control parameters in a deterministic nonlinear feedback network are tuned up (for example, when information or energy flows are increased), the behavior of the network follows a bifurcating path in which it continues to display regular, stable patterns but they become increasingly complicated. The new discovery is that past some critical point in the level of the control parameter, the system is attracted to, or caught up in, a paradoxical attractor that is both stable and unstable at the same time, an attractor lying in the borders between stability and instability. This "strange attractor" is now called chaos. Although it was known to Poincaré at the turn of the century, its significance has only recently been understood (Lorenz, 1963).

The strange attractor has a precise mathematical meaning. Chaos is an attractor in the sense that all nearby trajectories are drawn into its orbit, but it is strange in that two arbitrarily close points within the attractor may diverge away from each other and yet remain within the attractor; this is identified by a positive Lia-punov exponent, which measures the exponential rate at which nearby trajectories separate (Doyne Farmer and Sidorowich, 1988, p. 102). The trajectories separate because of the property of sen-sitive dependence on initial conditions, which means that tiny changes may be escalated into major differences. By *chaos*, math-ematicians generally are referring to low-dimensional chaos, a pat-tern of evolution displayed by a deterministic system with many variables, whose flow is restricted to a small space that folds back on itself. Chaos usually has a fractal dimension, that is, a dimen-sion of less than 2 or 3 (Kauffman, 1993, p. 178). The system gen-erating chaos is deterministic and in that sense its behavior is not random, but the specific outcome is indeterminate and in that sense, perhaps, its behavior is random. This, of course, is coun-terintuitive, with potentially major significance.

An example of a strange attractor is given in Figure 2.2, which depicts the trajectories open to a simplified model of the weather system—Lorenz's famous butterfly attractor (1963). It can be seen that by setting boundaries or constraints, a strange attrac-tor defines the space within which a system may move and speci-fies a shape to the movement. Thus the weather system is bounded or constrained—heat waves do not occur in the Arctic, nor do snowstorms at the Equator. The weather system is also bounded by the cycle of the climate, with temperatures tending to be high in the summer and low in the winter, for example, and it follows a shape specified by the attractor, first swirling around one lobe of the attractor and then suddenly switching to the other. These shapes can be seen quite clearly in satellite pictures of the earth.

The constraints of boundary and shape provide the system with order and stability while it operates within the strange attrac-

Figure 2.2. The Lorenz Butterfly Attractor.

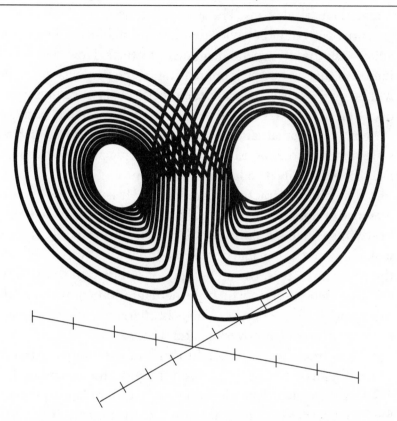

tor. However, within these constraints, the specific state of the weather is free to move where it will, or rather where tiny chance changes drive it. This makes specific weather patterns unpredictable over the long term: tiny changes can be escalated into qualitatively different patterns of weather. This unpredictability introduces instability or disorder into the system but also opens it to immense variety. The system's "choices" are no longer limited to a selection from a small number of equilibriums; the range of choices within the boundaries and shape of the attractor is now infinite.

This example makes it clear how we can describe chaos in nonmathematical terms. The strange attractor is an archetype, a potential pattern of behavior that has the stability of boundaries and shape, that is, general qualitative features. However, actualization of that archetype is unpredictable: the particular form that will be realized depends upon the precise experience of a system over time. The chaos archetype is an irregular or fractal potential pattern whose actualization occurs through a process in which the system flips autonomously between negative and positive feedback, providing its own internal constraint.

The chaos attractor is paradoxical. It is the simultaneous presence of stability in archetypal or dispositional form and instability in specific actualization. Chaos is also the only state in which a system is capable of novelty and endless variety because the other attractors, the archetypes of stability and instability, consist of repetition in which the actualization always coincides exactly with the archetype. Chaos is, therefore, an archetype of novelty, creativity, innovation, and surprise.

In a simple way, one might think of the strange attractor chaos as a phase transition between stability and instability. This will be a useful approximation when we return to human systems, but strictly speaking it is not correct. In the march to chaos described above, a system bifurcates continually until it reaches the strange attractor. Just before it does so, it may pass through a phase transition in which global and local short-term order coexists with chaos. This is the true phase transition, described as *the edge of chaos*.

Chaos theory, therefore, demonstrates how systems can lead to extremely complicated, even totally unpredictable, behavior even though they are very simple, in the sense that they are driven by small numbers of rules in the absolutely fixed schemas that are common to all agents (Gleick, 1988; Stewart, 1989; Ruelle, 1991; Briggs and Peat, 1989). We now turn to the theory of dissipative structures, which focuses on how systems use disorder to generate new order through the process of spontaneous self-organization.

Dissipative Structures and Spontaneous Self-Organization

The following example indicates what is meant by a dissipative structure, the process of self-organization, and the meaning of emergence. A liquid is at thermodynamic equilibrium when it is closed to its environment and the temperature is uniform throughout it. The liquid is then in a state of rest at a global level; that is, it has no bulk movements, although the molecules move everywhere and face in different directions. In equilibrium, then, the positions and movements of the molecules are random and hence independent of each other, with no correlations, patterns, or connections. At equilibrium nothing happens; the behavior of the system is symmetrical, uniform, and regular. This means that every point within the liquid is essentially the same as every other point, and that at every point in time the liquid is in exactly the same state as it is at every other time. Time and space do not matter.

When the control parameter heat is turned up and the liquid is pushed far from equilibrium, the system uses positive feedback to amplify small fluctuations throughout it. Therefore, applying heat to the base of a layer of liquid that is close to thermodynamic equilibrium sets up a fluctuation or change in the environmental condition in which the liquid exists. This temperature change is then amplified or spread through the liquid. The effect is to break the symmetry and cause differentiation within the liquid. At first the molecules at the base stop moving randomly and begin to move upward, those most affected by the increase in temperature rising to the top of the liquid. That movement eventually sets up convection, so that the molecules that are least affected are displaced and pushed down to the base of the liquid. There they are heated and they then move up, in turn pushing others down. As the molecules move in a circle, the symmetry of the liquid is broken by the bulk movement that has been set up and each point in the liquid is no longer the same as all others: movement is up at some points and down at others.

After a time a critical temperature is reached and a new structure emerges in the liquid. The molecules move in a regular direction, setting up hexagonal cells, some turning clockwise and others turning counterclockwise: they self-organize. What this represents is long-range coherence. Molecular movements are now correlated with each other as though they were communicating, and a degree of connectivity is established. However, the direction of each cell's movement is unpredictable and cannot be determined by the experimenter. The direction the cell takes depends upon small chance differences in the conditions that existed as it was formed. As further heat is applied to the liquid, the symmetry of the cellular pattern is broken, other patterns emerge, and eventually the liquid reaches a turbulent state of chaos—evaporation. Movement from a perfectly orderly symmetrical situation to one of some more complex order occurs through a destabilizing process—through the system being pushed away from stable equilibrium, which takes the form of a point attractor, through bifurcations, where stable equilibriums take the form of periodic cycles, and so on toward deterministic chaos. The process is clearly one where destruction makes way for creation of the new.

Thus, self-organization is a process that occurs spontaneously at certain critical values of a system's control parameters and in which the agents of the system organize themselves to produce a new pattern without any blueprint. This is a truly bottom-up process of change. Emergence means that the pattern produced by this self-organization cannot be explained by the actions of the agents or reduced to the agents' behavior; something new happens and true synergy results. The new pattern that emerges is a dissipative structure: it easily dissolves if the system moves away from critical points in its control parameters. An equilibrium structure requires no effort to retain its structure and great effort to change it, whereas a dissipative structure requires great effort to retain its structure and relatively little to change it.

Prigogine (Nicolis and Prigogine, 1989; Prigogine and Stengers, 1984) has established that nonlinear chemical systems are changeable only when they are pushed far from equilibrium, where they can become dissipative systems. A dissipative system imports energy and information from the environment that then dissipate through the system, in a sense causing it to fall apart, but it also has a structure that takes the form of irregular patterns, and it is capable of renewal through self-organization as it continues to import energy and information. A dissipative system is essentially a contradiction or paradox: symmetry and uniformity of pattern are being lost but a structure still exists; the dissipative activity occurs as part of the process of creating a new structure. A dissipative structure is not just a result, but a system or process that uses disorder to change. It is an evolving interactive process that temporarily is manifested in globally stable structures.

Thus, when we introduce nonlinearity, positive feedback, and constraints into a system, the result is to hold the system far from equilibrium in a state of some instability. The system is prevented from becoming adapted to its environment, and this enables it to amplify small changes. This amplification, in turn, makes it possible for the whole system to change. Stability dampens and localizes change to keep the system where it is, but operation far from equilibrium destabilizes the system and opens it up to change.

Let us consider now the principal insights that the theories of chaos and dissipative structures give us about the dynamics of deterministic nonlinear feedback networks in general.

Properties of Deterministic Nonlinear Feedback Systems

Simulation and analysis of deterministic feedback networks and dissipative structures, as well as laboratory experiments with physical and chemical examples of these structures, have identified a number of fundamental properties that are common to all such systems no matter whether the agents comprising them are ants, points on a weather grid, molecules in a fluid, or anything else. These properties will be discussed under the following five headings:

1.   Space for novelty: the paradox of stability and instability
2.   The source of instability
3.   The source of stability
4.   Dialectical evolution
5.   Causality and predictability

Space for Novelty: The Paradox of Stability and Instability

The first property of major importance is that deterministic nonlinear feedback systems are capable of novelty and endless variety, akin to creativity, when their control parameters are set at the critical levels that produce the strange attractor chaos or a phase transition at the edge of chaos. Two general classes of control parameters seem to exist for deterministic nonlinear feedback systems: (1) levels and rates of flow of energy or information and (2) levels of interconnectivity between agents in a system. Chaos and the state at the edge of chaos lie in the borders between system stability and instability: in a sense they lie at the edge of system disintegration. Here, the behavior of a system is paradoxically stable and unstable at the same time; this bounded instability is the ground from which novel forms of behavior emerge.

Novel behavior takes the form of dissipative structures that emerge when some constraint holds parameter values at their critical points. These dissipative structures use positive feedback to amplify fluctuations in their environment in order to disrupt existing patterns of behavior, break symmetries, and create differentiation across time and space. The result is irregular, fractured, or fractal patterns of behavior that might include deterministic low-dimensional chaos. This symmetry-breaking differentiation creates the possibility of emergent new kinds of chemical and physical reactions. As a result, dissipative structures display great individual variety within overall irregular categories, archetypes, or dispositions.

The Source of Instability

When a deterministic nonlinear feedback system is operating in the space for novelty, it is capable of escalating tiny changes into qualitatively different patterns of behavior—the property known as sensitive dependence on initial conditions. This positive or amplifying feedback possibility introduces irregularity and unpredictability into the behavior of the system, which constitute the instability or disorder that is found in the overall order of behavior in the strange attractor. Dissipative structures also display sensitive dependence on initial conditions by amplifying small changes in their environments and spreading waves of change across the system. This makes it possible for small changes to lead to major qualitative changes in physical or chemical structure. A deterministic feedback system, therefore, has one source of instability—its propensity to amplify tiny changes.

The Source of Stability

When a deterministic nonlinear feedback system is in the vicinity of any stable equilibrium attractor, negative feedback will ensure that it returns to that stable equilibrium state. Stability in its equilibrium sense is a state that has precise, predetermined, specific forms, and it is produced and sustained in a relatively simple manner through negative feedback. When a system is in the space for novelty, however, specific patterns of behavior are realized through a rather complicated experiential process that combines both negative and positive feedback. Any stability in the emergent irregular patterns is produced by the tension between negative and positive feedback, in which one provokes while the other restrains. The resultant stability consists of the emergence of an irregular pattern, in the sense that it is not programmed in advance. The precise actualization can occur only when the system is operating, and the outcome is thus a surprise that nothing in the preceding situation can account for. For example, nothing about two hydrogen atoms and one oxygen atom, the building blocks of water, can account for the fluidity, opacity, and taste of water. Water is thus a phenomenon that emerges from the interaction of hydrogen and oxygen.

One source of stability at the edge of system disintegration is thus the tension between negative and positive feedback, the constraint that they place upon each other. The other source of stability is the structure displayed by dissipative systems and that is the result of the process of emergence. Hence, whatever causes emergence to take place is a source of stability. Emergent order occurs when parameters reach critical values, causing the system to operate within or at the edge of deterministic chaos. Here, iterative nonlinear feedback has a stretching, folding, mixing action that makes behavior complex in that an initial pattern is being continuously reorganized and transformed. This initial pattern is sustained and spread in a similar form throughout the system, resulting in more than one similar pattern. In this sense, redundancy is being built in by the operation of the system, and emergent order relies crucially on this redundancy (Goldstein, 1994b). The stability in chaotic behavior is thus crucially dependent upon redundant patterns—the retention of patterns that are similar to each other. Order emerges as a result of inefficiency and surplus resource.

New patterns can only emerge once small changes or random fluctuations have been amplified and spread across a system in a destabilizing manner as an essential prelude to some new form of stability. The system is then actually utilizing randomness, chance, and redundancy to produce a new stable pattern. Paradoxically, randomness, redundancy, and chance are causes of emergent order and hence sources of stability when systems operate in the space for novelty. Dissipative structures use symmetry-breaking disorder as the source of new order.

Therefore, two sources of stability exist in deterministic feedback systems. The first is constraint, provided by negative feedback, for example. The second, self-organization, is cooperative activity that spreads redundancy and produces emergent outcomes.

Dialectical Evolution

When a deterministic nonlinear feedback system operates in the stable and the unstable zones, it follows regular, predictable, and predetermined time paths toward an exact actualization of the equilibrium archetypes. However, in the strange attractor and the phase transition preceding it, the behavior of a system emerges through experiencing a dialectical process—a continual rearrangement of the paradox of coexisting stability and instability, the mixing and folding action within boundaries referred to above. Time and space matter and history is important because dissipative systems are not uniform but differentiated. The dialectic between stability and instability, change and constancy, is what drives the evolution of dissipative systems.

Causality and Predictability

If we consider the specific trajectory of a deterministic nonlinear feedback system operating in the strange attractor or the phase transition preceding it, it is clear that the links between a specific cause and a specific effect, between action and long-term outcome, are lost in the complex interaction between agents in the system and in the escalation of tiny changes in that interaction. The system's specific behavior cannot be designed or controlled;

instead, that behavior emerges. Because these causal links are lost, long-term predictability of specific outcomes is impossible. Note that I am not saying that no causal links exist. They are there but they cannot be traced either backward or forward in time. To be able to trace them we would have to be able to identify every tiny change that might escalate and measure all of those changes with infinite accuracy. Since these conditions are impossible to fulfill, we cannot trace cause-and-effect links when a system is in the space for novelty, and therefore we cannot make long-term predictions. However, it takes time for tiny changes to escalate. A system in the phase transition or the strange attractor has a momentum driving it from its past, and this makes short-term predictability possible even though long-term predictability of specific outcomes may be lost.

When a deterministic nonlinear feedback system is in the space for novelty, the usefulness of the notion of causality and hence the possibility of predictability is largely confined to the nature of the system rather than to its specific behavior. The notions of causality and the possibility of prediction do not have to be abandoned; rather, they must apply to different phenomena and at different levels. First, once the equations describing a system have been identified, the point at which each bifurcation occurs and the onset of chaos itself can be predicted. A causal link exists between the state of the control parameters and the general dynamics of the system—a predictable route from the stable zone through the chaos phase transition into the unstable zone.

Second, although we cannot determine what causes any specific emergent pattern in the space for novelty, we can talk about the causes of patterns in general and the causes of emergence itself (Goldstein, 1994b). The tuning up of the control parameters, the increase in the rates of information and energy flow through the system, and the iterative, interactive feedback of behavior in a nonlinear manner together lead to emergent chaotic patterns with their stable and unstable features.

Third, we may predict the potential, the archetypes, even though we will be unable to predict the form in which the archetypes will be realized. We may be able to quantitatively predict the boundaries of the strange attractor and to qualitatively say something about its shape and the archetypal behavior patterns it gives rise to but, in general, we can predict relatively little about the chaos archetype other than that it is a general potential pattern of behavior that is actualized by experience in an unpredictable manner. For specific systems, however, we will be able to say more. The weather system's archetypal behavior has already been commented on. Precisely what we are able to predict about archetypal behaviors therefore depends upon what we know specifically about the system we are talking about. But, always, we will be unable to predict the specific actualizations.

Despite specific long-term unpredictability, then, the behavior of nonlinear feedback networks operating in the space for novelty does display patterns, and even though they are irregular, they can be recognized and even predicted in archetypal form. This is a hopeful outcome, because where before we might have thought events to be random, we can now see that apparently random events might have recognizable, qualitative, irregular, archetypal patterns. We can understand and explain more than we could before, even though we have to recognize limits to predictability. The properties of deterministic nonlinear feedback networks are summarized in Figure 2.3.

Conclusion

The discoveries of the chaos attractor, the phase transition at its edge, and the dissipative structures that emerge in it are of major significance because they require a shift in the whole way we view the world. The dominant perspective of the physical and chemical world is one in which deterministic laws produce determinate outcomes: the universe moves according to some grand blueprint that leaves no room for the truly novel. We have much to discover

Figure 2.3. Properties of Deterministic Nonlinear Feedback Networks.

I   A space for creativity
   • A phase transition between stability and instability, either low-dimensional chaos
     or the phase transition before it or some other bifurcation, always in a sense at the
     edge of system disintegration
   • A state of paradox
   • Actualization of archetypes
   • Creative destruction
   • A critical point for the control parameters: rate, level of energy, information flow,
     degree of agent connectivity

II The sources of instability
   • Amplification of tiny changes

III The sources of stability
   • Constraint
   • Cooperation, redundancy, and self-organization

IV Dialectical evolution
   • Continual rearrangement of paradoxes of stability and instability

V   Causality and predictability
   • Specific long-term evolution is radically unpredictable but archetypal patterns and
     short-term changes are predictable

and much will seem novel to us, but it will have been there from
the beginning. The discoveries of chaos and dissipative structures
shift the perspective to a physical and chemical world in which
deterministic laws yield indeterminate outcomes: the universe
moves according to self-organizing processes that utilize instabilities to render systems changeable and capable of true novelty.
Much of what we can discover has not been there from the beginning but is yet to happen: the universe is truly paradoxical and
continually creative.

    We also find immediate implications for our understanding
of organizations. At the start of Part Two, I pointed out that scientific management and manipulative forms of behaviorism
assume that if a competent system, consisting of detailed sets of
deterministic rules, is designed in an environment that does not

change, and if everyone is persuaded to obey those rules, then it will be possible to realize a comprehensive shared intention relating to the future development of the organization: we will be able to get it to do what we want. We can now say quite unequivocally that this is not true, and we can say this because our new understanding of deterministic systems tells us that we can get such a system to do what we want only if what we want is an endless repetition of what it has already done. If we are at all interested in novelty, and that, after all, is one of the key features of life, the system will have to be designed to operate in the space for novelty, where its long-term future is unpredictable and emergent and hence cannot be intended in any comprehensive way.

However, human systems are not deterministic, much as some people would like them to be. They are quite definitely adaptive, and we turn now to see what the science of complexity has to say about such systems.

3

Adaptive Feedback Networks: *Self-Organizing Learning Systems at the Edge of Chaos*

At its simplest, an adaptive nonlinear feedback system is a network consisting of a large number of agents, each of whose behavior is determined by a shared schema consisting of a few rules that are fixed over time and that apply to all agents without exception. However, in contrast to deterministic nonlinear feedback systems, even the simplest adaptive system has some purpose, namely, to perform some task. It follows that, unlike agents in deterministic systems, agents in all adaptive systems adjust their behavior in light of its consequences for their purpose. In other words, adaptive systems learn, at the very least, in a simple single-loop manner, whereas deterministic systems do not. For example, a flock of birds is an adaptive system in that it consists of many agents, perhaps thousands, who follow simple rules for examining the behavior of their neighbors in order to fly in formation without crashing into each other. They learn by simple reflex conditioning to adjust their position if they get too close to each other.

72

This kind of behavior can be simulated using models of adaptive systems called cellular automata (Von Neumann, 1963; Burks, 1970; Wolfram, 1984). These and all other simulations of adaptive systems are computer models of networks of agents, where each agent is a schema taking the form of a computer program. That program is, of course, a set of operational instructions that determines how an agent inspects the state of each neighboring agent and responds to this state in order to perform some task. The instructions are coded in computer language in the form of bit strings, sequences of 0s and 1s—that is, arrangements of symbols. Organisms are constructed of genes, also an arrangement of symbols, which form a set of instructions to produce physical forms. Human minds are arrangements of imaginal symbols into operational rules, or schemas, that produce thoughts, feelings, and behaviors. Groups and organizations are networks of agents, all of whose thoughts, feelings, and behaviors are driven by such schemas, as we saw in Chapter One. It follows that bit strings, interacting with each other in a computer's memory, can model some aspects of interaction in living adaptive systems.

An illustration of cellular automata is given in Figure 3.1, and its resemblance to a human organization as depicted in Figure 1.3 is obvious.

Reynolds (1987) simulated the flocking behavior of birds with a computer program consisting of a network of moving agents, called Boids, each following universal rules requiring it to inspect its position and its neighbor's position and speed, and to alter its behavior in the light of that information. With no more than this, the Boids learned to flock, to part around obstacles, and to regroup afterward. No central program determined the flocking strategy and no agent was in charge, instructing the others what to do. Instead, a simple form of self-organizing learning produced the emergent outcome of flocking behavior. We can think of that emergent outcome as an implicate, archetypal property of

Figure 3.1. Cellular Automata Network with Three Agents.

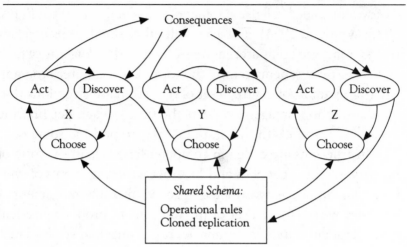

Schema: –Shared only
            –Reactive rules
            –Evolves through random mutation and competitive selection only

Agent
Structure: –None

a certain set of rules that is realized when the rules are systemati-
cally applied in an iterative, nonlinear-feedback manner.

Another example of the operation of an adaptive system is
provided by the trail-laying behavior of ants. Ants set off from their
nest in search of food, and those who find it lay down trails of a
chemical called a pheromone. Other ants learn to follow the trail
and find the food. This behavior has also been simulated using cellular automata called Vants. In the Vants simulation (Langton,
1986), each agent moved across a grid according to rules such as "If
you move into a square colored blue, then turn right and change
the color of that square to yellow." As they did this, the Vants left
colored trails that other Vants could follow just as ants do. The simulation started from a random position in which the Vants simply

moved without pattern. They had no "boss" or central program-mer once the table of rules had been established, and yet, through bottom-up self-organization, they produced emergent patterns of behavior out of the chaos of randomness—they learned to follow a trail. This bottom-up process and its emergent outcomes are fun-damental properties of the process of adaptive nonlinear feedback.

More Complex Forms of Adaptive Feedback Networks

Rather more complex adaptive systems consist of networks of agents that are capable of reproducing themselves and that have the much more general purpose of simply surviving and reproduc-ing. These agents' schemas are more complicated in that two sets of rules exist: (1) a set of operational instructions that require agents to examine their neighbors and act in a particular way and (2) a set of replicating instructions that require agents to copy their operational and replicating rules so as to create other agents. This is the cloning method of replication, which produces an exact copy of the parent agent subject only to random copying errors.

In these more complex systems, the opportunity to replicate is always constrained in some way by the availability of some kind of resource. The opportunity any agent gets to replicate is, there-fore, linked to the success that agent has in carrying out its oper-ational rules to perform the task of obtaining resources. This success defines an agent's fitness for survival, which can be mea-sured and then used in a fitness function to determine the agent's chances of selection for replication. The result is a neo-Darwinian replication process in which agents randomly mutate and are then competitively selected for replication according to their fitness for some purpose, that is, according to their fitness function.

Replication makes it possible for individual agents to develop different schemas. Any population of agents comes to consist of agents following partly their own unique individual schemas, partly schemas they share with a few others, and partly schemas, such as the replication rules, that they share with all other agents in the system. This differentiation of schemas opens up the possibility of changes in operational rules over time—that is, evolution. More complex learning thus becomes a possibility, but only through chance mutations.

Even More Complex Forms of Adaptive Feedback Networks

An even more complex adaptive system is one that employs crossover replication rather than cloning. Here the schema rules for reproduction require an agent to find a mate, copy half of its operational and replication rules, and then splice them to half of the mate's operational and replication rules. This mixing of schemas leads to much greater diversity in agent schemas than random mutation and competitive selection do. Highly differentiated, unique individual schemas can now evolve, as can partly and wholly shared schemas. Complex learning and evolution are not purely matters of chance changes selected by competition but instead flow from the competitive-cooperative process of cross-fertilization. Such cross-fertilization can take place in genes, ideas, or bit strings in a computer.

This kind of complex adaptive system is illustrated in Figure 3.2, and it can be compared with Figure 3.1 and also with Figure 1.3, which depicts a human organization.

An ecological system, such as the pond in my garden, is an example of a complex system that employs crossover replication. The pond system consists of interacting subsystems, each of which contains a number of agents. The fish constitute one such subsystem, with all the fish following mainly shared schema rules for swimming about the pond and finding a specified form of food. Frogs, newts, insects, and predator birds make up other subsystems that mainly behave according to their own subsystem-wide schemas. The subsystems interact with each other and coevolve,

Figure 3.2. Complex Adaptive System with Three Agents.

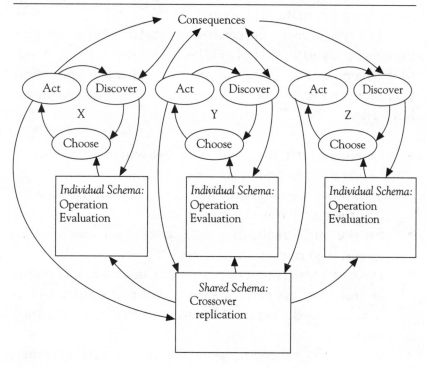

Schemas: –Individual and shared
–Reactive and anticipatory
–Shared: evolve through crossover replication
–Individual: changes through learning

Agent Structure: –None

each subsystem depending upon the others, at least to some extent, for food and survival. The frogs, for example, have evolved, or learned, a survival strategy involving the development of a sticky substance on the tongue that traps insects. However, if this strategy becomes too successful, few insects may be left and the frog population might decline. The whole system also shares some schema rules; for example, all agents share crossover replication. No doubt individual rules also exist for each fish, frog, and newt. In structural terms such a system is no different from one made up

of firms interacting in an industry or national economies interacting in an international system.

This type of ecosystem can be simulated on a computer using
the genetic algorithm (Holland, 1975; Goldberg, 1990), a network of computer programs that reproduce themselves according
to crossover replication rules. An example of such a simulation is
Ray's Tierra (1992). Here, the experimenter:

- Determined that the evolution of this system would initially
  be driven by random mutations.
- Set some general task for the agents and the requirement
  that they survive as a species, that is, replicate.
- Set the initial replication rules, a schema common to all
  agents, requiring agents to clone.
- Defined a fitness function, that is, the schedule of points
  awarded for task performance according to which agents
  were allocated computer time to carry out their replication
  rules.
- Introduced a constraint taking the form of scarce computer
  time that worked as follows: Agents were required to post
  their locations in the computer memory on a public notice
  board. Each agent was then called upon in turn, according
  to a circular queue, to receive a slice of computer time for
  carrying out its operational and replication tasks.
- Introduced a further constraint on the agents' life span.
  Agents were lined up in a linear queue according to their age
  and a "reaper" lopped off some of them, generally the oldest.
  However, by successfully executing their programs and thus
  increasing their fitness, agents could slow down their move
  up the linear queue, whereas flawed agents rose quickly to
  the top.

The agents, as part of a system, were then left to learn how to perform the task, that is, to develop their own survival strategies.

The simulation was set off by introducing a single agent consisting of eighty instructions. Within a short time the computer memory space was 80 percent occupied by agents, but then the reaper took over and prevented further population growth. After a while agents consisting of forty-five instructions appeared, but they were too short to replicate. They overcame this problem by attaching themselves to longer agents and borrowing some of their code in order to replicate. This strategy increased their fitness because they needed less computer time in their normal operations, leaving more time for replication using borrowed code. In other words, parasites had emerged.

However, if the parasites destroyed too many hosts in order to replicate, they also destroyed their own ability to replicate and declined. In the simulation, the parasites suffered periodic catastrophes. One of these catastrophes occurred because the hosts stopped posting their positions on the public notice board and in effect hid, so that the parasites could no longer find them. Some hosts had, thus, immunized themselves against parasites by using camouflage as a survival strategy. But in hiding, the hosts did not retain any note of their position in the computer memory, so they had to examine themselves to see if their position corresponded to the position that was being offered computer time before they could respond to that offer. This increased the time they needed for normal operations and reduced their time available for replication. Although it was not perfect, this strategy worked in a good enough way so that the parasites were nearly wiped out. The parasites then developed their own memories and did not need to consult the public posting board. Once again it was their turn to succeed.

Later, hyperparasites appeared in order to feed off the parasites. These were eighty instructions long, just like the hosts, but they had developed instructions to examine themselves for parasites and feed off the parasites by diverting computer time from them. The hyperparasites worked symbiotically by sharing reproduction code;

they could no longer reproduce on their own but required cooperation. Crossover replication had thus emerged spontaneously as a strategy for survival without anyone programming it in. This "sexual" cooperation was then exploited by opportunistic mutants in the form of tiny intruders who placed themselves between replicating hyperparasites and intercepted and used hyperparasite code for their own replication. The cheaters could thrive and replicate, although they were only twenty-seven instructions long. Next, the hyperparasites found a way to defeat the cheats, but not for long.

Note how this system produces periods of apparent stability followed by upheavals as particular strategies for the survival of either hosts or parasites emerge from spontaneous self-organizing processes that appear to be close to those of market competition. The experimenter is not introducing them and agents are not taking over and formulating a strategy. Instead, the strategies emerge unpredictably in a coevolutionary arms race that occurs in a dynamic, somewhat disorderly environment, driven partly by chance. First the strategy is to become small in size, but then parasites change the rules and the most successful strategy becomes feeding off others. Next the hosts change the rules and the better strategy is camouflage. The parasites change the rules of the game again and the best strategy becomes the development of a local memory. Competition and conflict emerge and the evolution of the system is driven by agents who are trying to exploit each other, but the game can go on only if neither side succeeds completely or for long in that exploitation.

Note also that this system produces diversity in a spontaneous, emergent way that has not been programmed in and that this is vital for the continuing evolution of the system and its ability to produce novelty. Through an internal process of spontaneous self-organization, this system produces an emergent predator-prey dynamic, behavior that is paradoxically both cooperative and competitive. In a similar manner the system spontaneously produces crossover replication, again an activity that is cooperative and competitive at the same time. Adaptive systems learn as a whole system and the introduction of predator-prey and cross-fertilization dynamics enhances the learning capacity of the total system, making it capable of generating more novelty and complexity. Both predator-prey dynamics and crossover replication introduce a tension between cooperation and competition—a kind of disorder, but one that clearly assists system-wide learning. Simpler systems that rely only on random mutations and competitive selection cannot produce the same degree of diversity, and it is critical levels of diversity that enhance further learning.

Three important questions arise from the points noted in the last two paragraphs. First, why are tension and disorder so important in complex learning? Second, is the process of evolution that is produced by the Tierra kind of simulation an example of punctuated equilibrium, with long periods of stasis, or equilibrium, before the system jumps suddenly to a new equilibrium? Or, third, is some rather different change process going on? We will look for an answer to the first question by exploring the nature of fitness landscapes and then will consider the second and third questions.

Fitness Landscapes

In a community of evolving systems, such as those in my garden pond, those in the Tierra simulation, and those in an industry or an international economy, the suitability of a survival strategy pursued by one system—its fitness—depends upon the survival strategies being employed by other related systems—their fitness. For example, we use antibiotics as a survival strategy against viruses, but the response of the viruses is to mutate resistant strains; our antibiotic survival strategy only works until the virus changes its survival strategy. One firm uses a strategy of low-cost standardization until another changes the rules and follows a strategy of customization. In each case what makes one fitter simultaneously damages the fitness of the other. It is also quite possible for one system to pursue a strategy that improves both its own and another's fitness. For example, a firm could adopt a strategy of close cooperation with a supplier that could benefit them both. The key point is that complex systems and their agents are always locked into interactive games, and the success of one play strategy always depends upon the play of others.

We can model the notion of fitness using the concept of a fitness landscape (Kauffman, 1993). For a particular system—call it X—the fitness landscape covers the array of all possible survival strategies open to it. The shape of that landscape is defined by the survival strategies that all other systems in the community are pursuing. Suppose that X adopts a particular survival strategy and the survival strategies of those it interacts with are such that X moves toward extinction—for example, X takes an antibiotic but the virus has mutated. That strategy is represented by movement into a valley. If another strategy improves system X's survival chances—X takes a new antibiotic—it could be represented by movement up toward a peak. If firm X pursues a strategy of low-cost standardization and no others are adopting customization, the strategy represents a peak. If some others are customizing, firm X's strategy leads it down into a valley. In this way, the fitness landscape is configured with a range of peaks and valleys, whose heights and depths represent just how advantageous or dangerous the strategy is in light of the given repertoire of strategies being pursued by the other systems. A fitness landscape is illustrated in Figure 3.3.

Assume that system X is evolving, that is, changing its survival strategy, while all the others continue to use the same survival strategies. Then X's evolution can be thought of as a journey across the fitness landscape, with the purpose being to find the highest peak. In other words, the process is one of trial and error to find a strategy, in relation to the strategies of the others, that maximizes X's survival chances.

Figure 3.3. A Fitness Landscape.

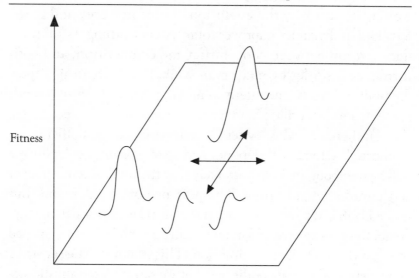

Fitness

If system X evolves in a steady, smooth manner, taking tiny experimental steps to produce progressive improvement, it is highly likely to get stuck on the first peak it comes to, because each subsequent smooth, small step from a peak can only lead downhill, reducing fitness. System X will avoid this, because the rule of logical incrementalism is to only take small steps that result in improvement, that is, to only go uphill. Consequently, system X will never discover a higher peak. Discovering a new peak requires accepting a decline in fitness and efficiency before a subsequent improvement. Because it is rather unlikely that the first peak encountered by a system will be the highest—the fittest— the procedure of moving smoothly across the landscape in small incremental steps is not an effective one.

However, if system X takes a rather erratic, disorderly walk in which it sometimes stumbles and rolls downhill, it is much less likely to get trapped in the foothills and much more likely to chance upon a new mountain. This is the same as saying that the system should not seek adaptation or equilibrium but should follow strategies that hold it away from them, at the edge of chaos. Now we can see just why the evolution of predator-prey and cross-fertilization dynamics improves total system learning. Both introduce tension between cooperation and competition, and both introduce disorder by mixing up symbols and creating unpredictability. This is equivalent to moving across the fitness landscape in a messy, erratic manner.

Furthermore, when system X changes its strategy, other interconnected systems will respond, and system X's fitness landscape will heave about, making it unlikely that the total system will ever settle into an equilibrium. The presence of disorder, and thus unpredictability, plays a very positive role in keeping a system more flexible and responsive and in preventing it from becoming trapped in a less than satisfactory situation. This is akin to the sensitive dependence on initial conditions that we saw in deterministic systems in that small erratic movements will allow a system to stumble into different areas of fitness. However, a system's sensitivity must be limited, for if small differences always allowed large changes, the system would have no stability and would fall apart. We can see that instability comes from sensitivity to small changes, but where does stability come from? This is where a notion called canalization, produced by self-organization, comes in.

Canalization and Lock-In

Kauffman (1991, 1993) has demonstrated how self-organization is closely related to a process of canalization or "lock-in." Some rules in an agent's schema tend to perpetuate or "lock in" a particular form of behavior. For example, if agent A has a rule stating that it will do z if agents B, C, or D do y, then A will perform z much more frequently than if the rule is to perform z only if B does u, C does w, and D does y. The first rule is canalizing—it relatively easily keeps B's behavior constant and stable, moving in a kind of fixed canal—but the second rule is not, because the conditions for sustaining stable behavior are more onerous. Canalizing rules, therefore, preserve constant behavior because they involve redundancies: continuity in A's behavior relies entirely on D in the second rule but not in the first, because C and D are doing the same job as D, at least as far as A is concerned. This duplication of functions gives stability to the system, making it much more robust in the face of turbulent change. This is, of course, anathema to efficiency, but it does promote greater stability because behavior is locked in, making a system rather insensitive to small changes in the environment.

When the agents following canalizing loops are linked by feedback, the feedback will tend to spread the behavior favored by the canalizing functions, providing walls of constancy where a network remains frozen. Thus, the canalizing rules in schemas spread order or stability; to put it another way, they spread redundancy, moving the same behavior around the system—and this redundancy creates islands of stability.

Evolution to the Edge of Chaos

In his development of the concept of fitness landscapes, Kauffman argues that agents and systems jointly tune their landscapes to operate at the edge of chaos. They design their own games and make their own rules, tuning the games they play to operate where they can find both sensitivity to small changes and the stability provide by the amplified redundancy of canalization. The state at the edge of chaos can be described in terms of fitness landscape shape; it occurs when landscapes are neither too smooth nor too rugged. Let us consider why this must be so.

Agents coevolve through a process of spontaneous self-organization, and as they do so they deform each other's fitness landscapes. If they all have smooth landscapes, it is easy for any agent to climb to its peak, but it is also easy for rivals to do the same thing. As each agent climbs its peak, however, it deforms the fitness landscapes of others, and because this is easy to do, the landscapes of all the agents will be constantly changing, rapidly and violently. We then observe huge avalanches of extinction. When it is easy for all agents to improve fitness, the system becomes highly unstable. If, on the other hand, the landscape is extremely rugged, with many low peaks (Kauffman, 1993), it will also be easy for each agent to climb a peak and deform the landscapes of others. Because the peaks are low, any agent reaching one can easily be displaced by others it interacts with. Once again we observe huge avalanches of extinction as the whole system changes violently.

In between, however, when the fitness landscapes of the agents are neither too smooth nor too rugged, the system will be changeable, but not violently so. We would then expect to observe many small avalanches of extinction and few large ones. Such a distribution is known as a power law. Because we observe such power laws in both natural and human systems (Kauffman, 1993), it is plausible to claim that all systems evolve to the edge of chaos. If the system moves away from the edge it will set off huge avalanches of extinction, and this will move it back to the edge again. Very smooth landscapes are highly redundant, and very rugged, or highly random, landscapes have no redundancy. The edge of chaos, therefore, has some canalization and redundancy, but not too much.

Punctuated Equilibrium or More Complex Learning Processes?

In the Tierra simulation, we saw periods of apparent stability in which hosts and parasites simply followed the same survival strategies until, suddenly, one or the other would change, with the new strategy very quickly supplanting the first one. This would require a response from the rivals; then, after a period of turbulent and revolutionary change, the system would calm down again into another stable period without much change in survival strategies.

According to some researchers (Gould, 1989), fossil records seem to indicate that this is how life evolved on Earth. This process has been described as punctuated equilibrium—the notion that systems tend to equilibrium, then one component of the system upsets things, and a furious readjustment follows that restores a new equilibrium. At least one important simulation (Hillis, 1992) provides evidence that would lead us to question whether this is what happens in complex adaptive systems.

Ramps and Punctuated Equilibrium

Ramps (Hillis, 1992) simulated a battle for survival between a host species called Ramps and parasites called anti-Ramps. This simulation revealed long periods of stasis in which each species followed more or less the same survival strategy, roughly maintaining its position, followed by sudden changes in strategy with short bursts of rapid progress for one of the two species. The system seemed to evolve in the manner postulated for punctuated equilibrium. Closer examination, however, revealed a pattern of development that is far more complicated than punctuated equilibrium.

In the simulation, a Ramp is a string of bits or binary numbers. At any one point in the simulation the string has a particular configuration reflecting the history of crossover replications it has been subjected to. Parts of the string are dominant in that they constitute the set of instructions that the agent is currently using to carry out its current survival strategy. This dominant schema, however, does not take up the whole string; it also has redundant bits not currently being used that we might call a recessive schema.

It was observed in the Ramp simulation that although the dominant elements stayed the same for some time and agents carried out their survival strategies in the same repetitive manner from generation to generation, the recessive part had movement, a kind of play. The redundant or recessive bits were changing as a result of crossover replication while the dominant bits were being passed on largely unchanged. All the change was concentrated in the recessive, redundant parts, those that were not required to perform the day-to-day tasks. These redundant parts in the Ramp simulation quietly accumulated into groupings of coadaptive bits until they reached a critical point; then they suddenly took over from the dominant schema. The operating instructions of the agents immediately changed across most of the population as they all pursued a new survival strategy.

It looked like a sudden jump from one equilibrium state to another, but this is not what was happening. Instead a random, rather messy, chance, competitive, and cooperative self-organizing process was going on behind the scenes set by the dominant schema, which finally produced major changes in the visible operating instructions of the population of agents. It was as if a shadow system was subversively plotting to replace the currently operating visible system.

To see this dynamic process as a sudden leap to a new equilibrium is to miss a point of major significance, namely, that behind the scenes, in the redundant part of the schemas, a very important evolution was taking place through a mechanism, crossover replication, that had disorderly, nonadaptive aspects. The parallel with Prigogine's theory of self-organization (Prigonine and Stengers, 1984) is clear. Prigogine's theory depicts a sequence starting with fluctuations that keep a system away from equilibrium adaptation to its environment; then amplification of these fluctuations causes some kind of instability throughout the system, followed by a critical point at which spontaneous self-organization suddenly produces an emergent new order. The parallel with the shadow informal system of an organization and the disruptive nature of double-loop learning is, I suggest, striking and will be taken up in later chapters.

The discussion of complex adaptive systems so far could quite easily convey the impression that these systems have an inherent ability to learn that is always positive. This impression must be corrected by stressing the possibility of maladaptive learning.

Ackley's AL and Maladaptive Learning

In a very sophisticated simulation known as AL (Ackley and Littman, 1992), an artificial world was created in which agents with neural network brains had to avoid obstacles and find food. Initially they had to rely on trial and error to discover that plants were good to eat. That information was converted into a bias for a particular kind of action—a tendency to approach plants. In later generations this tendency to approach plants became automatic; the neural networks passed on in replication were configured in a way that brought it about. What had originally been learning became instinct and atrophied into skillful behavior, below the level of the agents' "awareness." This happened because from time to time mutations in the operational schema caused some agents to approach food automatically. This was a fitness criterion that was rewarded, and those agents reproduced more.

Similar instinctual behaviors to avoid carnivores developed, constituting a submerged, instinctual element of inherited neural networks, a kind of "unquestioned assumption." However, because the agents avoided carnivores, they rarely came into contact with them. Therefore, the learned avoidance of carnivores atrophied. Indifference and even a positive view of carnivores evolved because they were so rarely encountered. This lack of encounters also deprived the carnivores of food, leading to a reduction in the population and even less chance of encounters. What happened was that a well-adapted operational schema was shielding an atrophied or maladaptive evaluation schema. Their efficient actions led the agents into the illusion that carnivores either were of no consequence or were benign. This put the agents at the mercy of any chance shift in the balance of the population or in the operational schema. A sudden chance surge of carnivores or a tendency for agents to approach them would tip the balance and allow carnivores to attack agents, perhaps even driving them to extinction.

This simulation demonstrates the dangers of adaptation, which can be seen as a form of skilled incompetence that includes acting upon unquestioned assumptions and using atrophied learning skills. The simulation also points to the paradoxical nature of the system's evolution: shielding by the operational schema frees up neural networks to do other things and to become more efficient, but such efficiency carries with it the danger of too much order and adaptation, reducing learning and therefore effectiveness.

The Nature of Complex Adaptive Systems

A great many more simulations of complex adaptive systems have been done and written up (see, for example, Levy, 1992; Waldorp, 1992; Casti, 1994; Cohen and Stewart, 1994; Goodwin, 1994; Kauffman, 1995), and they all convey much the same message that we have considered above. The key features of such systems are summarized in Figure 3.4 (Gell-Mann, 1994); their properties will be reviewed in the next section. The close resemblance to the depiction of an organization given in Figure 1.4 is immediately obvious. The key difference lies in the structure of the agents: in human systems agents have emotions but in simulations of complex adaptive systems they do not.

Properties of Complex Adaptive Systems

In the last chapter we saw that deterministic nonlinear feedback systems are driven by fixed schemas that are universally applicable to all the agents that comprise them. Neither the system nor its agents has any purpose and the agents have no capability for

Figure 3.4. Key Features of a Simulated Complex Adaptive System.

A complex adaptive system:
- Has a basic purpose of performing tasks and surviving
- Consists of networks of large numbers of interacting agents
- Interacts with an environment consisting of other complex adaptive systems and therefore coevolves
- Interacts in an iterative, nonlinear manner
- Discovers, that is, acquires information about the systems constituting its environment and information about the consequences of its own interaction with those systems by employing feedback
- Chooses, that is, exercises a kind of free will to identify and select regularities in the feedback information it acquires and then condenses those regularities into a schema or model of its world, in effect selecting one of a number of competing models that might "explain" the regularities and yield effective rules of behavior for coping with that world
- Acts according to its schema rules in relation to the systems that are its environment
- Discovers the responses its action provokes, as well as the consequences of those responses
- Uses this information to adapt its behavior, that is, to perform simple or single-loop learning
- Revises its schema so as better to adapt, that is, to perform complex or double-loop learning

The key to the whole process lies in the schemas, as follows:
- Agents may have unique individual schemas.
- Agent behavior may also be conditioned by common shared schemas.
- Schemas may consist of simple reaction rules, more complex rules requiring formation of expectations and taking anticipatory action, performance evaluation rules, and rules for evaluating schema rules themselves.

Agent's internal structure is as follows:
- None

sensing and evaluating their own or their neighbors' states. Therefore, no learning occurs of the simple type in which agents adjust their behavior according to that of neighboring agents, nor does any complex learning occur in the sense of altering the schema: feedback operates mechanistically with a state in one time period determining the state in the next. The key property of such systems is that very simple schemas can generate very complicated behaviors; at critical points in that complication, in a particular space (as it were), the system uses instability in a process of spontaneous self-organization to produce emergent novel patterns of behavior. These new patterns of behavior emerge unpredictably, without any prior overall design.

The first part of this chapter has described the simulation of adaptive feedback networks with a purpose: survival through performance of some task. Agents' behavior is driven by both individual and shared schemas that involve sensing and evaluating their own and their neighbors' behavior. These schemas change over time though learning processes. The differences between deterministic and adaptive systems are summarized in Figure 3.5.

Despite these differences, however, complex adaptive networks display much the same kind of key properties as deterministic systems:

1. Space for novelty: the paradox of stability and instability
2. The source of instability
3. The source of stability
4. Dialectical evolution
5. Causality and predictability

We will now review each of these properties.

Space for Novelty: The Paradox of Stability and Instability

Studies of adaptive systems show that they are creative when they occupy what we might think of as a space for novelty at the edge of chaos. What does this mean?

The Phase Transition at the Edge of Chaos. The term *chaos* tends to be used in a rather different way by those writing about adaptive systems and those writing about deterministic systems. The

Figure 3.5. Key Features of Deterministic and Adaptive Nonlinear Feedback Networks.

	Schemas	Nature of the Phase Transition	Process and Product
Deterministic Systems			
Chaos and dissipative system theory	Small number of fixed rules applied to all agents mechanistically without learning	Low-dimensional deterministic chaos + dissipative structures	Mechanistic, interactive feedback producing spontaneously self-organizing patterns
Adaptive Systems			
Cellular automata	Small number of reactive rules that change through random mutation and selection according to feedback on action success. Single-loop learning	Edge of chaos	Self-organization· producing emergent patterns
Genetic algorithms	Large number of reactive and anticipatory rules that change through crossover replication. Double-loop learning	Maximal effective and potential complexity	Self-organization producing emergent patterns

latter use the term in the very precise mathematical sense of low-dimensional deterministic chaos. This is a particular form of bounded instability that results from the sensitivity of a deterministic system to some, but not all, tiny changes in initial conditions or control parameters. That sensitivity leads to a combination of underlying recognizable, self-similar patterns in unpredictable specific behavior. This is clearly not the same as the popular usage, in which *chaos* means utter confusion. In the literature on adaptive systems, the term *chaos* is used to describe a state in which behavior is sensitive to all tiny changes in control parameters, and such sensitivity leads to the complete loss of recognizable pattern. This is high-dimensional chaos, which has much the same meaning as in the popular usage.

However, researchers studying complex adaptive systems have shown that such systems display a phase transition at the edge of this high-dimensional chaos similar to the one that sometimes is displayed at the edge of low-dimensional chaos in deterministic systems, including the following:

- Kauffman (1993) showed that Boolean networks (types of cellular automata) are capable of continuous variety and novelty only when agents are connected richly enough to drive the system to the edge of chaos but not so much that they drive it beyond into chaos. He also showed that when the degree of diversity in agent schemas was low, the system tended to stability; when it was tuned up, the system was driven to the edge of chaos; and when diversity became too great, the system was driven into high-dimensional chaos.

- Langton (1992) showed that cellular automata are capable of novelty at intermediate levels of the lambda parameter, which measures the rate of information flow and retention in a system. At these intermediate levels, information moves freely around a system but not so freely as to render information retention impossible.

- Wolfram (1984, 1986) independently identified four categories of behavior for cellular automata: stable, periodic, chaotic without pattern, and richly complex. A system displays continuing variety only when behavior is richly complex.
- Gell-Mann (1994) showed that complex adaptive systems function when effective and potential complexity is maximal, a state between the ordered and disordered zones of operation. I will define effective and potential complexity below.

The notion of bounded instability thus applies to adaptive feedback systems as it did to deterministic systems: the former is a state that has both pattern and unpredictability and is described as the edge of high-dimensional chaos; the latter is also a state with both pattern and unpredictability and is described as low-dimensional chaos, or the phase transition at the edge of that chaos. Both deterministic and adaptive nonlinear feedback systems can produce novelty only in the space between stability and instability.

As mentioned above, some researchers use the term *complexity* to define the space for novelty. Gell-Mann (1994) gives a useful clarification of the different meanings of complexity and in doing so provides insight into the nature of the space for novelty. He distinguishes between algorithmic, effective, and potential complexity. Suppose that a system operates in an environment that is highly disorderly in the sense that it is random. Information about that environment is so irregular that its description cannot be compressed or summarized, only reproduced in full. Few if any regularities will occur, so any schema that might be extracted will be short and of limited usefulness in the adaptation task because it will be able to encompass only a limited part of the environment.

In other words, at this extreme the information content is enormous (in technical language, the algorithmic information complexity is maximal), but only a short computer program (schema) is required to describe the regularities. If effective complexity is defined in terms of the length of the schema, then it is low when the environment is random, although the algorithmic information complexity is very high. For example, the schema might be a mean and a standard deviation that will allow the boundaries around the environment's behavior to be established, but nothing more. This obviously has a very limited usefulness in terms of guiding behavior. A system trying to adapt or learn in these circumstances will not be able to extract many regularities, nor will it be able to predict much in specific terms. Randomness equals high information complexity but low computational or low effective complexity and therefore has a poor ability to develop effective behavioral schemas.

Suppose now that a system operates in an environment that is highly orderly, in the sense that the systems constituting it behave in a perfectly regular manner. It will be very easy to compress, or summarize, the behavior of such an environment. A short computer program, or schema, can reproduce it. Here, where the algorithmic information complexity is very low, the effective complexity—the length of the schema that captures the regularity—is also very low. In this situation, however, nothing much happens, nothing much changes, and little learning or adapting is needed.

A complex adaptive system, therefore, can adapt only when effective complexity is sizable, that is, in "conditions that are intermediate between order and disorder" (Gell-Mann, 1994, p. 116). Although we started off considering effective complexity as a property of the environment, note how it has become an essential feature of a system adapting in an environment: effective complexity is defined in terms of the length of the adapting system's schema, and as such it is an internal property of the system just as much as it is a feature of the environment. This insight, along with the notion that systems coevolve, should lead us to seriously question the dominant way of thinking that distinguishes sharply between a system and its environment and explains a system's behavior in terms of adaptation to changes in the environment.

However, effective complexity has to be supplemented by the notion of potential complexity. This is the potential that complex adaptive systems possess for "creating a great deal of new effective complexity" (Gell-Mann, 1994, p. 70) from only a modest change in their schemas. An example of this is provided by humans, whose genome (biological schema) varies only slightly from that of apes but who have much greater effective complexity in terms of behavioral schemas.

Thus, the space for creativity in an adaptive system is a phase transition at the edge of chaos, at the edge of system disintegration. It is characterized by paradox in which archetypal behavior is actualized through a process of creative destruction that occurs when a system's control parameters are at critical levels. We will consider each of these further elements of the space for novelty.

A State of Paradox. Bounded instability is an essentially paradoxical space of simultaneous stability and instability. This basic paradox is expressed in various simulations of complex adaptive systems as follows:

- Information both flows freely and is retained.
- Schemas display both diversity and conformity; they are neither too long nor too short.
- Agents are richly but not too richly interconnected.
- Behavior is both predictable and unpredictable.

- Behavior has pattern but that pattern is irregular.
- Freedom of shape and movement exist, but within the constraints of boundaries and overall archetypes.
- There is stability in the archetypal form, but instability in the actualization of that form.
- Efficient operational schemas mask maladaptive evaluation schemas. This allows more efficient performance of the current primary task but it renders the system vulnerable to a change in the strategies pursued by any other system it interacts with. Hence, efficiency and effectiveness exist in tension with each other.
- Destruction takes the form of amplifying feedback that breaks symmetries, and creation takes the form of spontaneous self-organization that produces an emergent new order.
- Dominant schemas sustain the orderly performance of the current primary task, the current survival strategy; recessive schemas develop a replacement for dominant schemas and thus undermine and subvert them. The space for novelty is, therefore, characterized by the tension between sustaining the status quo and replacing it.
- Both competition and cooperation exist.
- Both order and disorder exist.
- Fitness landscapes are intermediate between smooth and rugged.
- Fluctuations keep a system away from equilibrium while canalization or lock-in keep a system on a spatial or temporal path that, in a sense, takes the system to equilibrium.
- The same complexity is a property of both a system's external environment and its internal nature, in the sense that its schema models the environment it interacts with.

Actualization of Archetypes. In the space for novelty, schema rules contain an implicate, immanent order taking the form of archetypes that are unfolded, or made explicit, by the iterative operation of nonlinear feedback. For example, some rules lead to flocking behavior, whereas others always produce trail-laying behavior. The actualization of the archetype is sensitively dependent upon the precise interactive experience of the system.

Creative Destruction. In the phase transition, a dominant symbol system or schema drives the performance of the current primary task, whereas movements in a recessive symbol system or schema prepare possible replacements for that dominant schema. In this sense the space for novelty involves one system operating in an undermining, potentially subversive manner in relation to the other. Creative change is made possible by destruction. The definition of the phase transition as a point of self-organized criticality with large and small extinction events again underlines the intimate connection between creation and destruction.

A Critical Point for Control Parameters. Complex adaptive systems are driven by three control parameters: the rate of information flow through the system, the richness of connectivity between agents in the system, and the level of diversity within and between the schemas of the agents. As these control parameters are tuned up, adaptive nonlinear feedback networks pass from stability through a phase transition at the edge of chaos into true chaos— internally unconstrained, patternless instability. A system occupies the space for endless variety, novelty, and creativity only at critical points in parameter values with enough disorder to prevent the system from becoming trapped in some local equilibrium to the detriment of its long-term development to higher fitness peaks, but also with sufficient containing structure and order to prevent it from falling apart into patternless behavior.

The Source of Instability

Adaptive systems operating in the phase transition at the edge of chaos display instability for three reasons.

Sensitive Dependence on Initial Conditions. When an adaptive system operates in the phase transition, small perturbations in the environment can be amplified by positive feedback to force major changes in the system's evolution, making its future unpredictable (Rasmussen, Knudsen, Feldberg, and Hindsholm, 1990; Cohen and Stewart, 1994).

Competition. Competitive interaction between coevolving systems makes it highly unlikely that they will settle into any equilibrium state. Predator-prey dynamics are inherently destabilizing. Furthermore, the adoption of erratic, unstable behavior patterns that rivals are unable to predict is a powerful survival strategy that is bound to be discovered by learning agents. Crossover replication is partly competitive; it also mixes up the code of two agents, making it a matter of chance, to some extent, whether any individual "offspring" resulting from this process will be an improvement.

Exposure to Creative Tension Set Up by Recessive Schemas. The recessive schema of a system develops potential replacements for the dominant schema that sustains current stability. This tension between two different components within the same schema, with diametrically opposed tasks, is a source of instability. It does, however, also provoke vital learning processes behind the facade of a stable dominant schema.

The Source of Stability

Three sources of stability occur when a system occupies the space for novelty; they are the opposites of the three forces of instability.

Constraints. The first source of stability is a complex system's built-in constraint on the operation of amplifying feedback and its escalation of tiny changes. This constraint may take the form of negative feedback. Another constraint takes the form of canalization, which basically prevents a system from responding in a major way to tiny changes. Canalization spreads redundancy as the same behavior is spread around the system; this redundancy creates islands of stability. In the organizational literature, this is referred to as loose coupling, a form of interaction that preserves flexibility and thus stability in the face of major change (Perrow, 1972, 1984).

Cooperation. Crossover replication is a source of instability in that it mixes up code from one generation to another, but it is also a source of stability in that successful code tends to cohere into blocks that are unlikely to be scrambled by the mixing process. Although the predator-prey dynamic is mainly destabilizing, it may also introduce stability, because in order to survive in competition, agents may evolve cooperative strategies in which the survival of one depends upon the survival of others. This is canalization or lock-in.

The major cooperative source of stability, however, lies in a system's inherent ability to self-organize in a spontaneous manner, in other words, to cooperate rather than competing and thus to adapt to change through a process of learning.

Protection from Creative Tension by Dominant Schemas. Simulations of complex adaptive systems also highlight another source of stability—dysfunctional learning. When agents succeed in achieving a very high level of adaptation, that is, when their operational schemas are operating with great efficiency, complex learning skills become atrophied. Efficient operational schemas tend to shield maladaptive evaluation schemas, resulting in a kind of skilled incompetence, the continued acting upon unquestioned assumptions. Efficient actions lead agents into an illusion of a predictable environment that puts them at the mercy of any chance shift in that environment. So when the operational schemas of agents are very efficient, that is, when dominant schemas face no challenge, complex learning skills become atrophied. Systems may thus display stability because of some failure in the learning process.

Dialectical Evolution

The simulations indicate quite clearly how linear, progressive incremental patterns of evolution result in systems becoming caught on local fitness peaks, where they are highly likely to be destroyed by the novel strategies developed by other systems. Instead, the most effective evolutionary path is a dialectical one, driven by the tension between contradictory forces, in which these forces are continually rearranged. Thus, the dialectical process of cooperation and competition, order and disorder, leads to more effective learning. This happens because such a process keeps a system in some state of fluctuation, preventing it from being trapped in a local optimum, an equilibrium state that is less than universally optimal, whose predictability opens the system up to exploitation by rivals.

A far less obvious dialectic also exists between the currently dominant way of behaving embodied in the observable operating instructions of agents in a system, on the one hand, and the recessive, redundant, currently concealed ways of behaving on the other. While the dominant mode of operation is addressing the task in an obviously orderly manner, more complex double-loop learning is occurring behind the scenes in a part of the system that is in continuous flux and is not adapted. This behind-the-scenes learning, involving a subversive process of cooperation and competition, plays the role of unsettling the system, disturbing it from stable equilibrium, and keeping it at the edge of chaos. A feedback network seems to encourage the development of the recessive, redundant bits until they reach a critical point, when they suddenly take over so that the operating instructions of the agents change across most of the population at the same time. It is as if a shadow system is subversively plotting to replace the currently operating visible system.

Causality and Predictability

Simple systems generate outcomes that are either highly predictable or completely unpredictable: either they have clear-cut links between cause and effect or no links occur and behavior is random. Any single complex system is the opposite of this: its behavior is predictable in some respects but unpredictable in others. In some cases, causal links can be identified; in others, the sequence of causal links tends to become lost in the complexity of interactions. A community of systems made up of complex subsystems, all of which are evolving schemas for describing and predicting one another's behavior, is obviously highly unlikely to approach a steady state, yet simple observation shows that these communities normally display impressive degrees of order. So what is predictable and what is not?

Complex systems produce highly stable generic forms (Goodwin, 1994), category features (Cohen and Stewart, 1994), or taxonomies. Thus global patterns, broad category features, or archetypes are predictable when a system is complex. However, the specific forms are radically unpredictable because they are always open to unexpected novelty. This radical unpredictability is the foundation of system creativity (Goodwin, 1994). In complex systems, agents design their actions utilizing short-term rationality, but system-wide, long-term patterns or strategies emerge.

Thus, once we understand the configuration of a network and its dynamics, we can predict the generic shape of the behavior that system will produce and identify the archetypes associated with it. In principle, this enables us to design a particular type of network in order to generate selected kinds of archetypal behavior. However, within this generic shape, the realized form of the archetype cannot be intended by the designer of the network. Instead, the specific form emerges through the spontaneous self-organization of the agents—through actual specific experience—and is thus unpredictable. In principle, we can design a network with certain archetypal potentials, establish the conditions required for it to be set at threshold conditions, and push it into the phase transition of bounded instability, but we cannot determine the specific form of the generic pattern. That specific form will emerge. The creative, innovative, novel aspects of any realized version of a generic form are radically unpredictable.

So we can *predict the dynamics* and explain why they occur as soon as we know the condition of the control parameters. Also, we can predict that self-organization will occur in the phase transition at the edge of chaos and that it will produce some emergent pattern. Furthermore, according to Kauffman, we can predict that at least some adaptive networks will evolve to the edge of chaos through feedback, whether they start in the stable or the unstable regime.

In addition, we can *predict and recognize archetypal behaviors*. For example, the particular schema specified in the Boids simulation discussed above will always produce the archetypes of flocking behavior, but if we want to know the precise form this flocking will take, we have to run the program. The particular schema specified in the Vants simulation always produces the archetype of trail-laying behavior, but if we want to know which trail will be laid, we have to run the program. Note that this kind of prediction is not based on cause-and-effect reasoning; it is based on repeated experience with a particular kind of schema. Thus, one kind of prediction requires us to know a cause-and-effect link, whereas another form of prediction relies on past experience of the general forms of behavior produced by a particular system. This latter kind of prediction depends on pattern recognition ability, the ability to reason by analogy and intuition, rather than on analytic reasoning.

Even where prediction is impossible, experience of the operation of a system allows us to build up a capacity for recognizing patterns in the behavior of that system as they emerge, provided, of course, that patterns exist. The presence of structure and pattern at the edge of chaos, though unpredictable in specific form, makes it possible to cope even in the absence of predictability. If we cannot design a long sequence of actions with known outcomes, once we recognize a pattern we can at least design our next action in a sensible manner. The properties of nonlinear feedback systems are summarized in Figure 3.6. By comparing this figure with Figure 2.3, you can see how adaptive systems have the same general properties as deterministic systems. What is added is an additional control parameter and further sources of both stability and instability.

Figure 3.6. Properties of Adaptive Nonlinear Feedback Networks.

I   A space for creativity
   • A phase transition between stability and instability at the edge of system disintegration
   • A state of paradox
   • Actualization of archetypes
   • Creative destruction
   • A critical point for the control parameters of energy and information flow, agent connectivity, schema diversity

II The sources of instability
   • Amplification of tiny changes
   • Competition
   • Exposure to creative tension set up by play in recessive schemas

III The sources of stability
   • Constraint
   • Cooperation and redundancy
   • Protection from creative tension by dominant schemas

IV Dialectical evolution
   • Small incremental, progressive changes are a poor learning strategy but tension between contradictory forces provokes more effective learning

V   Causality and predictability
   • Specific long-term evolution is radically unpredictable but archetypal patterns and short-term changes are predictable

Conclusion

Over the past few decades, scientists have been exploring the properties of complex adaptive systems, primarily in biology and ecology, their concern being to explain how life might have originated in a prebiotic soup of chemicals and then evolved to the complex forms we find today. Complexity theory thus seeks to explain how systems might start from a random or disorderly state and yet produce complex order. Computer simulations of complex adaptive networks demonstrate that it is possible for the order of new survival strategies to emerge from disorder through a process of spontaneous self-organization. The order arises from nonlinear feedback interaction between agents, where each agent "does its own thing" without any overall blueprint or prior program. The computer simulations suggest that nonlinear feedback, operating at critical points in system parameter values, causes spontaneous self-organization among agents, which in turn causes new patterns of behavior. It seems that a self-organizing capability is an inherent property of a complex adaptive system operating in certain conditions.

PART THREE

MAPPING THE SCIENCE OF COMPLEXITY ONTO ORGANIZATIONS

Chapter One set out in Figure 1.4 the key features of human systems, and Chapter Three did the same in Figure 3.4 for the complex adaptive system simulations that complexity scientists have been studying. These figures are reproduced here (Exhibit 1) to show how closely the key features of the complex adaptive simulations map onto human systems.

Comparison of these two figures makes it quite clear that human systems have the same basic structure as all other complex adaptive systems, and therefore we would expect them all to display a phase transition at the edge of chaos that contains both disorder and constraint on that disorder. The disorder is required to prevent the system from being trapped on a local fitness peak and the order is required to keep it from falling apart. The only difference between complex systems in general and human systems consists of the four points that relate to the specifically human nature of the agents in a human system. Consider now, in

Exhibit 1. Comparison of Key Features of a Human System and a Complex Adaptive System.

Key Features of a Human System	*Key Features of a Complex Adaptive System*
A human system:	A complex adaptive system:
• Has a basic purpose of performing tasks and surviving	• Has a basic purpose of performing tasks and surviving
• Consists of networks of large numbers of interacting agents	• Consists of networks of large numbers of interacting agents
• Interacts with an environment consisting primarily of other human systems and therefore coevolves	• Interacts with an environment consisting of other complex adaptive systems and therefore coevolves
• Interacts in an iterative, nonlinear manner	• Interacts in an iterative, nonlinear manner
• Discovers, that is, acquires information about the systems constituting its environment and information about the consequences of its own interaction with those systems by employing feedback	• Discovers, that is, acquires information about the systems constituting its environment and information about the consequences of its own interaction with those systems by employing feedback
• Chooses, that is, exercises an element of free will to identify and select regularities in the feedback information it acquires and then condenses those regularities into a schema or model of its world, in effect selecting one of a number of competing models that might "explain" the regularities and yield effective rules of behavior for coping with that world	• Chooses, that is, exercises a kind of free will to identify and select regularities in the feedback information it acquires and then condenses those regularities into a schema or model of its world, in effect selecting one of a number of competing models that might "explain" the regularities and yield effective rules of behavior for coping with that world
• Acts according to its schema rules in relation to the systems that are its environment	• Acts according to its schema rules in relation to the systems that are its environment
• Discovers the responses its action provokes, as well as the consequences of those responses	• Discovers the responses its action provokes, as well as the consequences of those responses
• Uses this information to adapt its behavior, that is, to perform simple or single-loop learning	• Uses this information to adapt its behavior, that is, to perform simple or single loop-learning
• Revises its schema so as better to adapt, that is, to perform complex or double-loop learning	• Revises its schema so as better to adapt, that is, to perform complex or double-loop learning

**Exhibit 1. Comparison of Key Features of a
Human System and a Complex Adaptive System, Cont'd.**

Key Features of a Human System	*Key Features of a Complex Adaptive System*
The key to the whole process lies in the schemas, as follows:	The key to the whole process lies in the schemas, as follows:
• Agents have unique individual schemas.	• Agents may have unique individual schemas.
• Agent behavior is also conditioned by common culture, a schema shared with all or some other agents.	• Agent behavior may also be conditioned by common shared schemas.
• Schemas consist of simple reaction rules, more complex rules requiring formation of expectations and taking anticipatory action, performance evaluation rules, and rules for evaluating schema rules themselves.	• Schemas may consist of simple reaction rules, more complex rules requiring formation of expectations and taking anticipatory action, performance evaluation rules, and rules for evaluating schema rules themselves.
Agent's internal structure is as follows:	Agent's internal structure is as follows:
• Agents and groups of agents get caught up in sequences of responses driven by emotion and aspiration, inspiration and anxiety, compassion and avarice, honesty and deception, imagination and curiosity.	• None
• Agents share a common purpose but also develop their own individual mental purposes, leading to tension between conformity and individualism.	
• Some agents are, or become, more able and/or more powerful than others and apply force and persuasion, whereas others follow.	
• Agents are conscious and self-aware, that is, they can adopt the role of observer and think systemically.	

a very general way, whether this difference makes it pointless to map the properties of complex adaptive systems in general onto organizations in particular. In other words, is it possible for these four characteristics to change the dynamics of a human system so much that they eliminate the phase transition or remove the disorder in the transition without removing the creativity? To put it another way, can humans be creative in an intentional, harmonious manner? Or have they no option but to rely on paradoxical operation at the edge of system disintegration?

The Presence of Paradox

Tensions between (1) creative inspiration and the need to contain the anxiety aroused by it, (2) rationality and all the other emotions humans feel, and (3) belonging to a group and being an individual are all examples of the paradoxes to be found in human systems and, as we have seen, the presence of paradox is a key feature of operation at the edge of chaos. Including these peculiarly human aspects of agents can only make interactions more complex and unpredictable and render the dialectical evolution more novel and surprising. They represent an increase in potential complexity. These human factors certainly cannot overcome the need for a paradoxical space for novelty, nor can they overcome sensitivity to tiny changes, because they are themselves paradoxes and mechanisms for escalating tiny changes.

Power Differentials and the
Roles of Leaders and Followers

Can agents who acquire more power than the rest remove the connection between disorder and creativity? Perhaps creativity in the rest of nature has to rely on some kind of mess, but is it possible for powerful human leaders to make it different in human systems so that creativity can come about in an orderly, planned manner? The answer to this question seems to be "yes and no." Let us take the "no" part first.

A powerful agent could remove the need for disorder in the creative process altogether by consistently identifying higher fitness peaks in the fitness landscape of the system being led. Is this possible? The answer must be no, for no matter how powerful, determined, or brilliant any agent is, that agent will be unable to consistently identify higher fitness peaks, simply because the shape of the landscape is being determined by others in a very complex cooperative and competitive interaction. Other powerful agents in competing systems will be trying to do exactly what the powerful agent is trying to do, namely, to identify the fitness peaks. They will make it impossible for each other to succeed in their endeavors. Power differentials will, therefore, have to be exercised in the space for novelty at the edge of chaos, where both order and disorder are present, if a system is to remain changeable and creative. Furthermore, a system that is part of a competitive-cooperative suprasystem and wishes to survive will have to remain creative simply because others will keep changing the rules for survival. The need for some degree of disorder does not disappear simply because some agents lead and others follow. Now let us take the "yes" part of the answer.

A few powerful agents could face the disorder of the creative space and shield followers from it. All the double-loop learning required to reach new fitness peaks would then have to be performed by the small number of powerful agents, while the others simply carried out instructions until their schemas were changed by the most powerful agents. We would expect this to reduce the capacity of the system as a whole to learn, but this might not be the case if anxiety levels were reduced by this use of power differentials. Nevertheless, it does seem likely that a small group of powerful agents would have more difficulty in escaping from the kind of maladaptive learning behaviors exhibited in some of the simulations surveyed above. We will consider later the psychological effects of a few holding all the creativity and anxiety for the many.

What we see, then, is that power differentials cannot remove the fundamental dynamics of a nonlinear feedback system, but they will affect its learning capacity in one way or another. In fact, the powerful can push their whole system away from the edge of chaos into the stable zone by setting up systems of behavior for other agents and inspiring or forcing them to obey. However, such systems will then be incapable of novelty and will eventually fall to rivals who change the fitness landscape—perhaps the centrally planned societies of the former Eastern bloc are evidence of this.

The Impact of Consciousness

Could a perceptive agent move into the role of observer, think systemically, and identify a higher fitness peak toward which the system could then move intentionally, making disorder unnecessary? The complex system simulations surveyed in previous chapters strongly suggest that this is not possible. The fitness landscape for any system is determined by the strategies of the other systems with which it interacts. Every time the other systems change their survival strategies, the fitness landscape changes. Complex system simulations consistently show the spontaneous development of cooperative and competitive structures, taking the form of cross-over replication or cross-fertilization and predator-prey dynamics. Some of the other systems with which our observer agent's system interacts are therefore highly likely to be competitors. Simulations show that competitors soon learn the advantages of adopting surprising moves that their rivals cannot predict. Changes in agents and systems resulting from cross-fertilization, which depends partly on chance, are also, by definition, not fully predictable. Furthermore, if systemic thinking is possible for an agent in one system, it is likely to be possible for some agents in rival systems. They too will be trying to foresee higher fitness peaks and design strategies to climb them, but their ability to do so will depend upon the predictability of the strategies that the first agent is adopting. Every move each agent makes deforms the fitness landscape of the others.

In the presence of competition, then, it will be impossible for observers in any system, even the most powerful of systemic thinkers, to foresee how the fitness landscape is going to heave about, because other powerful competing systemic thinkers will be doing their utmost to make this impossible. Without such fore-sight, higher fitness peaks cannot be intentionally identified. In fact, it is not at all clear that systemic thinking, adoption of the observer role, will be stabilizing at all. It seems even more likely that as agents in rival systems compete using systemic thinking, they will increase the rate at which fitness landscapes heave about. Systemic thinking may well increase the disorder rather than remove the need for it. The only way around this would be for powerful systemic thinkers to agree to cooperate for the common good and abandon all competitive behavior. Human history to date leads us to be rather skeptical of this possibility, at least for the foreseeable future, and the experience of centrally planned economies raises some doubt about attempts to remove competi-tion from a system altogether. It seems that we can escape the conclusion that we constitute complex systems driven by a coop-erative and competitive dynamic only if we persuade ourselves to believe in some kind of utopia of either the extreme centrally planned kind or the extreme market forces kind, the extremely altruistic kind or the extremely selfish kind.

Suppose, then, that the need is accepted for a space for nov-elty that is a paradoxical mixture of stability and instability. Would an observer skilled in systemic thinking be able to overcome any of the other four properties (stability, instability, dialectical evolution, and lost links between cause and effect) identified for nonlinear feedback networks? No matter how skilled a systemic thinker is, it will be impossible to overcome sensitivity to tiny changes, a prime property of the edge of chaos, simply because it is impossible to detect all tiny changes and measure them with infinite accuracy. Such an agent would presumably not want to remove the sources of stability, and it therefore follows that systemic thinking cannot overcome the nature of causality and the kind of predictability that is possible in nonlinear feedback networks operating at the edge of chaos: long-term specific outcomes will not be predictable but general archetypal behaviors may be and, if not, such patterns will at least be recognizable to perceptive observers when they occur. Systemic thinking, I suggest, makes it possible to understand and explain the dynamics of feedback networks but not to alter or remodel them. Human consciousness and self-awareness cannot alter the fundamental nonlinear feedback nature of the complex adaptive system that each of us is and that we all construct as soon as we interact with each other.

Summary

In general, the peculiarly human nature of agents in organizations does not provide grounds for doubting the applicability of the general properties of nonlinear feedback networks to organizations. Human systems are adaptive nonlinear feedback networks and there is every reason to believe that the five properties (space for novelty, stability, instability, dialectical evolution, and lost links between cause and effect) identified for such networks in general will apply to human systems in particular.

What the peculiarly human features do seem to add is potential complexity; they make the operation of human systems more complex and unpredictable rather than less so. It may be useful to think of these peculiarly human features as additional control parameters. In human systems, the rate of information flow, the level of diversity in schemas, and the richness of connectivity among agents all remain as control parameters, but further control parameters are added. As will become clear in later chapters, these take the form of power differentials and levels of anxiety containment. It will be argued that large power differentials and high levels of anxiety avoidance produce stable human systems, whereas very small power differentials and high levels of uncontained anxiety all produce explosively unstable human systems.

Map E. Creativity Lies at the Edge of Disintegration.

4
However, we will find that the new framework resonates with our experience and enables us to see that we can accept lack of foresight and control without inevitable anarchy, thereby enabling us to hold the anxiety rather than defend against it and so avoid it. We will find that this is essential to creativity and innovation.

3
Since we will find much that is inherently unpredictable, we will be anxious and fearful of failure.

2
We will find that the new framework enables us to understand what can be foreseen and what cannot, when we can agree and when we cannot.

1
We need to develop a new framework to make sense of life in organizations.

1a
Organizations are networks consisting of large numbers of agents—people—who interact with each other according to a set of behavioral rules we can call a schema. A dominant part of this schema drives current survival strategies, the primary task carried out by an organization's legitimate system. But there is also a recessive part that drives playful and destructive behavior in a shadow system that may or may not support the legitimate (see Figure 1.1). Schemas change in organizations; that is, organizations are systems that learn in complex ways. We can describe groups, minds, and even brains in similar ways.

PART ONE

5
This has radical implications for management research and practice.

PART FOUR

HOW CAN WE MAKE SENSE
OF OUR EXPERIENCE OF
LIFE IN ORGANIZATIONS?

1b
The science of complexity explores the nature of deterministic (see Figure 2.1) and adaptive (see Figures 3.1 and 3.2) networks. The latter—complex adaptive systems—are networks of large numbers of agents who interact according to schemas that contain both dominant and recessive parts. The key discovery complexity scientists have made about complex adaptive systems is that they are creative only when they operate in what might be called a space for novelty. This is a phase transition at the edge of chaos, that is, at the edge of system disintegration. The state is a paradoxical one that is both stable and unstable at the same time, driven by contradictory dynamics of both competition and cooperation, both amplification and constraint, both exposure to creative tension and protection from it. Such systems evolve dialectically with radically unpredictable outcomes. The coevolving process is that of self-organizing creative destruction and reconstruction in which a recessive schema undermines a dominant one to produce emergent outcomes (see Figures 2.3, 3.4, and 3.5). These are systems that learn in complex ways and they are ubiquitous in nature.

PART TWO

1d
This will allow us to specify a new framework for making sense of life in organizations.

PART THREE, cont.

And so we escape the vicious circle.

7
Because we are learning in complex ways, we need no longer depend upon "savior" recipes.

1c
For about half a century now, psychoanalysts have very clearly understood that individual minds are creative (a) when they occupy the depressive position, that is, when they can hold paradox in the mind; and (b) when they can use transitional objects to play (see Figure 4.1). These mental states are intermediate between neurotic defenses and psychotic fantasy—genius is literally at the edge of madness. It has also been understood for a long time that groups of people, both small and large, can perform creative work only when they occupy a psychic state between heavily defensive behavior and psychotic, basic assumption behavior (see Figure 5.1). Since organizations are collections of groups, the same points apply to them (see Figure 6.1). We can map the properties of complex adaptive systems in general onto human systems (see Figure 6.2) and it is clear that human consciousness, determination, and intention cannot alter these fundamental dynamics.

PART THREE

6
The new framework leads us to focus on self-reflection and learning from experience at all levels in human systems and gives greater insight into what we actually do in organizations, rather than what we say we do or what we believe we are supposed to do.

Map F. Organizational Creativity Flows from the Tension Between Legitimate and Shadow Systems.

4
However, we will find that the new framework resonates with our experience and enables us to see that we can accept lack of foresight and control without inevitable anarchy, thereby enabling us to hold the anxiety rather than defend against it and so avoid it. We will find that this is essential to creativity and innovation.

3
Since we will find much that is inherently unpredictable, we will be anxious and fearful of failure.

2
We will find that the new framework enables us to understand what can be foreseen and what cannot, when we can agree and when we cannot.

1
We need to develop a new framework to make sense of life in organizations.

1a
Organizations are networks consisting of large numbers of agents—people—who interact with each other according to a set of behavioral rules we can call a schema. A dominant part of this schema drives current survival strategies, the primary task carried out by an organization's legitimate system. But there is also a recessive part that drives playful and destructive behavior in a shadow system that may or may not support the legitimate (see Figure 1.1). Schemas change in organizations; that is, organizations are systems that learn in complex ways. We can describe groups, minds, and even brains in similar ways.

PART ONE

5
This has radical implications for management research and practice.

PART FOUR

HOW CAN WE MAKE SENSE
OF OUR EXPERIENCE OF
LIFE IN ORGANIZATIONS?

1d
Organizations are complex adaptive systems and they, too, are creative and innovative when they occupy a space for novelty at the edge of chaos or disintegration. This is a state in which people play in an organization's shadow system with concepts and actions that in the end undermine their legitimate system in the sense of changing it. Organizations transform themselves through tension between the legitimate system and its shadow; this is the essence of organizational learning or extraordinary management (see Figure 7.3). Such real-time learning, or self-reflection, is a self-organizing process that produces radically unpredictable, emergent outcomes. It operates in tension with the intentional processes of the legitimate system—ordinary management (see Figures 7.1 and 7.2).

PART THREE, cont.

1b
The science of complexity explores the nature of deterministic (see Figure 2.1) and adaptive (see Figures 3.1 and 3.2) networks. The latter—complex adaptive systems—are networks of large numbers of agents who interact according to schemas that contain both dominant and recessive parts. The key discovery complexity scientists have made about complex adaptive systems is that they are creative only when they operate in what might be called a space for novelty. This is a phase transition at the edge of chaos, that is, at the edge of system disintegration. The state is a paradoxical one that is both stable and unstable at the same time, driven by contradictory dynamics of both competition and cooperation, both amplification and constraint, both exposure to creative tension and protection from it. Such systems evolve dialectically with radically unpredictable outcomes. The coevolving process is that of self-organizing creative destruction and reconstruction in which a recessive schema undermines a dominant one to produce emergent outcomes (see Figures 2.3, 3.4, and 3.5). These are systems that learn in complex ways and they are ubiquitous in nature.

PART TWO

1c
For about half a century now, psychoanalysts have very clearly understood that individual minds are creative (a) when they occupy the depressive position, that is, when they can hold paradox in the mind; and (b) when they can use transitional objects to play (see Figure 4.1). These mental states are intermediate between neurotic defenses and psychotic fantasy—genius is literally at the edge of madness. It has also been understood for a long time that groups of people, both small and large, can perform creative work only when they occupy a psychic state between heavily defensive behavior and psychotic, basic assumption behavior (see Figure 5.1). Since organizations are collections of groups, the same points apply to them (see Figure 6.1). We can map the properties of complex adaptive systems in general onto human systems (see Figure 6.2) and it is clear that human consciousness, determination, and intention cannot alter these fundamental dynamics.

PART THREE

7
And so we escape the vicious circle.

Because we are learning in complex ways, we need no longer depend upon "savior" recipes.

6
The new framework leads us to focus on self-reflection and learning from experience at all levels in human systems and gives greater insight into what we actually do in organizations, rather than what we say we do or what we believe we are supposed to do.

When these control parameters operate at intermediate levels, human systems move to the edge of chaos where they are capable of novelty. Human dynamics do not alter the general properties of nonlinear feedback systems; they simply add potential complexity and more control parameters.

The chapters in this part seek to locate the space for novelty in human systems and explore the process of evolution in that space. In Chapter Four through Six, we will be following step 1c in Map E, locating the space for novelty in the human mind, in the human group, and at the level of organizations. Then, in Chapters Seven and Eight, we will move on to step 1d in Map F, to develop a complex adaptive system theory of organization and to show how it might be used to illuminate the experience of life in two organizations.

4

The Space for
Creativity in a Mind

The most consistent and striking insight that comes from nearly all studies of nonlinear feedback networks, both deterministic and adaptive, is that all of these systems seem to display a space for novelty, or creativity, located just at the edge of system disintegration. The human brain and the human mind are both quite clearly complex adaptive networks and so are human groups, organizations, and societies. Does this property of a creative space at the edge of disintegration map onto human systems? It is not difficult to see that the answer to this question is most probably yes.

The most immediate and convincing link between the science of complexity and human behavior that I am aware of lies in psychoanalytic theory, particularly the object relations theory of Melanie Klein and Donald Winnicott's notion of transitional objects. I will first give a brief summary of their theories and then examine the relationship between them and the aspects of the space for creativity in complex adaptive systems that are listed in Figure 3.6.

119

Psychoanalytic Explanations of Individual Creativity

Both Klein's theory of object relations and Winnicott's theory of transitional objects identify a psychological position that is in some sense transitional and paradoxical and that humans must occupy if they are to be capable of learning and creativity.

Object Relations Theory

On the basis of her extensive clinical work with children, Klein (1975a, 1975b, 1975c) developed a theory of the development of an infant and argued that this pattern of development underlay later adult behavior. Her theory explains how creative behavior comes about and what role it plays in the human psyche.

Infants are born with an innate capacity for recognizing and relating to certain objects and activities—a concept bearing some resemblance to Jung's notion of the collective unconscious (Gordon, 1993). It is as if infants arrive with brains already "wired up" to enable the actualization of particular potentials, or archetypes. Examples of such potentials are the action of sucking to feed and an ability to recognize and relate to the object that feeds. No training is necessary: the potential for this kind of recognition and this kind of activity is already there, awaiting actualization by particular opportunities and experiences. These experiences in effect actualize the potential, the actualization taking the form of a mental object. Through experience of feeding and of the object that feeds, the infant develops a mental representation of this object. This is clearly a feedback process: the experience of a "real" object is fed back into a preexisting potential, activating it in a particular way that then affects how the object is related to and experienced; that experience then feeds back to reinforce or change the mental representation of the object.

Infants thus develop mental representations of reality through a feedback process in which they project a mental image of an object onto the object and then introject the experience of the object in some way. The process is nonlinear, because a great many mental representations of any given real object are possible. In this manner, the mind of an infant becomes populated with mental objects, actualizations of archetypes, that interact with each other in a feedback manner to generate inner fantasies and interact with outer real objects in a process of projection, identification, and introjection through which the inner objects develop some link with outer reality.

Research has shown that the human brain is a complex adaptive system taking the form of a neural network (Minsky, 1968), and the above is a convincing argument that right from the beginning the human mind, which we might well think of as an emergent property of brain-body interaction (Damassio, 1994), is also a complex adaptive system. At the earliest stages of development, however, infants are incapable of distinguishing between what is inside and what is outside their mind, that is, between internal fantasies and external realities. The earliest fantasies are those of omnipotence and omniscience, in which infants experience a fusion between themselves and the world. It is as if they believe that they are the center of everything, everything exists for their benefit, and they control everything. Satisfaction of an infant's every need confirms these fantasies; the infant feels an archetypal comfort, security, and love, whereas any frustration of needs is experienced as persecution and arouses archetypal fear, anger, violence, and hate, and hence great anxiety.

Maturing is a process of separating what is inside the mind from what is outside, a differentiation of the individual from the world of which she or he is a part, as well as a differentiation of an ego from a fused unconscious. This process of separation and differentiation requires the gradual abandonment of fantasies of omnipotence and omniscience. This can be done only if the infant experiences some frustration; if nothing but satisfaction is experienced, the infant will have no need to abandon the fantasies. The process of maturing, therefore, provokes anger, violence, fear, and hatred and is accompanied by great anxiety. It appears that the prime generators of this anxiety are the tensions between:

- Love on the one hand and hate on the other
- Omnipotence or dominance on the one hand and needy dependency or submission on the other
- The drive to separation, differentiation, or individuation on the one hand and the longing for a continued state of fusion, ultimate belonging, or conformity on the other

If these tensions lead to too much anxiety, the infant will not be able to bear the maturation experience; with too little anxiety, the infant has no need to embark upon it at all. The management of anxiety is therefore a matter of great importance from the very start of life. One method of management lies in the skill of a carer who knows just how much to frustrate the infant and how much to hold him or her; this is Winnicott's notion of the "good enough mother" (Winnicott, 1965, 1971). The good enough mother has an instinctive ability to know when to frustrate the child and then when to hold the child so as to keep the anxiety level from rising too much. In this way, through a feedback process, the child increases his or her tolerance for anxiety and is able to cope with the existential tensions referred to above.

However, infants must also develop their own internal methods of managing anxiety if they are to mature; they do this by developing defense mechanisms. The earliest, most primitive of these defenses appear also to be archetypal potentials that infants are born with. The first of these mechanisms is splitting. Strong hateful feelings are split off from comforting, loving feelings and projected onto different mental objects so that the mind becomes populated with differentiated good and bad objects. As infants begin to develop a perception of an inner mental life and an outer real world, the objects perceived in the real world are also subject to projection and are split into good objects, which are highly idealized, and bad ones, which are greatly denigrated, denied, and attacked in fantasy. They also develop the fantasy that attacked objects will attack back, so bad objects are also feared.

Klein called this the schizoid-paranoid position. Here anxiety is defended against by projection and splitting and by fantasies of attacking and destroying, which unfortunately are accompanied by fantasies of being attacked and destroyed. Projective identification is also used, in which the person into whom the infant's feelings are being projected actually feels those feelings on the infant's behalf— hence the carer's ability to empathize. If the infant can utilize these inner defense mechanisms sufficiently and if the good enough experience holds, the infant has the possibility of maturing. However, if the anxiety is too great, the container too weak, the infant will not be able to bear the maturation experience and will become locked into continued massive use of the primitive psychotic defenses: splitting, projection, and projective identification.

Even when maturation does proceed normally, continued moderate use is made of projection and introjection as well as projective identification; in moderate form they are part of the normal feedback process of relating to others. More than this, we can say that no individual ever completely leaves behind the schizoid-paranoid position. That is why Klein called it a position rather than a stage of development. We all retain that position at some level in the mind and we are all liable to regress to it when exposed to too much anxiety. High levels of anxiety place human beings in psychotic states, that is, in relatively undifferentiated states of mental disintegration in which the ego is weak and easily shattered and in which little separation exists between mental contents and the real world.

The primitive defenses of splitting and projection perform the task of defending the infant against anxiety, but they also have a disadvantage. First, the fantasy attacks on bad objects arouse the fear of retaliation, and second, as the infant matures the realization grows that the good and bad objects in the mind relate to the same object—in reality, usually the caregiver. At some stage, thought to be about six months, infants must start dealing with the paradoxes of life, one of the earliest being that of loving and hating the same person. When the infant reaches the stage of realizing and beginning to hold ambiguity and paradox, then, according to Klein, the depressive position has been reached. The term *depressive* might involve some depression, but this is not its main feature. It is a position in which the infant can hold ambiguity and paradox without being overcome by anxiety. Once again, this is a position rather than simply a developmental stage, because people can and do move in and out of it all their lives, just as they can and do move in and out of the schizoid-paranoid position.

If the infant reaches the depressive position and can recognize that the loved object coincides with the object that is hated and attacked, she or he may possibly feel guilt for the previous fantasies of hateful and destructive attacks on the bad object, which now turns out also to be good. This guilt gives rise to the need for reparation, a need that Klein believed lies behind all creative activity; our urge to be creative arises from a deep, unconscious need to make reparations for our own destructiveness. If early attempts at reparation are accepted and received with love by the carers, this is experienced as forgiveness. The cycle of guilt, reparation, love, and forgiveness that underpins creativity is thus developed and sustained by a feedback process.

A failure to experience forgiveness will raise anxiety levels, and this will have to be defended against by deploying various defense mechanisms. Later developmental failures, such as an inability to deal adequately with the realization of an exclusive relationship between parents, will also need to be defended against. Defense mechanisms will normally take the form of rigid behaviors that make it unnecessary to hold ambiguity and para-dox or feelings of separation and exclusion. In other words, fail-ure to develop the capacity to hold the depressive position takes the form of rigidly defensive patterns of behavior such as depres-sion and mania.

Transitional Objects

Winnicott further clarified the creative process in individuals. From his clinical work with small children, he identified devel-opment with a process of separation from the carer, and he stressed the vital importance of good enough holding by the carer in this process. He defined the good enough carer as one with a fine judgment of how much to gratify the child to sustain a suffi-cient degree of security, and how much to frustrate the child to provoke exploration of, and relation to, the environment. That fine balance comes from the instinctive empathy the carer has with the child. Good enough holding enables children to cross the boundary of their own mind and begin to explore, relate to, and manipulate the real world outside their mind.

However, eventually the child has to develop his or her own holding mechanisms, since reliance cannot be placed on the carer to do this all the child's life. Winnicott proposed that such hold-ing mechanisms take the form of what he called transitional objects. As they mature, children develop the ability to compen-sate for short absences of their carer by forming a very powerful relationship with some special object such as a blanket or a teddy bear. Winnicott suggested that this object stands for the carer: it is treated for short periods as if it were the carer, providing enough security for the child to continue exploring the environment. In this sense the object is a transitional one: it is a transition from a present carer to an absent one; it stands for the carer although it is not the carer. This is how the child begins to use symbols, the start of all language and reasoning powers.

The teddy bear soon comes to stand for anything the child wants it to be, providing experiences of play that develop the imagination and the ability to manipulate symbols. It is through this experience of play that the child learns and develops imaginative, creative powers. The child discovers how to control and manipulate objects outside the mind, first by manipulating the transitional object and then by controlling real objects. The play takes place in a transitional space between the inner fantasies of the mind and the outer reality of a concrete world, as depicted in Figure 4.1. Here the child holds ambiguity and paradox: the transitional object is one thing but stands for something else. In this sense the transitional space is close in meaning to the depressive position (Miller, 1983; Gordon, 1993).

Figure 4.1. Zones of Operation for an Individual Mind.

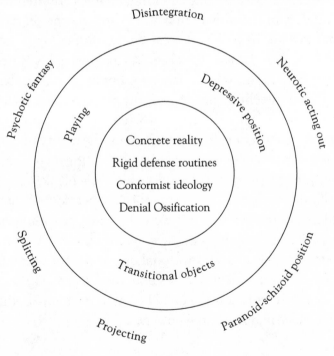

Play continues to be a major source of learning, and it continues throughout life to be closely associated with creativity. When individuals are able to play, to manipulate symbols, and to occupy the transitional space and use transitional objects, they are able to be creative. Winnicott argued that the transitional space continues throughout life to be the area in which people develop cultures, myths, art, and religion.

The Match Between the Science of Complexity and Psychoanalytic Explanations of Creativity

Now let us consider how much the above explanations of creativity at the level of the individual mind have in common with the science of complexity. The work of both Klein and Winnicott makes it very clear that the mind is a nonlinear feedback network, a complex adaptive system, and that a space or set of conditions exists in which the mind is potentially creative: that space is the depressive position in Klein's terms and the world of transitional objects in Winnicott's. Together these notions define a mental space for novelty with characteristics that are remarkably similar to those we have already identified for other complex adaptive systems. These are:

1. A phase transition
2. A state of paradox
3. The actualization of archetypes
4. Creative destruction
5. A critical point for control parameters

Each of these characteristics is now considered.

A Phase Transition

The human mind clearly has an unstable zone just as other complex adaptive systems do. Each human mind has the potential for regression to psychotic levels, that is, to defensive behaviors that were developed early in life before the paradoxes of the depressive position were encountered and that are retained at some level in all our minds. Regression to these levels is activated in perfectly normal people when they experience high levels of anxiety. Here, in a sense, the mind disintegrates: the ego is weakened, as is reality testing, and behavior is driven by fantasies of a psychotic, splitting, paranoid kind. This is the unstable, disintegrative zone for the nonlinear feedback network that is the human mind. It is not a paradoxical, ambiguous state, but rather a massive avoidance of such a state.

Also like other complex adaptive systems, the human mind has a stable zone. Each mind employs a collection of defensive behavioral mechanisms that are activated by anxiety and that take the form of highly rigid, unambiguous, concrete behaviors into which individuals become locked against their conscious wills in order to avoid anxiety. In between psychotic episodes, psychotic patients may develop highly rigid behaviors such as checking, for example, compulsive searching for needles in chairs, or bouts of binging and vomiting, to defend against further episodes. This is the stable zone for the nonlinear feedback network that is the mind. It is not a paradoxical, ambiguous state, but a massive avoidance of such a state.

Psychoanalytic explanations also make it clear that a phase transition exists between the stable and unstable zones of the human mind just as it does for all other complex adaptive systems. Each mind is potentially capable of functioning in the depressive position, in which it is able to hold anxiety and accept fundamental ambiguity and paradox. In this state, the urge to make reparation in the form of creative work can be realized. This is a kind of phase transition between disintegrative psychotic behavior and neurotic acting out on the one hand and rigid defensive behavior to prevent such disintegration on the other.

The space for creativity in the human individual is the depressive position: individuals may be creative only insofar as they can move from the stable zone of rigidly defensive behavior into the depressive position without tipping over into disintegrative psychotic and neurotic behavior. Psychotically and neurotically ill people do not seem to be able to hold the depressive position: they swing from disintegrative episodes to rigid, repetitive behaviors and back again. Anxiety governs which zone a mind will operate in. If uncontained anxiety levels are turned up, the mind either retreats into rigidly defensive behavior to avoid the anxiety altogether or disintegrates into psychotic fantasy or neurotic acting out. When anxiety is adequately contained, even at high levels, the mind is capable of holding the depressive position, the creative space at the edge of chaos. In other words, the control parameter that determines where a mind will operate is the level of uncontained anxiety it is subjected to.

Winnicott's theories provide an important insight into the space for creativity in the human mind and also show how the space for novelty is a phase transition. Playing, the basis of human creativity, takes place in a transitional space between an individual's rather disorderly inner fantasy life and the relatively orderly outer reality the individual encounters, the tasks and routines she or he follows in the real world. Playing is the process of manipulating transitional objects, objects that are one thing but stand for another. Creativity is also play because it is closely connected to the ability to use symbols and analogies, to construct and use metaphors—in other words, to allow one thing to stand for something else. Creativity, therefore, requires a feedback process between inner fantasy and outer reality. And, once again, the ability of an individual to operate in this space, rather than operating exclusively in an unstable inner world or a rigid outer world or swinging erratically between them, has to do with how effectively anxiety is being contained, both internally by the individual and by the environment he or she operates in. Individuals will be able to live in the transitional space only if they can rely on a good enough internal holding mechanism and a good enough external holding environment (Stapley, 1994).

For an individual human mind, then, the edge of chaos has a clear location and essentially the same kind of clear meaning as any other nonlinear feedback system. It is a zone between system disintegration on the one hand and system ossification on the other, as depicted in Figure 4.1.

A State of Paradox

The space for novelty in the human mind, as with all other complex adaptive systems, is one in which paradox is held and endlessly rearranged rather than resolved. This is exactly what the depressive position means and it is the essence of play. The main paradoxes that are so dialectically rearranged throughout the life of an individual relate to:

- The capacity to both love and hate the same object
- The urge to separate from others and individuate and the longing to fuse and lose oneself
- The capacity for destructiveness and the creative urge to make reparation
- The need for the safety and comfort of the known and the desire for the exciting and the unknown
- The desire for the rational, the functional, and the factual, on the one hand, and the longing for the aesthetic, the emotional, and the sacred on the other

The Actualization of Archetypes

Freud, Klein, Winnicott, and Jung and their followers have shown that every mind is the result of a developmental process, an evolutionary trajectory, flowing from a feedback process in which experience actualizes archetypal behaviors. Each human mind is uniquely different because of the often small differences in the history of that person's experience that cause the archetypes to be actualized in unique ways.

Creative Destruction

As in the case of the symbol system in computer simulations of complex adaptive systems, the symbol system of the mind can be thought of in dominant and recessive terms. Some of the mind's schemas engage current reality, driving the performance of the current primary task and defending against current anxiety, in a dominant symbol system. A natural and necessary resistance to changing this occurs in the interest of performing current tasks as efficiently as possible. The rest of the mind's symbol system, the recessive part that is not engaging current reality, is the part we use to fantasize and dream with, in fact to play with. Transitional objects are thus much the same thing as the recessive symbol system of the mind, where creativity mainly occurs. The recessive symbol system and transitional objects are in tension with the dominant system because they are building up potential replacements for the dominant system.

Changes in the recessive symbol system may simply stay as play, or they may be translated into replacements of the dominant symbol system. This allows innovation, that is, a change in system behavior, to occur. However, we only apply the labels *creative* and *innovative* if the resulting behavior actually turns out to improve fitness. Creativity, then, is a change in the pattern of symbols in the mind that eventually turns out to produce behavior that increases fitness, and innovation is that behavior. Changes in the recessive symbol system are potential creativity. If these changes replace existing dominant symbol systems, then performance of the current primary task changes; this is potential innovation. If that innovation actually improves fitness, we can say that innovation and creativity have actually taken place. In these respects the mind displays the same property of creative destruction, the same interplay between competing parts of schemas, as any other complex feedback system.

A Critical Point for Control Parameters

The previous sections have shown that theories already exist that see the human mind as a complex adaptive system capable of the same dynamic progression as other complex adaptive systems: they have a stable zone, an unstable zone, and a phase transition between them. The control parameter that moves the mind between these zones is primarily whether the level of anxiety is avoided or contained. The critical point occurs when there is enough anxiety to provoke exploration but enough containment to prevent the mind from shutting down.

How the Human Factor Enters into the Comparison

The procedure we are adopting in this part of the book is to try to map the general properties of complex adaptive nonlinear feedback networks onto particular human systems, checking at each stage to ensure that the essential characteristics of being human do not in some way render the mapping invalid. We have identified the space for novelty in the mind and found it to have the same essential characteristics as any other complex adaptive system. We now need to ask whether the structure of human agents changes this conclusion. In other words, we need to explore whether the human tensions identified in Chapter One—those between inspiration and anxiety, individualism and conformity, leadership and followership, and participant and observer roles—render the dynamic properties of complex systems in general inapplicable to human systems in particular.

Klein's object relations theory focuses very clearly on the first three of these dynamics. The equivalent of a leadership-followership dynamic within an individual mind is the domination-submission tension that is characteristic of the schizoid-paranoid position. The individuation-conformity dynamic is essentially what the separation-fusion tension discussed above is all about. And the inspiration-anxiety dynamic is at the center of the phenomena that object relations theory deals with. Anxiety arises from fears concerning separation and differentiation, losing individuality under the domination of others, and inherent destructiveness. All creativity has destructive elements. In other systems we saw symmetry breaking as an essential part of the production of novelty. In the human mind old schemas have to be destroyed to make way for the new. Hence the dynamic of creativity and inspiration versus anxiety. We can see from considering the effects of these three essentially human dynamics in an individual mind that they do not enable humans to alter or overcome the dynamic progression of nonlinear feedback, nor do they make it possible for humans to avoid the edge of chaos if they are to be creative. Instead the three human dynamics identified above lie at the very heart of what the edge of chaos means for an individual mind: they are peculiarly human manifestations of nonlinear dynamics.

But what of the participant-observer dynamic, the fact that a human mind can reflect upon itself? Self-reflection is the same thing as thinking systemically: it is a process in which the human mind understands something of the whole system that it is. Such self-reflection, perhaps assisted by a psychoanalyst, does not allow anyone to alter the facts of disintegrative psychotic fantasy or the rigidly defensive behavior that all of us experience to one degree or another, and it does not remove the depressive position or the need to occupy it if one is to be creative. Instead, successful self-reflection renders an individual more capable of accepting these facts and holding the paradoxes of the depressive position. Self-reflection does not remove the edge of chaos or the need to locate there; rather, it makes it more possible to stay at the edge of chaos. It creates new knowledge about one's own mental processes and is double-loop learning in that it is a process of questioning and changing the rigidly defensive or wildly disintegrative schemas that lie below the level of immediate awareness.

I suggest that at the level of the individual human mind there is a striking mapping of the main property of nonlinear systems, the space for novelty, onto the human mind, and this mapping is reinforced and given richer meaning rather than being made invalid by the essentially human characteristics of the mind. Nothing about our capacity to form individual mental purpose, our strength of will and determination, our intelligence, or our souls can overcome this dynamic. In fact, it lies at the heart of what it is to be human.

Conclusion

I have suggested that the schema of an individual mind may be thought of as consisting of two subsystems: a dominant symbol system and a recessive symbol system.

The Dominant Symbol System

The dominant symbols form the rules that drive current engagement with external reality and thus the performance of current primary tasks, they defend against the anxiety that task performance or any creative threat to it arouses without incapacitating the ability to work, they evaluate task performance, and they use evaluations to improve performance. The rules are expressed as routines, habits, procedures, theories in-use, checking and control behaviors, customs and rituals, and so on. Previous learning is, in effect, stored in the form of these routines, which are then used to perform tasks (Nelson and Winter, 1982). Task performance may be improved through practice, that is, through using feedback on how well performance achieves its purpose without changing any of the dominant schema. This is single-loop learning. It sets up no mental tension because it involves no destruction of the dominant symbol system.

The Recessive Symbol System

The recessive symbols form the rules that govern play. Because play is not the engagement of current reality but the use of real objects in fantasy, it cannot be driven by the dominant symbol system and so must reflect the contents of the recessive symbol system. That system forms speculations, images, dreams, metaphors, analogies, fantasies, espoused theories, myths, and inner representations of outer real objects. In other words, the recessive schema consists of the repertoire of thoughts and behaviors available to an individual but not currently being used to engage reality. The recessive symbol system governs the inner life with which an individual engages others in play and in speculative, exploratory dialogue. This exploratory dialogue is the process of double-loop learning, which constitutes creativity. Innovation is new learning embodied in the performance of novel primary tasks or novel ways of performing old tasks; it requires alterations in the dominant part of the schema. For innovation to occur, parts of the dominant symbol system must be replaced, a process of destruction and creation that is bound to cause mental tension.

Creative work, or play, may proceed in the recessive symbol system and then suddenly be manifested as a major change in the dominant system and revolutionary behavior, or the two processes of creation and innovation, both involving destruction, could continually feed into each other, resulting in gradual changes in the dominant symbol system and incremental behavioral change. In both cases, however, two symbol systems are operating in tension with each other: play in the recessive system builds up potential destruction and renewal of at least parts of the dominant system. If we can keep it as "only a game," if we can keep the creative destruction in the recessive symbol system, then the anxiety inherent in that creative destruction is fairly easy to contain for most people. However, as soon as it looks as if the game will become real and the play threatens to spill over into the dominant symbol system, anxiety rises and defensive behaviors are erected: we attempt to kill our own learning as an alternative to killing comfortable and beloved current ways of behaving.

Therefore, at the level of the individual, the creative act of play and any subsequent innovative change in behavior both flow from tension and conflict between a dominant symbol system and a subversive recessive symbol system in the mind.

All humans are potentially capable of the creative and innovative behavior just described, but they can actualize the potential only when they are able to hold the depressive position, that is, when they can hold ambiguity and paradox in the mind, particularly in regard to preserving current ways of thinking in the interest of efficient performance of the current primary task, on the one hand, and destroying them in the interest of creativity, on the other. To put it another way, individuals can actualize their inherent creative potential only when they are able to operate in the transitional space between rigidly defensive behavior and psychotic fantasies, where they must hold the anxiety of destroying and replacing symbol systems. This is a state of tension between the dominant symbol system and its shadow recessive system.

However, potential creativity and innovation become actual creativity and innovation only when they help an individual to survive better in his or her environment, that is, to climb higher up a fitness peak or, better still, to climb up a higher peak. The fitness landscape for an individual is determined by the behavior of those to whom this individual is linked in his or her network—usually one or more of the immediate groups of which he or she is a part. Creativity can therefore never be an individual process but must always involve interaction with others in a group. We turn to this in the next chapter.

5

The Space for Creativity in a Group

In the last chapter we saw how an individual has the capacity for creativity if she or he can occupy a mental space for novelty, which is defined as the depressive position and the world of transitional objects. The individual mind can then play, or manipulate the recessive symbol systems of the mind, to develop potential replacements for parts of the mind's dominant symbol systems. The latter constitute the systems that currently drive an individual's engagement with the real world and the performance of primary tasks, and in that sense we might think of them as constituting the "legitimate system" of the mind, whereas the recessive symbol system constitutes a kind of "shadow" system.

Creativity at the individual level clearly sets up a tension between play within the recessive, or shadow, symbol system and current reality engagement within the dominant, or legitimate, symbol system, simply because the former is always a potential replacement for the latter. Creativity within an individual mind is, in a very real sense, a subversive and destructive activity from the perspective of current ways of behaving: it impairs efficiency. On the other hand, creativity may be a constructive activity from the perspective of long-term survival: it may enhance effectiveness. In fact, we normally classify a change in an individual's symbol system as creative only if it does enhance long-term survival, in regard to either the life of the individual concerned, the time span over which he or she is remembered by others, or the life of the group of which he or she is a member.

Individuals who occupy the creative space have, by definition, an imaginative mental life: they are constantly playing and manipulating the recessive symbol systems of their minds, which are consequently in a state of continual flux, at the edge of chaos. However, not all of this play is creative: most of it may simply be frivolous, or may be defending against change, or may be even purely destructive. We can judge whether the play is creative only when it is translated into language and/or behavior, because it is only then that we can know whether it enhances fitness in the sense of long-term survival. Thus, rearrangements in the recessive symbol system of the mind must actually replace parts of the dominant system so that a change in behavior results before we can begin to conclude that something creative has occurred. The individual must actually perform double-loop learning, that is, change operational schemas. If this turns out to improve fitness— and it may take a very long time before this is evident—we may say that the original change in the recessive symbol system was creative and the consequent behavioral change was innovative.

Two aspects of this argument are of particular importance. First, the inherently destructive nature of both creativity and the innovation that might follow it means that they both arouse anxiety; unless this is contained, defensive mechanisms will be brought into play within the mind to put an end to the whole process. We all sometimes seek to destroy our own creativity and double-loop learning for fear of the destruction it will unleash. Containment of this anxiety requires an individual to have a strong ego structure and also to operate within a good enough holding environment. This environment is provided by the people in an individual's network with whom she or he has the closest links, namely, family, leisure, and work groups. This means that we cannot view creativity purely as an attribute of an individual. An individual is creative only if she or he is a member of groups that are capable of assisting in the containment of anxiety, although the degree to which individuals rely on groups for this purpose varies enormously.

The second aspect of the view that the last chapter presented on individual creativity is this. Whether or not any mental act is creative depends upon whether the resulting behavior is innovative. It is only innovative if it improves fitness, and that depends upon the response it evokes from those with whom the individual interacts. The mental act of an individual will turn out to have been creative only if it both counteracts the competing strategies of some members of the individual's network and elicits the cooperation, support, good opinion, and esteem of others in the network. In this sense as well, then, creativity is not simply an attribute of an individual mind, but a characteristic of a wider system: a group. In the end individuals can be said to be creative only if they can engage with the creative activity of others, in both some kind of competition and some kind of cooperation. In other words, we can only know that individuals have been creative if they succeed in engaging in some kind of dialogue that amplifies and spreads the manipulation in the recessive symbol systems of their minds. Ultimately, creativity, and thus innovation, lie in interaction within a group.

A group is a complex adaptive system just as an individual mind is. But where is the space for novelty for a group? What are the conditions required for individuals to engage with each other in the competition and cooperation that constitute the dialogue required for creativity to take place? How does a group provide containment for the anxiety provoked by the whole creative and innovative process? We turn once again to the psychoanalytic literature for answers to these questions.

Psychoanalytic Explanations of Creativity in a Group

At least two widely known theoretical frameworks relating to group behavior clearly show the features that the science of complexity would lead us to expect. The first is Bion's notion of basic assumption behavior in groups (Bion, 1961), and the second is the learning models developed by Argyris and Schön (1978). A brief summary of each of these frameworks is given in the next section, followed by a review of the extent to which they match the characteristics of the space for novelty in complex adaptive systems.

Basic Assumption Behavior in Groups

Building on Klein's work, Bion developed an explanation for group behavior based on his clinical work with groups. He distinguished conceptually between two intertwined aspects of group life. On the one hand, every group of people constitutes a work group in the sense that members come together to perform some explicit task, to construct something, to discuss something, or perhaps to entertain or be entertained. On the other hand, and at the same time, every group of people constitutes what Bion called a basic assumption group. By this he meant that whenever people relate to each other in a group, they do so within an emotional atmosphere. It is as if they also come together to serve some implicit emotional purpose: for example, as if they have come together to depend on someone, in which case they will display a basic assumption behavior of dependency.

Bion observed that when the emotional atmosphere takes the form of a low-level background, it can assist in the work task. For example, if the task is to learn, then a background emotional atmosphere among students of dependency on the teacher can aid in that task. However, if this basic assumption behavior comes to dominate the behavior of the group of students, it will make it impossible to learn: students will cease questioning and simply believe everything they are told. Domination by basic assumption behavior occurs when expected structures are removed and leadership expectations are frustrated, causing anxiety levels to rise dramatically. Groups dominated by this behavior cannot work or be creative.

When a group becomes predominantly a basic assumption group, it is incapable of performing its explicit task. Instead, it acts as if it has assembled solely to perform an implicit emotional task: to become dependent, or to fight, or to take flight from the task, or to rely on two of their number to find some magical solution, or to fuse with each other in some oceanic feeling of security (Turquet, 1974). These basic assumption behaviors are engaged in without conscious intention to do so—they constitute unconscious group processes. In this state, groups of people regress to the primitive psychotic defenses of splitting, denial, denigration and idealization, and projecting and projective identification that each member developed as an infant. The group displays behavior driven by primitive, psychotic fantasies, and this makes it impossible for them to work or be creative.

According to Bion, then, a group of people is capable of work and creativity when its members focus on the task within a functional background emotional atmosphere. In other words, groups are creative when they are able to operate at the edge of disintegration. This is a precarious state because fairly small increases in the level of anxiety can cause the group to be flooded with emotion, pushing it into a highly disintegrative zone of psychotic fantasy. It is very easy to experience the truth of these assertions and one's own strong propensity to engage in basic assumption behavior and psychotic fantasy by attending experiential group relations conferences run by, for example, the Tavistock Institute in the United Kingdom and the A. K. Rice Institute in the United States (Miller, 1989; Colman and Geller, 1985; Colman and Bexton, 1975; Gibbard, Hartman, and Mann, 1974).

So from Bion's perspective we can perceive a group of people to be a network of interacting agents driven by a circular feedback process between task performance and basic assumption behavior. The dynamics of that process, whether it is in a state of work or a state of emotional flooding, depends upon the level of anxiety group members are experiencing and how it is being contained. Further insight into the nature of group behavior is available in the learning models developed by Argyris and Schön (1978).

Models of Group Learning

Argyris and Schön distinguish between espoused and in-use schemas, that is, between the behavioral rules and assumptions that people publicly proclaim they use and the rules and assumptions that observation of their behavior indicates they are actually using. This distinction applies to any schema, but, importantly, it applies to the schemas that drive learning behavior. Argyris and Schön identified a popular, espoused model of learning that they called Learning Model II. The rules in this model are that people should cooperate and participate in a search for win-win solutions; gather the facts, generate the options, and hold all of them up for public discussion and testing; stand open to changing their mind in the light of that testing; and not use power or hierarchical position to obstruct the cooperative process. Clearly such a schema constitutes an instruction to perform double-loop learning.

The research, however, consistently shows that although this is almost always the espoused model, another model is actually employed to drive learning behavior. They called this Learning

Model I. According to this in-use model, people engage in group interaction in order to win and not lose; retain unilateral control of any situation to avoid embarrassing others or being embarrassed themselves and to contain the fear of failure; and restrict the effective participation in decision making to as few people as possible. Those who follow such a schema do not expose these assertions in public. Instead, they conceal their opinions and use factual information selectively to manipulate others. Rather than changing their mind, they resist and undermine any contrary evidence as well as contrary messengers.

The result is that people get trapped in single-loop learning, because the behaviors of the in-use Learning Model I clearly block any questioning or testing of assumptions that have sunk below the level of awareness. The in-use model is reinforced by covert politics and game playing: people employ Model I while proclaiming that they are employing Model II. However, they know that their own and others' proclamations are not true; they are all making untested assertions that they deny, but they hold such behaviors to be undiscussable. This undiscussability is itself undiscussable. In this way powerful, rigid, defensive group routines are built up that block double-loop learning. Argyris and Schön, however, warn of going to the opposite of Learning Model I. This is where power is dispersed so that all are equal, decision making and learning are open to participation by all, and all are free to expose their feelings and assertions about the others. The consequences described for such behavior are much the same as those that Bion calls basic assumption behavior and others (Cohen, March, and Olsen, 1972) call "garbage can" decision making—highly unstable conflictual behavior in which decisions are haphazard and what is learned depends primarily on chance.

To engage in double-loop learning, groups of people have to move from Model I to Model II while avoiding the opposite of Model I. This move requires them to destroy defensive routines and to endure being embarrassed, causing embarrassment, experiencing fear of failure, and feeling the anxiety of exposing assertions to public testing and holding themselves open to changing their mind. Avoiding the opposite of Model I means that only assertions that are relevant to the learning situation are held up for public testing and then only if they can be backed with evidence—it is the evidence that is being held up for public testing. This work on learning models is based on extensive observation of, and work with, groups of people who are trying to learn.

Now let us consider how the frameworks of Bion and Argyris and Schön relate to the space for novelty in complex adaptive systems.

The Science of Complexity and Psychoanalytic Explanations of Creativity

Both of the above frameworks for understanding group behavior postulate feedback processes between members who are interacting to form a group. In the Bion framework the interaction generates an emotional atmosphere and unconscious processes that affect the ability of the group to work, which in turn affects the emotional atmosphere. In the Argyris and Schön framework, the interaction generates covert political activities and defensive behavioral routines that affect the group's ability to perform double-loop learning. Both frameworks specify a set of conditions in which work, in one case, and double-loop learning, in the other, can take place. Consider now how closely these conditions match the characteristics of the space for novelty in complex adaptive systems. These characteristics are, you will recall, the following:

1. A phase transition
2. A state of paradox
3. The actualization of archetypes
4. Creative destruction
5. A critical point for control parameters

A Phase Transition

Bion postulates a highly stable zone for group behavior that occurs when a group operates within very familiar, clearly understood hierarchical structures according to clearly understood rules, procedures, and routines, all of which reduce anxiety to low levels. This is the group equivalent of the rigid defensive mental routines typifying the stable zone of individual mental operation. When groups of people work in the extremes of such a context, the emotional background is barely perceptible: what emotion there is takes the form of boredom and frustration that is largely repressed. Group behavior ossifies. Much the same picture is presented in the Argyris and Schön framework: people in a group employ the widespread in-use schema of Learning Model I, leading to behavior that is rigidly defensive. Cover-ups and implicit rules about what is discussable and not discussable considerably reduce the fear of being shown to be a failure and of embarrassing others and being embarrassed. Freedom from anxiety results in a zone of behavior that is highly stable but in which double-loop learning, the creative process, is impossible.

That same group of people, however, also has a highly unstable zone of behavior into which it can be plunged almost at a moment's notice. If hierarchical structures, clearly recognizable tasks, rules, procedures, normal social routines, and rituals are removed, the group is instantly plunged into basic assumption behavior, where members become very dependent, engage in fight-and-flight dynamics, seek salvation in pairing, and try to fuse with each other in the "good" group. In this state, behavior is driven for lengthy periods by fantasies of a psychotic nature and rational group behavior disintegrates. Basic assumption behavior at the level of the group is clearly closely linked to the unstable, psychotic zone of the individual mind. The Argyris and Schön framework has a similar phenomenon. When members of a group find that Learning Model I keeps them happily in the stable zone but blocks their learning, they tend to switch to its opposite. This leads to widespread participation in the learning process, equal distribution of power in accordance with a fantasy that all are equal, and freely exposed assertions about others on the assumption that total openness is required for learning. The research of Argyris and Schön (1978) and Cohen, March, and Olsen (1972) shows how this results in highly unstable behavior.

There is, however, a space between the stable zone of repetitive task performance accompanied by rigid defensive structures and the unstable zone of psychotic fantasy, a phase transition between group ossification and group disintegration. In this transitional space, basic assumption behavior occupies a background position, in Bion's terms, and Learning Model II is employed, in Argyris and Schön's terms. This is where work and double-loop learning—that is, creativity—become possible.

A group, then, has a space for novelty and, as with all other nonlinear feedback networks, that space is a phase transition between stable and unstable zones of behavior. In the case of groups, that phase transition is at the edge of disintegrative basic assumption behavior according to Bion's perspective and at the edge of highly defensive behavioral routines that preserve stability according to the Argyris and Schön perspective. Taken together, the space for novelty lies between basic assumption behavior and defensive behavioral routines. In this space, members of a group are capable of playing with ideas and proposals: they eagerly use imaginative constructs, analogies, and metaphors and develop myths and rituals. These dynamics of a group and the characteristics of its space for novelty are depicted in Figure 5.1.

A State of Paradox

The space for novelty identified above for groups of people is quite clearly a state of paradox just as it is for all other nonlinear feedback networks. When a group occupies the space between stable routines and psychotic fantasy, it is paradoxically governed by

Figure 5.1. Zones of Operation for a Group.

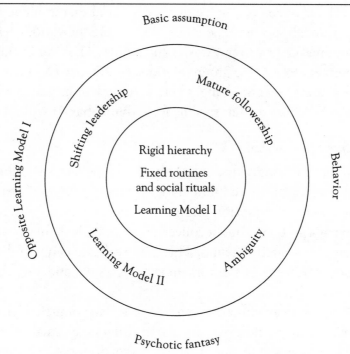

both routine and fantasy, and its evolution is driven by a dialectical process of rearranging the paradoxes. In the space for novelty a group of people is both stable and unstable at the same time. In order to perform the group's current primary task its members must conform, but in order to learn and improve future adaptation, they must utilize their differences. In other words, what is required for efficiency now, is the enemy of what is required for future fitness. Current efficiency and long-term effectiveness are enemies.

The Actualization of Archetypes

The distinction between archetypal behavior and its actualization applies quite comfortably to Bion's framework as well as that of Argyris and Schön. The basic assumption behaviors of dependency, fight-or-flight, pairing, and oneness are all archetypes, that is, potential behaviors of a broad qualitative kind that await actualization through specific experience. So, too, are the various defensive routines identified by Argyris and Schön. Thus, for example, an observer attending a group relations conference can regularly detect archetypal fight-or-flight behavior but will be quite unable to know in advance what specific form that behavior will take.

Creative Destruction

In a group, each individual retains his or her own unique schema but also utilizes a shared schema with other group members in order to make interaction and joint action possible. The total schema of a group is, thus, a collection of individual, fully shared, and partially shared schemas. This group schema can usefully be thought of in terms of a dominant symbol system and a recessive symbol system.

The dominant symbol system is the one that is most fully shared by group members and that consequently drives the actual, current, explicit behavior of the group, the performance of its current primary tasks, and the defenses against the anxiety that this arouses. This dominant symbol system is embodied in a group's routines—its procedures, customs, habits, rituals, control systems, policies, responsibility and authority definitions, task allocations, task-related roles, task definitions, and so on (Nelson and Winter, 1982). Some of these routines may be written down or expressed in some artifact, whereas others are implicitly understood. In other words, some of the routines constitute an explicit, formal system, whereas others constitute an implicit, approved, and widely shared informal system or culture; together they determine how individuals interact in a group and what they do as a group. I use the term *legitimate system* for these formal, widely shared, and approved informal systems.

A group may utilize feedback to improve its performance without making any changes in its legitimate system. In this way it acquires skill through practice and improves its efficiency: that is, it performs single-loop learning. A group may also make changes in the kinds of tasks it performs and how it performs them; that is, it may change its dominant symbol system. This is innovation, a behavioral change flowing from a process of double-loop learning that inevitably changes a group's legitimate system.

The recessive symbol system of a group consists of all its partially shared symbol systems and all the unshared parts of unique individual symbol systems, both dominant and recessive, that do not coincide with the group's dominant shared system. The recessive system is the repertoire of behaviors that is available to a group but that is not currently being utilized to engage reality and is not the current driver of actual group behavior in relation to primary tasks. Instead, the recessive system drives behavior that is not directly concerned with the current primary task but with tacit tasks having to do with emotional support, social interactions, political maneuvering, rumor generation, fantasizing, and myth manufacturing—in short, play—and thus potentially with much of the learning. Basic assumption behavior also becomes a dominant schema in the sense that everyone shares it. However, this sharing is not for carrying out work but for avoiding work altogether, and it is in the latter sense that basic assumption behavior might be thought of as part of the recessive schema and the shadow system. As at the individual level, we find the possibility of play located in a recessive system; in groups, it clearly constitutes a kind of unapproved informal system or shadow culture in that not everyone shares all of its contents or any shared contents have to do not with performing primary tasks but with avoiding or undermining them.

In the process of group creativity, members play in this shadow system, utilizing real objects in a fantastic manner, and take part in dialogues that use images, metaphors, and analogies to change the mental contents of group members. A group is creative when it changes parts of its recessive symbol system, destroying and replacing them; it forms new behaviors for the group repertoire even though they may not be used immediately. This directly involves individual schema change, because the unshared parts of individual schemas constitute most of a group's recessive system. The process thus cannot occur without tension and conflict between the individuals involved; some will be changing in directions that others do not agree with. The process of group creativity, then, is intertwined with that of individual creativity and is just as filled with anxiety.

A group of people may be highly creative and continually change the contents of the recessive system. However, for this to affect the task performance of the group and for innovation to occur, these changes have to become widely shared or incorporated into the dominant system. This process of securing widespread sharing is one in which the shadow system works to replace aspects of the legitimate system. Innovation requires the shadow system to work to undermine the legitimate system.

All groups of people are potentially capable of the creative and innovative behavior outlined above. However, this potential will be actualized only if a group can occupy the space for novelty. Just as at the individual level, a primary characteristic of the space for novelty is that a recessive symbol system works subversively behind the scenes to undermine and replace a dominant system.

A Critical Point for Control Parameters

In both the Bion and Argyris and Schön explanations of group dynamics, the key control parameter in moving groups of people between the stable and unstable zones of behavior and into the space for novelty is the level of the group's anxiety and the degree of its containment. Anxiety is tuned up by removing containing structures, such as Learning Model I behavior or conventional leadership. The group can be returned to the stable zone by re-erecting the containing structures and thus reducing the level of anxiety. However, when anxiety is at an intermediate level, at some critical point enough challenge and contention exist to provoke group members into some form of exploration, but also enough emotional containment of that anxiety to prevent them from being submerged by basic assumption behavior. At critical points of anxiety containment, groups of people can work and perform double-loop learning, avoiding both the psychotic fantasy of the unstable zone and the rigidly defensive behavior of the stable zone.

For individuals, as for groups of people, we see that the space for novelty has a clear meaning that is already identified in the psychoanalytic literature on group behavior and that this space has the same characteristics as other nonlinear feedback networks. Now, in keeping with the procedure established in the last chapter, we will consider briefly whether any of the characteristics that distinguish human agents from agents in other nonlinear feedback systems affect the mapping of the edge of chaos onto human groups.

How the Human Factor
Enters into the Comparison

This section explores how the space for novelty in groups of people is affected by the four dynamics discussed in relation to the individual mind in the last chapter.

Inspiration and Anxiety

As with the individual mind, creativity, inspiration, and double-loop learning in a group all inevitably generate anxiety because they shatter current shared group schemas and existing role patterns as a prelude to introducing new ones. And, as with the individual mind, the level of uncontained anxiety is the control parameter determining whether a group is in the stable zone, in unstable chaos, or at the edge of chaos in the space for novelty. It is only at critical levels of anxiety and its containment that inspiration is possible. Thus, anxiety and its containment do not nullify the properties of the space for novelty found in all nonlinear feedback networks; they simply add control parameters to the system. They paradoxically add both a spur and an obstacle to inspiration and creativity.

Conformity and Individualism

The edge of chaos for any nonlinear feedback system is a state of paradox. One of the most powerful paradoxes for any member of a group of human agents is how to be oneself and yet be a member of a group. This individuation-conformity dynamic is therefore a fundamental paradox in a human group. If it is resolved by all the members of the group becoming highly conformist, the group moves away from the edge of chaos into the stable zone. On the other hand, if the paradox is resolved by all members abandoning conformity for their own individuality, the group disintegrates and moves into the unstable zone. A group can be creative only if it holds the tension of conformity and individualism, which is only possible if the anxieties it raises are sufficiently contained.

Once again, this particular distinction between human agents and the agents in the computer simulations, which was considered in Chapters Two and Three, does not affect the existence or fundamental nature of the space for novelty; paradox is still sustained in the phase transition, the difference simply being the addition of yet another paradox.

Leadership and Followership

Creativity at the individual level is a process in which play in the recessive symbol system of the mind formulates replacements for parts of the mind's dominant symbol system, resulting in innovative behavior. But we judge the changes in schema and behavior to be creative and innovative only if they make the individual fitter in some way. Fitness is not an absolute but rather a property of interaction. Fitness landscapes are determined by all the agents in a system and all the systems in a suprasystem; survival depends on your own, your rivals', and your collaborators' strategies. Creativity and innovation, then, require both competitive and cooperative interaction between members of a group that leads to improved fitness for the group. Individuals are creative only insofar as they manage to engage the other members of a group in some kind of dialogue or other interaction. How does this amplification of individual creativity to a group level occur?

The key to this process, I suggest, lies in the manner in which the members of a group differentiate their roles into those of leaders and followers. An important insight into this process is available from participation in experiential group relations conferences, and it is on the basis of my participation in these conferences that I offer the following observations.

The process of differentiating roles into those of leaders and followers always arouses fear, anxiety, and envy. We seem to fear that we will lose our own individuality if we give up some of our authority to someone else, almost as if the choice were all or nothing, and we envy others who have more power than we do. When a group of people come together voluntarily and without any prior structure to perform a task, they therefore always resist appointing a leader, reasoning that all members can be equal and still perform the task. This is the defensive opposite Learning Model I behavior.

Eventually, frustrated at their inability to perform the primary task, the group may agree to appoint one of their number as the leader, with the rest somewhat warily taking up follower roles. This initial leader-follower differentiation is made in relation to the current primary task of the group or employment of the dominant schema, and it tends to be rather permanent. In carrying out the current primary task, the leader-follower role differentiation becomes institutionalized because it is the most efficient strategy to follow and because it is a highly effective way of containing the anxiety of group life. In fantasy, the leader-follower dynamic may well be experienced as the re-creation of the family structure, which may be why it contains anxiety. This is what we find, of course, in the "real life" that occurs outside group relations conferences—institutionalized leader-follower roles concerned with interactions around the current primary tasks of the group.

However, in parallel with this, another leader-follower role differentiation is going on, and it often takes members a long time to realize this; it seems that we most readily recognize leadership in its institutionalized, parental form. The other kind of differentiation occurs when a member of a group has a contribution to make and manages to attract and hold the attention of the group long enough to make it. During that period of time, this person is the leader and the others are followers. The leader-follower roles in this instance fluctuate, shifting from member to member according to a number of complex personality factors and potentials for contributing, as well as according to the prevailing emotional atmosphere in the group. This fluctuating differentiation in roles is provoked by and in turn provokes play within the recessive symbol system. It is thus intimately connected with double-loop learning, dialogue, and creativity, and the interactions it is concerned with have to do with emotion, exploration, and experimentation.

The two kinds of leader-follower role differentiations are not, of course, completely divorced from each other. Members with personalities that drive them to frequent contributions in the play area are also the most likely candidates for leadership in the primary-task area. And once leadership in the primary-task area has become institutionalized, the work leaders come to hold an enhanced status and authority in the play area.

If a group of people is to be creative, then, it must occupy the space for novelty and must be able to hold the consequent anxiety. This need to contain anxiety leads to the link between creativity and leader-follower role differentiation. Two basic strategies seem to be open to a group for coping with the anxieties of creative behavior: the first is specialization and the second is participation.

Occupying the Space for Creativity by Specializing. The specialization strategy is one in which a group differentiates its members into rather fixed leader-follower roles. Through projection and projective identification an innovative individual takes up the role of leader or articulator of a new narrative or image, and the others take up the roles of followers. The followers project their own creativity and authority onto their leader in return for the leader's tacit agreement to hold the anxieties of the transitional space, the paradoxes of the depressive position, on their behalf. In this way, they come to occupy the same transitional space as the leader: they are at the edge of chaos by proxy. The group will now be creative only if it allows the leader to be creative by continuing to play within his or her own mental recessive symbol system and to hold the depressive position. It will be innovative only if the leader is able to persuade, inspire, or force other members to replace their shared dominant symbol system with his or her own replacements. Thus, innovation can continue only while projections are held in place and the members continue to surrender their own creativity and authority. The tension between the legitimate system and the shadow system is located in the leader.

When the specialization strategy is adopted, a group may still occupy the space for novelty at the edge of chaos but now it is by proxy through the group's leader. The leader, however, can only remain in that role while the followers are prepared to follow and the leader is prepared to lead, in other words, while the contract between them is observed. The contract may be fully conscious or unconscious; it may be sustained by persuasion, by some kind of unconscious collusion, or through fear; and it may be quite short-lived or last a very long time.

The scope for breakdown here is obviously great. The leader may introduce a highly successful change in the legitimate system and then become identified with it. She or he may then resist any change in the legitimate system and, unless someone else is co-opted into the leadership role, creativity will dry up. Or the members may become locked into the first innovation chosen and the creative leader may then find it impossible to sustain the projections and persuade the followers to change the legitimate system. Innovation will then cease. Or the strain of holding the anxiety may become too great, resulting in neurotic leadership and hence neurotic followership (Kets de Vries, 1989). However, specializing the creativity of a group in one or a few people who occupy the space and hold the tension may work for a long time and has proved to be a successful strategy in many cases.

Occupying the Space for Creativity Participatively. The alternative route to occupation of the space for novelty involves widespread participation. This occurs when the differentiation of leader-follower roles takes on a shifting form determined by contribution. As one member takes up the leadership role, others project their creativity into him or her, but this is very short-lived and they take the projection back as soon as the member vacates the leadership role. In this way, all or most members take part not only in the creative play itself but also in holding the anxiety that the play generates. The play then becomes not one of unconscious projection and projective identification as much as a more conscious one of dialogue and self-reflection. The group as a whole engages in double-loop learning through which individuals change both the unshared and partially shared symbol systems in their schemas. This is a participative occupation of the transitional space, a more consciously shared group space rather than one that is apparently individual but is, in fact, an unconsciously shared group space.

In this strategy, the tension between the legitimate and the shadow group systems is not specialized but is borne by all or most members. This holds out a greater possibility of continuing creativity, and it is likely to make the translation from creativity to innovation easier because it is no longer a process of one or a few trying to convert the others—everyone has taken part in the creative process. However, it is still not a foregone conclusion that potential innovation will follow potential creativity or that a group will be able to continue holding the anxiety. The strategy of joint, conscious occupation of the space for creativity in a group may work sometimes but not all the time.

Impact of Power Differentials. Another important point should be noted about the leader-follower differentiation. Whenever this type of differentiation occurs, it always creates a power differential, no matter whether the differentiation is in relation to the dominant or recessive symbol systems or whether it is participative or specialized. This power differential introduces another control parameter into a group of human agents that is closely linked to anxiety. The manner in which power is used is one of the factors that causes a group of people to be in one dynamic zone rather than another. So if the leader-follower contract is a formally established, fully conscious one sustained by fear, the group is likely to operate in the stable zone. If this is what followers expect and accept, it can be a very effective container of anxiety but a complete block on double-loop learning and creativity. Here the followers do what the leader says, providing much scope for the neurotic leader.

On the other hand, if a vacuum in expected leadership exists, anxiety levels are likely to rise. We then find the nature of leadership being dictated by the basic assumption behavior of the group. If it is in a dependency mode, it will co-opt one of its members to become the dependency leader. However, unrealistically high hopes will be placed in this leader, who will then soon fail and be rejected, perhaps to be replaced by a fight leader. Here, in effect, the leader struggles to do the impossible that is unconsciously desired by the group, and this ensures both neurotic leadership and neurotic followership.

In the phase transition, the leader-follower relationship takes one of two forms. In the participative case discussed above it is ambiguous. The leader for the time being holds the boundary by being involved in the group process but not being sucked into it (Miller and Rice, 1967). Followers are mature and leadership tends to shift according to ability to contribute. The leader-follower contract is thus a flexible one, sustained by trust and respect, and this trust and respect, as well as the ability to articulate the issues, provides containment for anxiety. In the other form, specialization, one or a small number of people hold the ambiguity and anxiety more or less permanently. They then must be psychologically tough enough to avoid succumbing to neurosis or even psychosis.

As well as being a control parameter closely allied to anxiety containment, the leader-follower dynamic is also part of the definition of the edge of chaos for a group of people: it is a state in which paradox and anxiety are held either by a specialized elite or, participatively, by all the members. It is not a foregone conclusion which of these strategies for staying at the edge will be the most successful. The elite option has the advantage of much greater containment of anxiety for group members, but a much greater burden of both anxiety and creative ability on the leader. The possibility of neurotic leadership then becomes very real (Kets de Vries, 1980, 1984, 1989, 1991; Hirschhorn, 1990; Schwartz, 1990; Oberholzer and Roberts, 1995; Carr and Shapiro, 1995), and this propensity for neurosis also applies to followers, who may become bored, unfulfilled, and therefore less productive. The followers may then employ any retained creativity to disrupt the group, or they may take that creativity into activities outside the group (Trist and Branforth, 1951).

The participative strategy holds out the promise of much faster rates of creativity and innovation if it generates enough trust and respect to contain the anxiety. However, it is the specialization strategy that has been most frequently used in the past, at least in the West; it is the story of almost all entrepreneurial beginnings of firms and is the continuing story of most major corporations. Will it continue to be a successful strategy in a world that appears to be changing so rapidly and in which competitors may be using the participative strategy?

Taking account of the fact that human agents inevitably differentiate themselves into leader and follower roles by no means invalidates mapping the edge of chaos found in nonhuman feedback networks onto human groups. Such role differentiation provides a richer definition of what the edge of chaos means, and the consequent power differentials provide another control parameter for the human feedback network. A powerful leader may be able to shift a whole group out of the space for novelty into either the stable or unstable zones of behavior for groups. But no matter how powerful the leader, she or he cannot change what double-loop learning means or the fact that the creativity it produces is also destructive and so provokes anxiety. The paradoxical space for novelty must be occupied for creativity to occur, either by the leader alone or by all members, and this remains true no matter how powerful the leader.

Participant and Observer

In some of the computer simulations considered in Chapter Three, the agents could examine their own schemas as part of the process of learning. Human agents, however, can do more than this: they can reflect upon themselves as a group to understand the system they constitute. Does this invalidate the mapping of the space for novelty onto human groups?

We have seen that when a group of people operates in the stable zone, its learning behavior is being driven by Learning Model I, an essentially defensive structure. That schema forbids any kind of systemic thinking in the group situation. Individuals may privately reflect upon their own processes and on the group process and may even discuss them privately with each other, but the model forbids the group as a whole from discussing such matters. This ban on systemic thinking, on adopting the participant-observer role, effectively keeps the group in the stable zone. Much the same can be said of a group in the unstable zone: the basic assumption behavior characteristic of that zone makes self-reflection, even private self-reflection by members, a matter of great difficulty, and it is impossible for the group as a whole. This inability to examine its own processes keeps the group locked into its basic assumption behavior.

However, when a group of people can reflect upon their own group processes, when they can understand something about the system they constitute, then they are able to hold some of the paradoxes of group life, engage in double-loop learning, and become creative. Thus, the participant observer dynamic is only possible in the transitional space between stability and instability; it is part of the definition of the edge of chaos for groups of humans. At the edge of chaos people can reflect together on the system they constitute and hold the roles of participant and observer simultaneously. This ability is also what makes it possible for people to stay at the edge.

A group of people constitutes a nonlinear feedback network. The fact that they are human agents rather than bit strings on a computer adds a distinctiveness and a richness to what it means to be at the edge of chaos but does not alter any of the fundamental characteristics of the edge of chaos. The ability of some agents to become leaders and of groups to self-reflect does not enable humans to alter the dynamic progression of the system they constitute. No matter how clever the systemic thinker and how powerful, charismatic, and talented the leader, they cannot change the fact that groups can operate in stable zones, unstable zones, or at the edge of chaos. They cannot change the fact that double-loop learning and therefore creativity are possible only at the edge of chaos.

What both effective systemic thinking and effective leadership can do is to contain much higher levels of anxiety than would otherwise be possible, making it feasible for groups to be creative even when information flows, individual diversity, and connectedness are at very high levels. Systemic thinking and leadership are human strategies that make it more possible for us to survive at the edge of chaos than other species. The conclusion reached for the individual mind is also reached for a group of individuals.

Power and self-reflection cannot alter the dynamics and neither can the human link between inspiration and anxiety. We will now see the different ways in which a group may contain the anxiety of individuals.

Containing the Anxiety

The first way of containing group anxiety is for the group to impose structures on an individual that prevent him or her from occupying the space for creativity, the edge of chaos. Groups have powerful reasons for trying to do this because of the intimate connection between creativity and destructiveness, so they may contain anxiety by establishing structures that keep the individual members and the group as a whole away from the edge of chaos and safely in the stable zone. Learning Model I is one example of this. The process of socialization normally discourages individuals, as they grow up, from occupying the transitional space, from playing. Those adults who defiantly continue to play are likely to be labeled eccentric or mad, heretics or rebels, subversives or delinquents (Miller, 1983). This way of containing anxiety severely restricts the creativity of individuals and groups. A variant of this process has already been discussed, that of specializing creativity, of splitting it off and locating it in a few leaders. In this way most members of a group are protected from anxiety, but they are also blocked from the fulfillment of creativity.

The alternative method of containing anxiety so that a group of individuals can jointly stay at the edge of chaos relies first on the quality of the relationships that people in the group develop among themselves. In other words, for human agents it is not simply the extent of the connectivity but the quality of the connections that causes the system to operate at the edge. So if relationships have the quality of trust and compassion, if they are based on empathy and love, then they operate as very effective containers of anxiety. Given high-quality interconnectedness, a group can contain anxiety and stay at the edge of chaos.

The second way of containing anxiety without abandoning the edge of chaos is provided by the opportunity and capacity for honest self-reflection, that is, when members of a group jointly reflect upon and discuss the system they constitute. This is double-loop learning, a process that both provokes and contains anxiety.

The third way to contain anxiety involves the quality of leadership and the manner in which power is exercised. This is likely to happen when leaders avoid authoritarian behavior and getting sucked into group processes and exhibit a capacity for articulating issues and posing insightful questions; in this process, leadership moves among people according to their ability to contribute and power alternates between authority and influence. In all these cases, anxiety is not banished by a move to the stable zone; instead, ways are found to hold the anxiety, to feel it, to accept the destructive aspects of creativity and yet be able to continue working.

Finally, the reader is invited to note the self-similar nature of the spaces for novelty at the levels of the individual mind and the group. At both levels the containment of anxiety, not its removal, enables the individual and the group to occupy the edge of chaos. Both are states in which the tensions of inspiration-anxiety, individuation-conformity, domination-submission, and participation-observation can be held. And both are states in which recessive, or shadow, symbol systems work behind the scenes in tension with the dominant, or legitimate, symbol systems to change the dominant system. This seems to be the essence of the creative process for a nonlinear feedback network.

Conclusion

The space for novelty for a group of people lies between the defensive routines employed by people when they use Learning Model I, on the one hand, and basic assumption behavior, on the other hand. It is a paradoxical space in which people are their individual, different selves, yet conform enough to play. In this space, together, people can hold the anxiety of creative destruction because of the relationships of trust within the group; they are also assisted to do this because as a group they operate within a good enough holding environment, of which one major aspect is the existence of trust and another is an efficient legitimate system.

The defining characteristic of the space for creativity in a group is that it is a state of tension between a legitimate system seeking to sustain the status quo and contain anxiety in the interest of current primary-task performance and a shadow system seeking to undermine that status quo and replace it in the interest of increased fitness. The space for creativity exhibits the apparent stability of the legitimate system with the constant flux of the shadow system behind it. If the shadow system ceases to fluctuate and simply supports the legitimate system, the group moves into the stable zone away from the edge of chaos, away from the space for novelty. If the flux in the shadow system is accompanied by disintegration in the legitimate system, the group moves into the unstable zone, and the legitimate system's failure to contain anxiety leads to basic assumption behavior.

Members can occupy the space for creativity by proxy through an unconscious process of co-opting a leader, or they can occupy it jointly in a more conscious manner. If, through one route or another, a group is capable of occupying this space and, through the interplay of ideas, it changes the recessive part of its schema so that it replaces the currently dominant shared schema, then it will have succeeded in being both creative and innovative. Whether that innovation is a success or not will depend upon whether the changed behavior renders the group fitter, and that depends on the shape of the fitness landscape just as much as on the change in behavior itself. As with an individual, the fitness landscape is determined by others—the other groups and individuals that the group in question is relating to. Often, most of them will be within the same organization, so the effectiveness of an innovation in a group depends upon whether the group can also engage the creativity and innovation processes in other groups both within the organization to which it belongs and outside it. This brings us to the level of the organization.

6

The Space for Creativity in an Organization

Organizations are creative when their individual members learn and interact creatively with each other in groups. Organizational creativity and learning is, thus, the amplification and incorporation into shared schemas of individual and small-group creativity and learning and the containment of the anxiety that this process arouses. A theory of creativity at an organizational level must, therefore, explain this process of amplification and incorporation of schema changes and how the accompanying anxiety is contained. Given that creativity at the individual, group, and organizational levels is so inextricably intertwined, explanations of the creative process at each level must be clearly related to each other if they are to be useful. In fact, it would be reasonable to expect the explanations to be self-similar, that is, repetitions of similar qualitative process patterns at different levels. Indeed, the explanations presented in the last two chapters do demonstrate self-similar processes at the levels of the individual mind and the group.

165

As we saw in Chapters Four and Five, widely accepted, coherent explanations of creativity and innovation by individuals and groups that are found in the psychoanalytic literature have immediately obvious connections with the science of complexity, even though they were developed before that science, or at least independently of it. This cannot be said to apply at the level of an organization. The structure of this chapter, therefore, differs from that of the previous two. Instead of summarizing a few well-known explanations and then showing how they match the science of complexity, this chapter will take each characteristic of the space for novelty identified for complex adaptive systems in Figure 3.6 and ask whether the literature on organizational change, innovation, and creativity provides any support for its existence at the organizational level. In doing this I will be trying to use theoretical building blocks for managing and organizing that are already available in the literature in order to construct a complex adaptive system theory of creative organizational development.

The Science of Complexity and Explanations of Creativity in Organizations

The nonlinear feedback networks surveyed in Chapters Two and Three all display a space for novelty that takes the form of a phase transition between stability and instability. Chapters Four and Five identified spaces for creativity at the levels of both the individual and the group that take the form of a phase transition between rather rigid defenses and concrete ways of engaging current reality, on the one hand, and disintegrative behavior driven by fantasies of a psychotic kind on the other. There is, therefore, a convincing match between the space for creativity in physical, chemical, biological, and computer-simulated feedback systems; the individual mind; and the human group. Can we locate a similar phase transition at the level of the organization, continuing the pattern of self-similarity in the creative process from an individual to a group, and then to an organization? This section demonstrates that this can be done simply by putting together a number of well-known notions about organizations.

A Phase Transition

In demonstrating how the space for creativity at individual and group levels has the characteristics of a phase transition, extensive use was made of the distinction between dominant and recessive parts of schemas, a distinction displayed in simulations of the evolution of complex adaptive systems described in Chapter Three. This distinction can also be shown to apply at the level of the organization.

Every organization must perform a set of primary tasks, tasks that members must jointly carry out if they are to survive—that is, if they are to attract sufficient support from other systems they need to interact with. To perform its primary tasks an organization must have a system for carrying them out; as we saw in Chapter One, this is the purpose of an organization's legitimate system with its dominant schema. However, as we also saw in that chapter, people do not come together in organizations simply to perform primary tasks. While they work they also socialize with each other to form a shadow system. They may use this system to sabotage the primary task or to constitute a learning community that assists the legitimate system to function in the face of ambiguity and uncertainty by circumventing its rules. Members of an organization may use their shadow system for personal politicking or for organizationally useful political activity such as issue agenda building (Huff, 1988), or they may use it as a vehicle for organizational hypocrisy and irrationality in the interest of securing joint action (Brunsson, 1985, 1987).

Whatever it is used for, the shadow system is driven by recessive symbol systems, just as it is in groups. This organizational recessive symbol system consists of both the individual schemas of all members of an organization that are not shared with others and schemas that are partially shared within and across some groups, but not widely shared across the organization as a whole. The recessive symbol system of an organization is the repertoire of mental contents, as well as actual and potential behaviors, available to it but not currently engaging current primary tasks. The legitimate and shadow systems clearly interact with each other. Indeed, I suggest that the basic dynamics of an organization are determined by the manner in which these two systems inter-act. Let us consider the possibilities.

The purpose of an organization's legitimate system is to drive the performance of current primary tasks in the most efficient manner possible, that is, to engage with external reality. All legit-imate systems are cybernetic ones based upon negative feedback; they seek to steer and guide the performance of primary tasks, to sustain the status quo in the interest of efficient task performance, and to change the status quo in orderly and predictable ways to maintain that efficient performance. An efficient legitimate sys-tem is always an orderly, regular, stable equilibrium system that exists to actualize prior organizational intention. Because of this, it is a very effective container of the anxieties of individual, group, and organizational life: it delivers at least the illusion and some-times also the fact of certainty. The shadow system, however, has a potentially wider range of dynamics.

The dynamic that seems to be most widely commented upon, both in the literature and in practice, is the disorderly one: the shadow system can operate in a manner that directly sabotages the performance of the organization's primary task. Here it has the dynamics of anarchy, in which groups of members are submerged in basic assumption behavior, psychotic fantasies, and neurotic acting out, with mob behavior an ever-present possibility. The col-lapse of an organization under this pressure is held at bay only by the power and stability of the legitimate system. If the system fails in any way, the organization as a whole will display the dynamics of anarchy and disintegration. Only while the legitimate system holds the shadow at bay can the threat posed by an anarchic shadow be avoided.

However, the shadow system of an organization can also display the dynamics of great stability: this happens when resistance to change is located in the shadow system. This too is a dynamic that is widely commented upon: many point to how "illegitimate" resistance causes the failure of comprehensive culture change programs in organizations (Beer, Eisenstat, and Spector, 1990). Legitimate systems not only drive current task performance but also provide much of the current containment of anxiety. When people try to implement comprehensive plans to dismantle these defenses, the shadow system may well come into play to prevent this from happening, sabotaging the change but sustaining the stability of the status quo. It may exhibit rather sophisticated defensive systems, some of them unconscious, that are difficult to understand and access; Chapter Eight will give a practical illustration of this use of the shadow system in the case of Enigma Chemicals. When a defensive shadow system sustains the legitimate system, the organization clearly occupies a very stable zone, and that carries with it the danger of ossification. Even if the dominant symbol system begins to disintegrate, a powerfully conformist shadow system can counteract the disintegration for a long time, allowing the organization as a whole to continue ossifying.

This description of the dynamic possibilities open to an organization's informal system mirrors those that are open to a group as described in the last chapter. This is not surprising, because an organization's shadow system is simply a shifting set of small groups, of people coming together for one implicit purpose and then reforming for another. If they are all tightly locked into the same rigidly defensive behavior, then no matter how they shift, their groupings will continue to display much the same stable patterns of behavior. On the other hand, if an organization's shadow system is disintegrating into anarchy, then all of the small groups in that shifting pattern will display psychotic fantasies and basic assumption behavior. In other words, the dynamics of the shadow system so far are simply those of the small group writ large—and more dramatically. But the group has a third dynamic: the phase transition in which members are able to hold the anxiety of play and dialogue and perform double-loop learning without slipping into either ossifying defensive behavior or disintegrative psychotic fantasy. It follows that a third dynamic also exists for that shifting set of small groups that constitutes the shadow system of an organization.

The third dynamic occurs when some of the small groups in the shadow system are able to occupy the space between rigid defensiveness and psychotic fantasy. Then, at least in parts of the shadow system, groups can engage in the dialogues of double-loop learning. Parts of the shadow system will then be engaged in play within the organization's recessive symbol system; this constitutes potential creativity. This position at the edge of anarchy will be held most securely for an organization as a whole when the legitimate system is stable and functional, because then the anxiety provoked by creativity in the shadow system will be at its most contained. A disintegrating, weak, or inefficient legitimate system accompanied by a shadow system in creative flux may result in an entire organization being catapulted into the unstable zone.

This provides us with a clear meaning for the organizational space for novelty at the edge of chaos. It exists when at least parts of an organization's shadow system are in the space for group creativity and are operating in tension with a stable and efficient legitimate system, the tension arising from the fact that the shadow system has the potential for replacing the legitimate system. An illustration of what this means in practice will be given in the case of the aid agency in Chapter Eight. Figure 6.1 summarizes the different relationships between the legitimate and shadow systems of an organization and indicates the consequences for the dynamics of the organization as a whole.

Figure 6.1. Zones of Operation for an Organization's Shadow System.

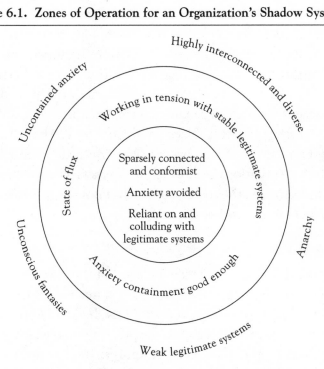

Highly interconnected and diverse

Uncontained anxiety

Working in tension with stable legitimate systems

State of flux

Sparsely connected
and conformist

Anxiety avoided

Reliant on and
colluding with
legitimate systems

Anarchy

Unconscious fantasies

Anxiety containment good enough

Weak legitimate systems

I am arguing, then, that it is primarily the state of the shadow system that determines whether or not an organization operates in the space for creativity at the edge of chaos, no matter whether the occupation is by the few on behalf of the many or jointly by the many. The space for creativity in an organization lies at the edge of organizational disintegration or anarchy. For an organization to occupy this space, its shadow system must be in a state of flux behind the stable facade of its legitimate system. The shadow must be working to undermine the legitimate system in acts of creative destruction.

When an organization is in this state, at least some of its members play by engaging in exploratory dialogue, utilizing analogies and metaphors, and employing self-reflection to develop new knowledge. This new knowledge is expressed as the replacement of parts of an organization's recessive symbol system in an act of creative destruction. If this change is then amplified through the organization to become a change in the dominant schema of the organization, potential innovation has occurred. Whether this potential turns out to be actual creativity and innovation depends on whether the changed behavior of the organization enables it to climb higher up a fitness peak or up a higher peak. The fitness landscape for an organization, however, is determined by the actions of the other organizations with which it interacts, that is, the actions of the industry and the society of which it is a part. We will return to this point at the end of this chapter.

A State of Paradox

The above discussion has made it clear that the phase transition is a state of fundamental paradox. In this state, a legitimate system strives to sustain the status quo while its shadow system seeks to alter it. Both of these forces must be present and operating in tension with each other if an organization is to be changeable enough but not so changeable that it falls apart into anarchy and psychotic group processes. The need for both efficiency and effectiveness exists despite the fact that they are the enemies of each other.

Organizational life, in fact, displays the same paradoxes as those listed in Chapter Five. The basic paradox of individualism and conformity is expressed at an organizational level as the paradox of decentralization and centralization. Competitive advantage also requires organizations to sustain paradox: a company cannot choose to compete on the basis of price with no regard for quality, nor can it compete on the basis of quality with no regard for price. Competitive advantage has to be based on both quality and cost, despite the fact that they pull in opposite directions.

The fundamentally paradoxical nature of organizations has long been recognized in the literature (Quinn and Cameron, 1988), which describes many more paradoxes (Hampden-Turner, 1990). Evidence shows that when organizations resolve the paradox, they eventually fail (Miller, 1990), whereas those that sustain the paradox and operate in nonequilibrium states are more likely to survive (Pascale, 1990). Once again creative and innovative organizations show the same characteristics as other complex adaptive systems.

The Actualization of Archetypes

The literature that deals with the content of organizational strategies displays a clear distinction between what can be thought of as archetypal organizational behavior and the actualization of that behavior. Typically, in the strategy content literature, we find a description of some general, or archetypal, strategy followed by one or more specific case studies, or actualizations, that illustrate it. So, for example, some classification of acquisition strategies will be set out—acquisition to secure vertical diversification; acquisition to secure horizontal diversification; related acquisitions; unrelated acquisitions; acquisition of low-technology, high-market-share companies; and so on. A few examples of companies following a particular strategy are given. Even though a number of organizations may follow the same archetypal strategic pattern, they never exactly replicate each other's experience. Instead, they actualize a slightly different pattern in a manner dependent upon the details of their own specific experiences.

Almost every organizational behavior pattern seems to display this relationship between a category, or archetype, and a specific realization that is unique for each organization. At one time or another every organization follows a pattern of decentralizing its operations, but no two do so in the same way. In fact, as organizations move through cycles of decentralization and centralization, they never repeat the pattern in the same way. This, once again, reveals the distinction between an archetype and its realization. Organizations display the same feature as all other complex adaptive systems—they repeat archetypal patterns as they evolve, but the actualization of those patterns is always different.

Creative Destruction

The discussion on the transitional nature of the space for creativity in an organization concluded that this space is a state in which an organization's legitimate system is stable and functional with at least some small groups within its shadow system remaining poised between rigidly defensive behavior and psychotic fantasy. As at the individual and small-group levels, this is a state of tension, because the shadow system is working to subvert the legitimate system. Creativity is play in the shadow system, the creatively destructive process of replacing parts of an organization's recessive symbol system, which holds out the possibility of innovation.

The dominant schema of an organization is its store or memory of previous learning. If an organization is to innovate, to perform new primary tasks and/or perform primary tasks in novel ways, then the dominant schema, and thus its embodiment in the legitimate system, must change. As with a group, any significant change in the dominant schema of an organization can occur only after some process of play in which the recessive symbol system has been manipulated and changed. Creative organizations change their recessive schemas through playlike learning activities conducted within their shadow systems. Innovation occurs when these learning communities, or play groups, acquire enough power to compete against and overcome those who are protecting the status quo (Duguid and Brown, 1991). Members of the play group can then install their changed recessive symbol system as a replacement for the dominant symbol system. Changes in legitimate systems do not usually happen purely through formal discussion within the systems themselves; rather, they follow a period of dialogue and political maneuvering outside the legitimate arena, in the shadow system.

Note that it is not necessarily the most powerful in the legitimate system who seek to sustain the status quo. They may have originally installed the legitimate system and been committed to it, but it not infrequently happens that they then seek to change it, only to be blocked by the obstruction of the majority. In this case, the parts of the shadow system operating in the space for creativity at the edge of chaos could well be the small group of the most powerful. In other cases, however, the most powerful members of the legitimate system might be working to keep it unchanged, and the less powerful may constitute the learning groups who are seeking to upset the balance of power and change the legitimate system. At the edge of chaos in an organization, learning and political activity are always intertwined.

The holding of the tension between the legitimate and shadow systems can be specialized: small groups of powerful elite may occupy the phase transition while others actualize the dominant schemas. Members throughout the organization then unconsciously project their creativity and authority into a few leaders and their destructiveness into others, and the formal structures and shared culture of the organization may institutionalize this pattern. Another strategy is to have a more widespread participative, conscious occupation of the organizational space for creativity. Both of these strategies for occupying the space for creativity have advantages and disadvantages, in terms of the ability to stay there and thus continue to be creative and the ability to translate creativity into innovation. Neither has any guarantee of success, and sometimes one strategy will work better than the other.

Suppose that an elite leader group is able to hold itself at the edge of chaos and produce creative changes in an organization's recessive schemas. How is it to get these changes into the dominant system? It may try to do so by making the hierarchical structures less definite, or by using fuzzy job descriptions to achieve more flexibility, or by mounting comprehensive programs of persuasion and reeducation. However, if the shadow system is highly defensive, such a loosening of the legitimate system is unlikely to have much effect. The shadow system will simply counteract what the most powerful are trying to do. It will require some highly anxiety-provoking shock to shake the shadow system from its rigid state, because the stable zone, like that of individuals and groups, is maintained by rigidly defensive behaviors and structures, particularly implicit, unconscious ones. The stable zone is a place of low anxiety; people are protected by legitimate systems, by their strongly shared defensive shadow system, and perhaps by a powerful sense of belonging. Anxiety is also low because ambiguity, uncertainty, and paradox are banished.

Now consider what is likely to happen if change agents are able to shock people out of this kind of conformist culture by plunging them into some crisis, while at the same time decentralizing the hierarchial structures and making the bureaucracy more flexible and less clear-cut. In other words, the defensive behaviors and structures are dismantled and people are exposed to ambiguity, paradox, and uncertainty. We would expect—and evidence supports this expectation—that anxiety levels would rise and many of the groups of which the organization is composed would be plunged into basic assumption behavior (Schwartz, 1990). This is a situation in which the legitimate system lacks clarity and discipline and is highly decentralized and disintegrating, and the shadow system is also in a disintegrative state. The organization then operates in the unstable zone; it is in anarchy or utter chaos. High levels of anxiety exist with little containment, and many things will be going wrong. The organization will be incapable of carrying out its primary task or of learning to change its schemas.

However, between the stable and unstable zones is the phase transition, the space for creativity. It has a stable legitimate system consisting of clear hierarchical structures and bureaucracies, supported by compliant, conforming behavior, on the one hand, and a shadow system, on the other hand, that is characterized by diversity, tension, and contention. The shadow system is in a state of flux and is working at undermining the legitimate system in the interest of change. Its tension, however, arouses anxiety; therefore, the diversity must not be too extreme, but must be contained by some relationships of trust. Furthermore, the very rigidity of the legitimate system, which the shadow system is seeking to subvert, is a most effective container of the anxieties that the process of subversion unleashes. As with all other nonlinear feedback systems, the edge of chaos for organizations is also a place of ambiguity and outright paradox, a process of creative destruction.

A Critical Point for Control Parameters

When the legitimate and shadow systems operate against each other, an organization is in the phase transition at the edge of chaos; it is only here that it is changeable, because it is only here that it is capable of double-loop learning. In double-loop learning, schemas are changed—the individual schemas of agent members and the schemas they share. Schema changes occur first at an individual interaction level, as an individual develops a new rule, stops referring to a previously shared rule, or interacts with other individuals to share a new rule. If these small changes occurring at an individual interaction level are amplified across a number of other individuals, we can say that a particular group of individuals has learned. If the schema changes of this group are amplified across many other groups so that they come to have a powerful effect at the organizational level, we may say that the organization has learned. In other words, organizations cannot be said to be learning if the groups and individuals they are composed of are not learning, and they cannot be said to be creative unless the groups and individuals they are composed of are being creative.

If an organization is in the stable zone, with an efficient legitimate system reinforced by a defensive shadow system, then by definition it bans the expression of difference and the questioning of assumptions. Groups within the organization are then also in the stable zone; they cannot engage in double-loop learning and the individuals of which they are composed are heavily discouraged from occupying the world of transitional objects. The whole learning mechanism is jammed from top to bottom. This process is exactly the same as the one demonstrated by Ackley's AL simulation, which was described in Chapter Three: an efficient operational schema is shielding an atrophied evaluation schema (Ackley and Littman, 1992).

If an organization is in the unstable zone—that is, it has a highly diverse, anarchic shadow system that is not at all contained by an efficient legitimate system—the whole organization will be suffused with basic assumption behavior. The anxiety of the groups of which the organization is composed will not be contained very much by organizational structures, and the organization's members will be immersed in basic assumption behavior. This makes it impossible for individuals to hold the anxiety of the depressive space required for individual creativity. Once again the learning structure is incapacitated at every level.

However, when the anxiety provoked by high levels of diversity is contained by efficient legitimate systems for carrying out current primary tasks, groups are able to occupy the space between rigidly defensive behavior and basic assumption behavior, and this in turn provides the containment to enable individuals to play in the transitional space of their minds. In an organization at the edge of chaos, the whole learning structure at lower levels is freed up to function.

Note that the legitimate system in an organization that is consistently at the edge of chaos rarely displays anything like the edge of chaos itself. Instead, the legitimate system displays stability, often for lengthy periods of time, and then suddenly changes to a new stable form in what looks like punctuated equilibrium. But behind the stable walls of legitimacy, the shadow system is always in a state of flux when an organization is at the edge of chaos, with political maneuvering and double-loop learning going on behind the scenes. Over some period of time, the shape of a change in the legitimate system is hammered out by political interaction and group learning processes; then, at some critical point, it emerges to replace the old legitimate system. This is the same phenomenon as the one revealed by the Ramp simulation (Hillis, 1992) discussed in Chapter Three. There a dominant schema was apparently suddenly replaced by a new one, but the process of fashioning the new one had been going on for some time in the recessive parts of the system's schema. This interaction between dominant and recessive schemas, between legitimate and shadow systems, may be a common characteristic of complex adaptive systems.

What determines whether an organization is at the edge or not? What pushes it from the stable zone, through the edge of chaos, and into the unstable zone? In other words, what are the control parameters? There seem to be five: the rate of information flow, the degree of diversity, the richness of connectivity, the level of contained anxiety, and the degree of power differentials.

Rate of Information Flow. As with all other nonlinear feedback systems, an increase in the flow of information tends to push an organization away from stability. Information will flow at a slow rate and be easy to retain in formal systems when the other organizations and individuals that constitute the environment are moving slowly. The first organization can then move at a leisurely pace across a rather stable fitness landscape. The faster the others change their strategies, however, the more the fitness landscape heaves about. This means that the information necessary to inform members about the changing landscape must flow more rapidly through the organization; this makes it more difficult to retain it in formal systems. At some critical point it becomes impossible for formal systems to retain enough information, and it becomes necessary to use the shadow system, the grapevine, which can retain faster flows of information because of its informality and the fact that information is retained and acted upon at local levels. Past the critical point, even the shadow system will be unable to retain enough information to enable the organization to cope with competitors' moves. This places great pressure on both the legitimate and shadow systems, tipping the organization into the unstable zone.

Degree of Diversity. As with other adaptive nonlinear feedback networks, the degree of diversity in schemas is another control parameter. The above discussion has shown how a defensive shadow system characterized by conforming members produces stable organizational dynamics and how increases in the degree of diversity among agents can rise to a point at which the organization falls into anarchy. At some critical point between these extremes, the organization has enough diversity to provoke learning but not enough to cause anarchy.

Richness of Connectivity. The dynamics of adaptive nonlinear feedback networks are also sensitive to the degree of connectivity between the agents in a system. Few connections bring stability and many bring instability, but between the extremes lie critical points where connections are rich enough but not too rich, and the result is endless variety in behavior. Studies of networks among human agents produce rather similar conclusions. Greater behavioral variety occurs when informal ties between people in a network are weak rather than strong. Ties are strong when people spend much time together, are emotionally involved, are mutually confiding, and provide reciprocal services. The effect of strong ties is to bind people together, making it more likely that behavior will be repetitive and uniform. Weak ties, on the other hand, provide bridges to other parts of a network through which variety may be imported into a cluster of people held together with strong ties (Granovetter, 1973). Other research, however, shows that strong affective ties increase feelings of security and can thus make a group of people more likely to change, so that strong ties may be more associated with variety in behavior (Krackhardt, 1992). Strong ties probably imply few ties, whereas weak ties probably mean a greater number of ties.

What the research indicates, then, is that at some critical point in the ranges of weakness to strength and many to few, the network is likely to produce great variety in behavior. With few and strong ties it will produce stable behavior—that is, too little variety for effective learning—and presumably with many and weak ties it will produce unstable behavior—that is, too much variety for effective learning.

Level of Contained Anxiety. Human systems have another control parameter—the level of contained anxiety. When anxiety is so firmly contained that it is avoided altogether, for example, by strict adherence to the requirements of hierarchy and bureaucracy, then an organization's shadow system operates in the stable zone. Members of an organization in this state may unconsciously behave as if they were members of a comfortable, secure family rather than members of a commercial organization. They will then resist change in a very effective manner; Chapter Eight provides a case study on Enigma Chemicals of just such an organization. When the anxieties of work and creativity are not sufficiently contained, an organization is swept by basic assumption behavior and psychotic fantasy, making any creative work impossible, and it operates in the unstable zone. Only when the anxiety of work and creativity can be experienced, but also held and contained in a good enough manner, is creativity possible.

Part of the good enough holding environment is provided by an organization's members themselves; the holding is good enough if they trust and like each other to a reasonable extent. Also, the manner in which power is used is an element in the environment for containing anxiety; this will be discussed below. Another element is the larger system of which an organization is a part—the industry and the society of which it is a member. Thus, the manner in which others in a society treat an organization affects the level of anxiety the organization experiences and what it then finds it must do to contain it; the Enigma Chemicals case in Chapter Eight will illustrate this. When an industry and society provide a supportive emotional environment for an organization, its members are able to hold higher levels of anxiety and therefore may be more creative. However, punishing, insecure, or highly pressurized societies are likely to drive organizations to create their own anxiety-containing structures at the expense of organizational creativity.

Degree of Power Differentials. Human systems have yet another control parameter—the degree of power differentials and the manner in which power is used. When power differentials are extreme and rather permanent, with a fixed elite wielding most of the power, and when that power is exercised as force or oppressive authority, then an organization's shadow system is driven deep underground and its members operate in fear. They may give up trying to undermine the legitimate system or they may plot in earnest to totally destroy it. Until that happens, the organization operates in the stable zone. On the other hand, if power is equally distributed and few people exert what power they have, then a power vacuum is experienced. This tends to raise anxiety levels and plunges an organization's shadow system into a disintegrative state. Because equal power distribution implies a weak legitimate system, the total result is an organization close to an anarchic state of disintegration with "garbage can" decision-making processes (Cohen, March, and Olsen, 1972).

In the spectrum ranging from concentrated power exercised in an authoritarian manner to equally distributed power that is hardly exercised at all, a critical point is reached where one can find both containment of anxiety through clear hierarchical structures and directing forms of leadership, on the one hand, and the freedom to express opinions and risk subversive, creative activity without fear on the other. At this point, an organization is in the space for creativity. Once again we find that when an organization is in the space for creativity it displays the same characteristics as all other nonlinear feedback systems; that is, the control parameters are at a critical point.

How the Human Factor Enters into the Comparison

We have now mapped the space for novelty onto organizations, and we have found that it has the same basic characteristics in an organization as it did in a group, in the mind of an individual, and in any other nonlinear feedback system: it is a phase transition between the stable and unstable zones of operation of the system that occurs when control parameters are at a critical point, a place at the edge of system disintegration in which paradox is sustained and in which archetypal behaviors are actualized through a process of creative destruction. Now, in keeping with the procedure we have been following, we need to examine whether the peculiarly human dynamics of anxiety-inspiration, individuation-conformity, leadership-followership, and participation-observation render the mapping invalid.

The first three of these dynamics have been woven so intimately into the explanation of what the edge of chaos means for an organization that we do not need to consider them further. These dynamics are descriptions of what the space for creativity means for a human system, and they also provide additional control parameters. Let us now consider the implications of the fact that human agents not only participate in an organizational system but are capable of observing its processes, reflecting individually and collectively on them, and affecting them. Can this ability to observe and reflect upon the system as a whole change any of the five characteristics of the space for creativity? Can human brilliance and determination, an individual mental purpose, make it possible for us to stay in the stable zone and still be creative, simply by intentionally exerting our will? Can we overcome the need for the anxiety and disorder that are experienced at the edge of chaos? Do human consciousness and self-awareness somehow enable us to alter the dynamics of the systems that we are and that we constitute with each other when we interact?

At the level of the organization, as at the levels of the individual mind and the group, the answer to these questions must be no. First, it is extremely difficult for members of an organization to sustain enough emotional distance from their roles as participants to also operate as observers. We seem to be able to do this only intermittently. But suppose that we did manage collectively to reflect upon our organizational system as a whole. Then a smooth move from one stable state to another could happen only if all the members of the organization who are currently conforming to a particular pattern of behavior could simultaneously agree to change to another pattern of conformity without any disagreement or conflict, for when disagreement and conflict appear, the system moves to the edge. The only way I can think of for this to happen would be if some powerful, charismatic person managed to change, suddenly and powerfully, the minds of all the other members of an organization. This is possible, but as far as I know it occurs only when fanatics show how they can lead bands of brainwashed followers; this frequently leads to death. The connection between creativity and destruction, the necessity of holding paradox in some space for novelty, seems to be inescapably part of the operation of nonlinear feedback systems, including those composed of human beings.

Even when we manage to reflect collectively on the organization we are a part of, we are still not able to alter the fundamental dynamics of that system. We cannot remove the fact that creativity involves the destruction and replacement of an organization's dominant schema and we cannot remove through self-reflection the anxiety this arouses, no matter how rationally the need for change is explained to us. No amount of systemic thinking, determination, and intelligence can remove the fundamentally paradoxical nature of creative organizational life. As at the group level, if members of an organization are able to reflect together on their own processes, they may be able to hold higher levels of anxiety and so be more creative, but they cannot alter the characteristics of the space they must occupy if they are to be creative. The characteristics of the space for creativity in human systems, ranging from the individual through the group to the organization, are summarized in Figure 6.2.

Figure 6.2. Characteristics of the Space for Creativity in Human Systems.

	Individual	*Group*	*Organization*
Phase transition	Depressive position Transitional space	A space between —Collusive, rigid, defensive blocks to learning —Basic assumption behavior	A space in the shadow system between —Defensive reliance on structures —Psychotic fantasy
Examples of paradox	Love and hate Destruction and reparation Conformity and individualism	Compliance and individuality	Compliance and individuality Centralization and decentralization
Actualization of archetype	For example, Oedipus complex	For example, fight-or-flight	For example, strategies of acquisition
Creative destruction	Replacing dominant schemas with ones developed in the recessive symbol system: a shadow system subverting its legitimate system		
Critical point for parameters	Information flows, degree of connectivity, degree of schema differentiation, level of uncontained anxiety, power difference		

Organizations as Components in a System

When members of an organization occupy the organizational space for novelty, they are able to engage in creative dialogue with which they may change their organization's recessive symbol system. This is potential creativity. If they succeed in amplifying that change throughout their organization, they may secure a change in their organization's dominant symbol system and thus in its behavior. This is potential innovation. These potentials become actual creativity and innovation only if the behavioral end product improves the organization's fitness. However, the shape and movement of the fitness landscape depends not only on an organization's own actions but also on those of the other organizations it interacts with, that is, the fellow members of the industry, the economy, and the society that it belongs to.

Creativity and innovation at an organizational level, therefore, are actualized when the organization concerned can engage the creative and innovative processes of other organizations by involving them in the competitive and cooperative process of dialogue. Organizations turn out to be creative and innovative only when they engage the creative processes of other organizations and so amplify the schema changes across industries, economies, and societies. Thus a space for novelty exists at the level of industries, economies, and societies. It is beyond the scope of this book to explore what that space is, but it is important to recognize that creativity and innovation are nested processes stretching from individual minds, through small groups and large organizations, to national and international industries, economies, and societies—and back down again to individual minds. Each level is itself a complex adaptive system that is a component of an even larger complex adaptive system, with behavior at each level ultimately affecting and being affected by behavior at all other levels to produce a coevolutionary trajectory through time.

The spaces for creativity at the level of an industry, an economy, or a society must have the same characteristics as those at the level of an organization, a group, or an individual. They too must be in phase transitions in which legitimate systems coexist in tension with their shadows, a tension arising from the fact that the shadow systems seek to undermine and replace the legitimate systems. This is a state of paradox in which archetypal patterns of behavior are realized through a process of creative destruction (Schumpeter, 1934). This phase transition occurs when industrial, economic, and societal control parameters are set at critical points and the control parameters are the speed of information flow, the extent of differences expressed and worked with, the richness of interconnections between agents in the system, the levels of contained anxiety, and the degree of power differences, as well as the way in which power is used.

The perspective suggested here has implications for the issue of governance, which is currently attracting a great deal of attention internationally. The debate about governance currently focuses primarily on arguments about which kinds of formal, legitimate systems are likely to produce the most effective governance of societies. From the systemic viewpoint of this book, that debate needs to shift to incorporate the role of shadow systems in effective governance, because it is in the tension between the legitimate and the shadow systems that creativity lies.

Conclusion

In our search for the space for novelty in human systems, we started at the level of the individual mind. We found that psychoanalytic theory and practice identify such a space, and, as with the other nonlinear feedback systems we have encountered, it is located at the edge of chaos. This space is the world of transitional objects and the depressive position that lies between the stability of concrete reality and rigid defensive routines, on the one hand,

and the instability of disintegrative psychotic fantasies on the other. The space is also a state in which the paradoxes of existence can be held in the mind and in which the mind can reflect upon itself. In this space, the mind is therefore able to play, to manipulate symbols, to rearrange paradoxes, and to perform double-loop learning, with its potential for creativity.

However, existential paradoxes cannot be held in the mind without tension, and creativity and destructiveness are intimately linked. Anxiety is thus an inevitable feature of mental life at the edge of chaos; the ability to bear that anxiety is a prerequisite for dwelling there. To contain such anxiety, an individual requires a strong ego structure and a good enough "holding" environment, which is to be found in the groups to which the individual belongs. The space for creativity, therefore, cannot be located simply at the individual level. An individual mind is a nonlinear feedback network that is part of a larger nonlinear feedback network of interacting minds. That network is made up of a set of minds coevolving competitively and cooperatively with each other.

Our search for the space for creativity, therefore, was lifted to a higher level, and we located a collective space for creativity for a group of interacting individuals. That space lies in the transition between the stability of rigid roles and routines and defensive learning schemas, on the one hand, and the instability of unconscious group processes, basic assumption behavior, and psychotic fantasies on the other. The space for creativity in a group is one in which members of the group can hold the paradoxes and ambiguities of their interaction and can jointly reflect on these paradoxes and on their own group processes in order to engage in double-loop learning. The key requirement for dwelling in this space is the ability of a group to bear the accompanying anxiety. Again, the space has an internal anxiety container, made up of the nature and quality of leadership and followership in the group together with the level of trust and liking, and an external holding environment that needs to be good enough, namely, the organization of which the group is a part.

This means that the search for the space for creativity must be lifted to the level of the organization. Here we also found a space with the characteristics to be expected of a nonlinear feedback network. That space is a phase transition between a stable zone, in which the legitimate systems of an organization are reinforced by rigidly defensive routines and fantasies in the shadow system, and an unstable zone, in which disintegrating legitimate systems are amplified by anarchic shadow systems. The phase transition, by contrast, is a state in which stable, functional legitimate systems exist in tension with subversive shadow systems. The result is a state of paradox, and when members of an organization are able to hold the anxiety of collectively reflecting upon these paradoxes and their own organizational processes, they are able to perform double-loop learning, the basis of creativity.

Holding organizational anxiety requires both internal and external containers. The internal container is provided by a culture of trust and particular patterns of power use. The external container must be provided by the society to which the organization belongs. This in turn means that our search for the space for creativity must be lifted to the levels of the industry, the economy, and the society. It is to be expected that at these levels, too, the space for creativity will display the same self-similar pattern as at other levels.

The individual and various collective spaces for creativity are, then, self-similar and all are at the edge of chaos, at the edge of system disintegration. Groups need to be a good enough holding environment for individuals, assisting them to live at the edge of their own individual chaos. Organizations do the same for groups and societies for organizations. From this perspective creativity is not an attribute of an individual but a property of a hierarchy of interlocking systems ranging from an individual mind nested in a group nested in an organization, which is in turn nested an economy and a society, which are nested in an international community, which is nested in the earth's ecology. The interaction between these nested systems is always circular, however, with one level affecting and being affected by the levels above and below.

Finally, when we think about creativity from the perspective of this complex adaptive system, what general conclusions might we reach about (1) the origins and (2) the outcomes of creativity? Where do the symbols in human recessive systems come from? Clearly, creativity is not the result of rearranging in different ways some fixed number of symbols that are given from the start. We create new symbols out of interactions between old ones—symbols breed rather like the agents in complex system simulations, and they breed through mental cross-fertilization. As a result, the total population of symbols increases over time.

The second question we may ask is whether creativity is inevitable. Do we have any guarantee that the outcomes will increase fitness or will be good in some sense? It does seem to be inevitable for variety and novelty to flow from the operation of nonlinear feedback systems. Certain forces may cause such systems to evolve to the edge of chaos, where they spontaneously produce variety and novelty that become increasingly complex. A universal law appears to generate more novelty and complexity in the universe, in a process that increases the fitness of the system as a whole as it becomes capable of coping with more and more complexity (Kauffman, 1995). However, this only applies to the system as a whole, with no guarantee that any part of the system will become fitter. All parts stand open to destruction as other parts increase their fitness, or so it seems.

At the human level, then, the complex system perspective offers no guarantee of continued improvement or even of continued survival. Occupation of the creative space at all levels of the total human system seems to be a precarious business, and we have no guarantee that this system will always remain there; it may move to ossification or disintegration while some other competing system that I cannot think of takes its place. Within the human system the same point applies. At any one time, large numbers of individuals and whole sections of societies seem to be ossifying in the stable zone while others are clearly disintegrating in an appalling way. However, agents who are at the creative edge and the human system as a whole are becoming more varied and more complex. As to whether this complexity and variety is creative, in a beneficial and good sense, is a matter of judgment. The point, from a complex system perspective, is that we have no guarantees that specific parts of any system will become increasingly fit or produce beneficial and good outcomes from the creative process that applies to the whole.

7

Evolution and Predictability in the Creative Space

The last three chapters have demonstrated how the first general property of nonlinear feedback networks, a space for novelty or creativity, can be located in human systems. This chapter completes the mapping process by identifying how the other four general properties listed in Figure 3.6 also apply to human systems. These are the sources of stability, the sources of instability, the dialectical evolution of the system, and the nature of causality and predictability.

First, an organizational framework for mapping the remaining properties of nonlinear feedback networks onto organizations will be constructed. Throughout, we have seen how all adaptive feedback networks evolve through processes that amount to single-loop and double-loop learning and how the space for novelty is where double-loop learning can take place. This distinction between the two types of learning and the need for both to occur at the same time is represented in Figure 7.1, which depicts a

192

distinction between what I have called ordinary and extraordinary management (Stacey, 1993). This follows Kuhn's important distinction between ordinary science, the solving of puzzles posed by a shared research paradigm, and extraordinary or revolutionary science, the replacement of the currently shared paradigm with a new one (Kuhn, 1970). This distinction clearly coincides with the one between single- and double-loop learning: ordinary management occurs when members of an organization carry out single-loop learning, learning within a constant shared paradigm, and extraordinary management occurs when they switch to double-loop learning, that is, when they alter their shared paradigm or some part of it.

In Figure 7.1, the solid loop at the center of the diagram depicts the circular process of ordinary management. It consists of an organization's dominant schema (step 1), embodied in its survival strategies (step 2), whose pursuit is a process of solving puzzles (step 3). In this manner an organization adapts its behavior according to how well it is achieving current perceptions of purpose.

However, as the last chapter made clear, creativity is a process of replacing at least some parts of the dominant schema through play in the recessive schema. That play is triggered by the anomalies thrown up by ordinary management. As managers go around the ordinary management loop, they uncover puzzles that must be solved if their organization is to survive. The puzzles are posed by and soluble within the current paradigm, but anomalies and contradictions are not. Because rationality is embodied in the dominant schema, contradictions of this schema cannot be dealt with in a technically rational way. Anomalies always expose the fundamentally paradoxical nature of an organization and raise pressures for synthesis. This need for synthesis is the driving force of the creative play within the recessive schema that eventually leads to replacement of the dominant schema or parts thereof, that is, to double-loop learning.

Figure 7.1. Ordinary and Extraordinary Management.

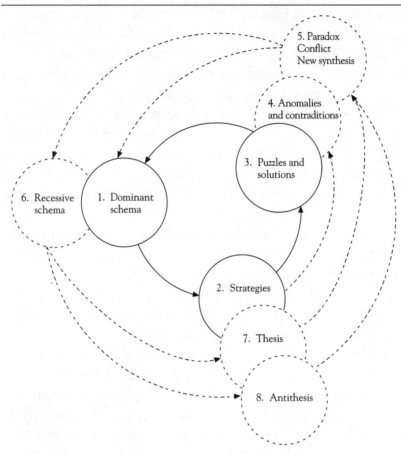

The dotted lines in Figure 7.1 represent this process, one in which anomalies (step 4) open up the basic paradoxes (step 5) that the current dominant schema has arranged or temporarily resolved; this activates play in the recessive schema (step 6), which may rearrange the paradox (steps 7 and 8). The recognition of paradox thus leads to pressure to rearrange it, but this can be only a temporary resolution, for the kind of existential paradoxes we are discussing here cannot be resolved permanently. The process of extraordinary management, therefore, is a creatively destructive one that may ultimately lead to replacement of at least some parts of the current dominant schema. This replacement need not be a major paradigm revolution, but it also can never be simply a progressively incremental change in survival strategies.

Organizations occupy the space for creativity when their members are fully engaged in both ordinary and extraordinary management, for only then do they face the fundamental paradoxes that are so characteristic of that space and only then are they in the phase transition, in which the recessive and dominant systems operate in tension with each other. It will be argued below that ordinary management is essentially a rather simple process and a primary source of stability, whereas extraordinary management is far more complex and paradoxical and is a source of both stability and instability. Let us consider now how this model of the management process can be used to map the remaining four properties of nonlinear feedback systems onto organizations.

The Sources of Stability

Three factors leading to stability in the behavior of nonlinear feedback networks were listed in the summary of the properties of such networks provided in Figure 3.6: (1) constraints that damp down change, (2) cooperation, and (3) protection from creative tension by dominant schemas, or maladaptive learning. Each of these can also be shown to be a factor leading to stability in organizations.

Constraint, Avoidance, and the Damping of Change

Figure 7.2 gives a graphic summary of an organization's ordinary management system. Ordinary management is the process of putting into practice the organization's dominant schema. This schema determines what agents in an organization discover about their organization's operation and its environment and how they do this. The dominant schema also determines what members of an organization will jointly choose to do and what methods they will use, then what actions they will undertake and how they will do this. Indeed, the existence of a dominant schema enables members to define rather precisely the meaning of discovery, choice, and action.

Because they share the basis of a rationality in the form of a dominant schema, members of an organization can discover, choose, and act in a rational manner: discovery consists of gathering and analyzing data (step 1); choice is setting objectives and generating, evaluating, and selecting the best options for achieving the objectives (step 2); and action is implementing the consequent plan (step 3). The second time around the loop, discovery consists of monitoring the actual outcome against the intended outcome expressed in the plan and feeding any deviation between them back into the choice procedure to identify corrective action. Choice and action then consist of choosing and carrying out this corrective action. The whole purpose of this technically rational decision making and this monitoring form of control is to remove surprises, to damp down change and keep an organization moving stably through time according to the joint, prior intention of its members.

Where objectives conflict and/or it is not clear what actions will lead to the realization of objectives, then the technically rational decision-making process must be supplemented by an overt political one. Choices between objectives and trial actions will be made on the basis of support from the most powerful coalitions—the current leaders of the legitimate system. This is depicted in the figure by the overt politics loop, which includes a reference to vested interests, the point being that while the dominant schema is governing what happens, the vested interests are unlikely to be disturbed. Overt politics will then maintain current vested interests (step 4) and not threaten existing coalitions and leadership structures (step 5), and it is these that will determine

Figure 7.2. Ordinary Management: The Source of Stability.

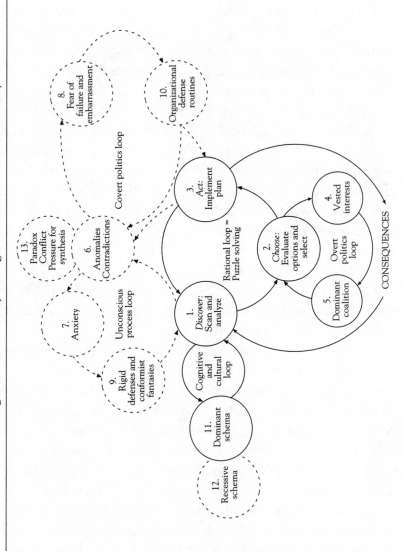

choices between conflicting objectives. Political decision making and control will then be further sources of stability in the system; they too take on a negative feedback form in which deviations from the current political program are damped down.

Ordinary management is, thus, a process of rational puzzle solution that constrains movement away from the status quo and a process of control that damps down surprising change, all in the interest of single-loop learning that improves the efficiency with which current tasks are conducted. However, dominant schemas are simplifications of reality, and as reality changes, they become inappropriate. In the course of conducting the ordinary management tasks of solving puzzles, members of an organization will inevitably uncover anomalies and contradictions (step 6), and if they focus on these they will have to face the fundamentally paradoxical nature of their organization and the need for a process of creative destruction of their deeply held beliefs about organizational life. Members, therefore, employ mechanisms to defend themselves against the anxiety that this arouses (steps 7 and 8), quickly finding a means of avoiding anxiety through avoiding any confrontation with anomalies and paradoxes. In this way, they sustain the stability of their system.

In Figure 7.2, this is depicted as the uncovering of anomalies that triggers anxiety (step 7), which is defended against by rigid routines and conformist fantasies (step 9). In other words, members react by sticking firmly to the hierarchy and the bureaucracy and by sharing their culture even more firmly. At an unconscious level, they may behave as if they are members of some comfortable family. An illustration of this is provided by the Enigma Chemicals case study in Chapter Eight. Thus, members of an organization may collude in unconscious processes that keep anxiety at bay by blocking access to double-loop learning. Playful activities in the recessive system that threaten the legitimate system are simply not permitted.

Furthermore, contradictions and anomalies, if they are attended to, arouse conflict between members, with the attendant fears of embarrassing others and being embarrassed, as well as of failing (step 8). Members of an organization quickly develop organizational defense routines, such as covert politics and game playing, to defend against this (step 10). They proclaim that they are following a particular and usually benign and participative mode of making decisions and controlling, when in reality they are doing the opposite. Everyone knows that this is going on, but it is undiscussable, as is the fact that it is undiscussable (Argyris, 1990). Once again the effect is to block true dialogue and play— that is, to block access to an organization's recessive symbol system. Figure 7.2 depicts how the recessive system (step 12) is not accessed, does not raise paradoxes (step 13), and therefore does not affect the dominant system (step 1).

Ordinary management enables members of an organization to become more and more efficient at carrying out the organization's current primary tasks using the current methods of doing so. It is an overwhelmingly stable form of management; it damps down surprising change through the use of negative feedback controls; it constrains members' thinking and acting by propagating strong conformist cultures and maintaining existing power structures; and it avoids anxiety, and thus double-loop learning and creativity, through the use of unconscious defense mechanisms and conscious covert politics.

How does ordinary management compare with the sources of stability in other adaptive nonlinear feedback networks? First, the summary of the properties of feedback networks in Chapter Three showed how stability was typically maintained by the operation of negative feedback constraining the destabilizing, amplifying operation of positive feedback. This is exactly what happens with ordinary management: it constrains the amplifying effects of anxiety and individual differences.

Chapter Three also emphasized the point that canalization or lock-in is a source of stability in all nonlinear feedback networks operating in the space for novelty. This phenomenon is clearly evident in the description of ordinary management processes. The dominant schema is locked in, primarily by the mechanisms that members of an organization utilize to defend themselves against anxiety: both unconscious group processes and the more conscious covert politics provide an immensely powerful canalizing force that locks members into existing patterns of behavior, even against their conscious wills. This is clear at individual, group, organizational, and even societal levels.

Cooperation

The second major source of stability and order in all nonlinear feedback systems is provided by cooperation between agents in the system, that is, by the universal tendency such systems have for spontaneous self-organization. The notion that human systems display spontaneous self-organization is, of course far from new: it is a central tenet of the Austrian school of economics as expounded by Hayek (1948, 1982).

Hayek saw the central problem facing any social science as that of explaining "how the spontaneous interaction of a number of people, each possessing bits of knowledge, brings about a state of affairs . . . which could only be brought about by deliberate direction by somebody who possesses the combined knowledge of all of those individuals" (Hayek, 1948, p. 79). Because it is impossible for anyone to possess such all-embracing knowledge, Hayek concluded that markets, like the rest of society, evolve as a result of human action, but not of human intention. He stressed the changeability of society arising from the activities of entrepreneurs who open up the possibility of satisfying requirements people did not know they had. He saw a market as a systematic discovery technique, the outcome of which could not be predicted. Outcomes, he claimed, depend upon an unpredictable mixture of effort, ability, and luck. (Mintzberg and Waters, 1985, make a similar point, as does Porter, 1990, both in relation to organizations.) Society was therefore seen as a system evolving unpredictably through a process of spontaneous self-organization by the agents who make up the society.

Schumpeter (1934) also emphasized the importance of enterprise. He saw profit as the reward for being one step ahead of the competition, a temporary monopolistic rent that came about precisely because markets were not in equilibrium. He saw success arising from a process of creating states of nonequilibrium in which firms were not adapted to their environment, in direct contradiction to the mainstream neoclassical economists who defined success as the achievement of equilibrium adaptation to the environment. And he explained the evolution of economies as occurring through a "perennial gale of creative destruction": for example, the introduction of the railways destroyed the viability of the waterways, and the development of small, gas-fired power stations destroyed the coal mines. (Pascale, 1990, makes a similar point.) Entrepreneurs cause and cash in on nonequilibrium, creating and profiting from uncertainty and instability (Parker and Stead, 1991).

Economists of the Austrian school, therefore, see organizations as systems that are part of a larger environmental system and that evolve through a process of creative destruction and spontaneous self-organization. Such evolving systems are in states of nonequilibrium, and their futures are unpredictable. Disorder is an essential part of the progress of the system. Organizational and environmental systems are so complex that agents within them cannot plan their long-term futures. Those futures emerge or evolve from the interactions between agents. The process of extraordinary management is the kind of spontaneous self-organization and creative destruction at an organizational level that was suggested by the Austrian economists at the level of the economy, and it is clearly both stabilizing and destabilizing at the same time. Here we will look at the stabilizing aspects, and in the next section we will turn to the destabilizing ones.

Figure 7.3 summarizes the key features of extraordinary management. It differs from ordinary management in two very important respects. First, the anxieties aroused by contradictions and anomalies (step 6 in Figure 7.3) are not avoided by the automatic erection of unconscious defense mechanisms. Instead, the paradoxes of organizational life are held in the minds of members who find it possible to contain the anxiety because they find themselves in a good enough holding environment (step 9). They therefore find it possible to engage in creative play and to access the organization's recessive symbol system (step 12 in Figure 7.3). Second, members manage to hold the fears of failure and embarrassment sufficiently to reflect jointly on their own group and organizational processes (step 11). In this way they can avoid covert politics long enough to engage in true dialogue, in the kind of play that enables them to access the organization's recessive symbol system. This means that members are working with the paradoxes of their own organizational life: there is a link from the recessive system (step 12) to paradox and pressure for synthesis (step 13), and from there back to the recessive system. In this way, the second loop is completed and an organization can engage in double-loop learning.

What is being described, therefore, is a legitimate system that is being driven by the dominant schema in the performance of current primary tasks and a vital shadow system that is engaged in potentially destructive play. But the result is not anarchy, because the very process of double-loop learning, of creative play in the shadow system, produces stability in the form of cooperation. Groups of people can learn in complex ways only if their members both cooperate and compete with each other.

Figure 7.3. Extraordinary Management: The Source of Stability and Instability.

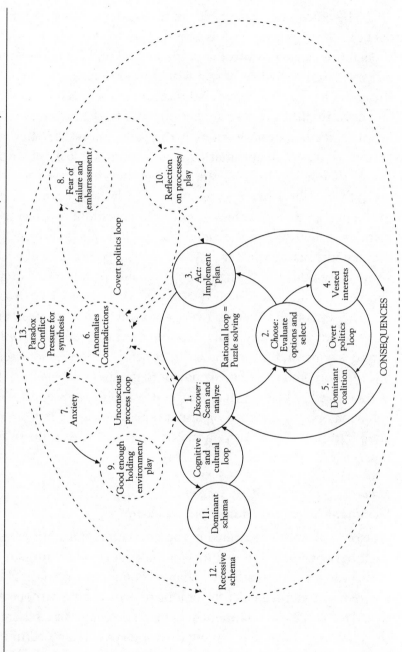

The process of creative play in the shadow system is spontaneously self-organizing. This is a form of controlled behavior even though no one is in control of it. Figures 7.2 and 7.3 both depict processes in the shadow system with dotted lines. In both cases, the activities involved have to do with unconscious interactions and covert politics. These are actions that by definition are not jointly agreed upon or dictated by the powerful; rather, they are actions that people automatically and spontaneously organize among themselves. In doing this, none of them are free to do simply as they wish. When people spontaneously engage with others in the play or dialogue that is central to extraordinary management, they must sustain the support of other members of the group they are interacting with. If they lose that support, they will effectively be excluded from their group. Because people are strongly affected by a fundamental need to belong, this requirement to sustain the support of others is a very powerful form of control, but it is exerted not by any individual but by the group as a whole. There is control, but no one is "in control." Spontaneous self-organization produces stable behavior in groups of people because of their need to belong; their cooperation constitutes controlled behavior. Spontaneous self-organization is a process of bottom-up cooperation and therefore a major source of the stability we observe in the behavior of organizations.

Protection from Creative Tension by Dominant Schemas: Maladaptive Learning

One of the features identified in the simulation of adaptive feedback networks is the possibility of maladaptive learning. This occurs when a particularly well-adapted dominant schema enables a system to perform efficiently for long periods of time without the need to change the dominant schema. The evaluative schemas then become atrophied, leaving the total system exposed in the event of sudden, unexpected changes. Exactly this kind of maladaptive learning is exhibited in human organizations, a matter discussed at some length in Chapter Five in connection with Learning Model I. In fact, the process of ordinary management described above always carries with it the possibility of maladaptive learning. When unconscious defense mechanisms and covert politics are used by members to defend against anxiety and fear of failure, the result is an inability to access the recessive symbol system and thus to perform double-loop learning. In this case, an organization continues to follow its dominant schema even though the rivals it is competing with have long since changed the fitness landscape. The history of industrial decline in Britain and parts of the United States reflects just such maladaptive learning.

Maladaptive learning produces stability because it allows the dominant schema to remain the same and thus permits organizations to follow their established patterns of behavior. They can go on in this way for long periods of time, the length of time depending upon how rapidly others are changing the fitness landscape. Miller's study of a number of companies (Miller, 1990) provides empirical evidence of this. Organizations display stable behavior for the same basic reasons as other adaptive nonlinear feedback networks do, and, as the next section will demonstrate, they display instability for the same reasons.

The Sources of Instability

In summarizing the properties of nonlinear feedback networks, Figure 3.6 listed three factors that account for the instability displayed by such systems when they operate in the space for novelty: (1) the process of amplifying small changes, (2) the operation of competition and the use of unpredictability as a survival strategy by other interconnecting systems, and (3) exposure to creative tensions set up by the recessive schema—that is, cross-fertilization and flux. It is not difficult to see how each of these factors applies to human systems.

Amplification of Small Changes

All the feedback systems described in Chapters Two and Three displayed positive feedback operating in the presence of some constraint, so that tiny changes could be amplified into major alterations of the system's state. This is a prime cause of the irregularity, disorder, unpredictability, and instability we observe in such systems. Human systems quite clearly display this property too, and it also accounts for much of the instability we find in human behavior.

Vicious (or virtuous) circles are immediately obvious examples of positive-feedback loops in organizations. For example, Gouldner's study of a gypsum plant in the United States (Gouldner, 1964) identified how senior managers sought to reduce tension between managers and workers by establishing impersonal rules to govern task performance. The rules, however, created norms for minimum performance and productivity dropped. This led to calls for closer supervision and closer control that increased the number of rules, and this in turn reinforced the minimum performance standards. In this way, unintended positive feedback caused a vicious spiraling circle of tighter controls, more tension, and lower productivity. Merton (1957) developed a similar model of organizations in terms of self-fulfilling prophecies.

Bandwagon effects and chain reactions are further examples of positive feedback. For example, the phenomenon of keeping up with the Joneses causes the demand for a product to spread as more and more people see that others have it. Through spreading and copying effects, a small gain in market share by one product can be escalated into market domination. So although Sony's Betamax is the technically superior video recorder, Matsushita's VHS recorder obtained a small market lead in the early days of market development. This led to more stores stocking titles in the VHS format, and that led to a further increase in VHS recorder market share. More retailers turned to VHS films, and so on until VHS dominated the market (Arthur, 1988).

Writers in the field of systems dynamics (Forrester, 1958; Senge, 1990) have demonstrated that nonlinearity and positive feedback loops are fundamental properties of organizational life. They make the point that the feedback structure of the system generates patterns of behavior, not just causes out in the environment, and that in complex systems, cause-and-effect links are circular, distant, and very difficult to identify. They also explain how behavior patterns can emerge without being intended and, in fact, often emerge contrary to intention, producing unexpected and counterintuitive outcomes.

Double-loop learning itself (Argyris and Schön, 1978) is destabilizing, positive feedback in that it is a process of conflict and dialogue that questions underlying assumptions and changes schemas. Organizational defense routines (Argyris, 1990) were cited in the previous section as causes of stability in organizations. However, these cover-ups and games can be disruptive and destabilizing instead of stubbornly sustaining existing practices. Greiner and Schein (1988) discuss the impact of overt politics on change programs and show how positive-feedback loops are activated by any attempt to change an organization in a fundamental way. This happens because change upsets the balance and nature of power, which provokes destabilizing power struggles as groups strive to maintain control. Bion's analysis of group behavior (Bion, 1961) can also be understood in terms of feedback loops. Regression to basic assumption behavior renders a group incapable of work, increasing the regression to basic assumption behavior, and so on, in a destabilizing vicious circle.

At the individual level, too, we are all familiar with our own susceptibility to major mood changes as a result of some small comment by another person, and we know how such mood changes affect our judgment and our subsequent actions. Positive feedback escalates small changes. We can see, then, that the operation of positive feedback with its amplification of small changes is ubiquitous in human systems, a feature particularly accounted for by the fact that human agents experience anxiety and fear of failure. The processes of ordinary management depicted in Figure 7.2 are all ones of negative feedback that damp down surprising change. While the unconscious defense mechanisms and the protective covert politics hold, the system will remain very stable, but it will be incapable of double-loop learning. However, the processes of extraordinary management are primarily of a positive, amplifying feedback nature. They spread awareness of contradiction and anomalies, they focus on paradox and conflict, and the whole shadow system operates in tension with the legitimate system, seeking to undermine it. The process of extraordinary management, the operation of the shadow system when it promotes double-loop learning, is therefore a source of instability for an organization as a whole, even though it is in some respects internally stable.

Competition

The exploration of adaptive feedback networks showed how such systems develop internal competition, or a predator-prey dynamic, because it enhances total system learning capability. Competition enhances learning by introducing instabilities that prevent a system from becoming trapped on a less than optimal fitness peak. Because one system is a component of a larger system within which it must compete with other components, it must continually adjust its behavior, developing new survival strategies to counteract those of its rivals. Competitive tension keeps systems on their toes, but the result is an irregular pattern of development for each component and for the system as a whole. We are all so familiar with the pressures of competition between our instincts and our conscience at the level of our own mind, and within the groups and organizations we operate in, that there is no need to say more. Competition is clearly a major feature of all human systems; it causes instabilities, on the one hand, and enhances learning, on the other, in the same way as in other adaptive nonlinear feedback systems.

Competition plays its destabilizing role internally within an organization in the sense that the dominant system is trying to sustain the status quo while extraordinary management is seeking to destroy it. Double-loop learning and creativity therefore require internal competition as well as the cooperation of spontaneous self-organization. The need for this internal competition comes, however, from the interaction with other organizations who are all competing for survival.

The Tierra simulation in Chapter Three showed how agents engaging in the competitive struggle for survival use the unpredictability of their own behavior as a survival strategy. In their fight to survive the onslaughts of the parasites, the host agents in Tierra stopped advertising their positions and, in effect, hid themselves. This put the parasites at a disadvantage because they could not predict where the hosts were. Neither, for that matter, could the hosts, so they had to use precious processing time to find out where they were each time they wanted to act. However, their lack of knowledge about their whereabouts was more than compensated for by the better survival chances that hiding gave them.

In human systems, individuals, groups, organizations, and whole societies engage in exactly the same kind of behavior for the same kinds of reasons. We conceal information from relatives, friends, and colleagues, as well as rivals and enemies, in order to maintain an element of surprise in our dealings with each other. Organizations keep their intentions secret, sometimes even from their own employees, to create an element of surprise in their dealings with other organizations. And, of course, the whole international espionage and counterespionage industry is built upon the recognized, if highly fantasized, value of secrecy and unpredictability as a survival strategy. Human agents work quite hard at making themselves and their immediate system unpredictable to others, and because they all are doing it, the result is total system instability.

Exposure to Creative Tension Set Up by Recessive Schemas: Cross-Fertilization and Flux in the Recessive System

The simulations of adaptive feedback networks show how they develop and use crossover replication. In a computer, this is the process of copying part of one agent's computer code and then mixing it with a copy of part of another agent's code. In an organism it is copying and mixing two agents' genes. In mental terms, much the same thing occurs when symbols from one component of the mind, say the conscious, are mixed with those from another component, say the unconscious: mixing real-world observations with dreams to create some new image is the essence of play in the transitional space. In human interaction terms, crossover replication is actually referred to as cross-fertilization; it happens when two or more individuals copy parts of their mental contents to each other and combine them to form new mental contents. In all of these cases, the crossover introduces irregularity and instability simply because it is not making selections on a progressive or rational basis but is mixing code, genes, and symbols in a somewhat haphazard manner. However, this enhances total system learning because it prevents a system from becoming trapped on a local fitness peak.

The simulations also demonstrate how most of the instabilities introduced by this crossover usually tend to be concentrated in the recessive systems: recessive computer code, recessive genes, or recessive symbol systems in the mind and shadows of legitimate systems in groups and organizations. These recessive systems are therefore in a state of continuous flux and are a primary source of the irregularity and instability we observe in a system's behavior.

It was argued above that an organization consists of a legitimate system driven by a dominant schema expressed as processes of ordinary management and a shadow system driven by recessive schemas expressed in processes of extraordinary management. It is when the latter is in a state of flux, opposing the legitimate system, that double-loop learning is possible, but that state of flux and the tension it causes are a source of instability for the total organization. Once again a close match occurs between human organizations and all other adaptive nonlinear feedback networks. Human systems are both stable and unstable for the same general reasons as those in any other adaptive nonlinear feedback system, and it is therefore not at all surprising that they should evolve in the same dialectical manner.

Dialectical Evolution

Nothing is new, of course, about the idea that human systems evolve dialectically. This view of history was formalized by Hegel and became the basis of Marxist explanations of the development of societies and economies. Recently researchers have called for more attention to be paid to dialectical models of the organizational strategy-making process (Chakravarty and Doz, 1992). This approach to understanding how organizations develop is the basis of Pascale's widely read book, *Managing at the Edge* (1990).

The sociologist Anthony Giddens (1979) argues that individuals are autonomous: they can choose their next action and what they choose to do will have some impact on what consequently happens—individuals can make a difference. Each individual, however, is not only autonomous but also dependent upon others. This paradox means that each individual's choice of a next action represents some rearrangement of autonomy and dependence. Through such choices, individuals interacting with each other build up a fund of mutual knowledge, which is largely tacit and embodied in institutions: that is, shared rules of conduct, social structures, patterns of relationships, procedures, routines, habits, rituals, and myths. These institutions, or the culture, embody the previous experience of a community of people—what they have learned together. The institutions then form the framework within which individuals will make subsequent choices, once again pulled in opposite directions by the contradictory forces of autonomy and dependence. (Karl Weick, 1969/1979, has developed similar models, and the impact of culture on strategy formation has been emphasized by, for example, Schein, 1985; Johnson, 1987.)

What Giddens puts forward is a continuous feedback system in which behavior unfolds or emerges from a dialectical process, as it does in the explanation of Pascale (1990). The regularities in behavior come about because each successive piece of behavior is conditioned by the institutions within which it occurs, but each time around the choices of individuals can also make a difference in that they can change the institutions. The circular nature of this interconnection between choice, action, and outcome leads to a complex connection between cause and effect (see also Forrester, 1958, 1961; Senge, 1990).

Consider an individual confronted with the need to make a choice in a situation that is well understood and has often been encountered before, not only by the person concerned, but also by those with whom he or she is interacting. In this repetitive situation, everyone is likely to choose to abide by existing institutions, thus keeping the situation close to certainty and making it possible for all the individuals to predict the long-term consequences of their next chosen actions. They all can then realize both their intended next actions and the intended long-term outcomes of those actions. The result will be the continuation of institutions in a largely unchanged form.

However, suppose that an individual faces a unique, ambiguous, uncertain situation. The institutions built up through shared experience with others will now provide very little, if any, guidance as to which action to choose. Furthermore, the individual will be most unwise to assume that others in the interaction, who are also faced with ambiguity and uncertainty, will act in accordance with the established institutions. In these circumstances, the individual will find it impossible to predict the consequences of her or his next action because they will depend on how others respond and what reaction those responses will in turn provoke. No one can be relied upon to act according to the institutions; therefore, no one will be able to predict the long-term consequences of her or his next action or intervention.

What we then have is a situation in which individuals can realize their next intended interventions but cannot realize any intended long-term consequences, because the inability to rely on the continuity of institutions removes clear-cut links between a specific cause and a specific effect. Institutional changes then emerge from the interaction process without prior shared intention on the part of those who are interacting.

Causality and Predictability

Organizations display the same kind of space for creativity as all other nonlinear feedback networks, a space that is paradoxically stable and unstable at the same time, for reasons that are always of the same general kind. All adaptive nonlinear feedback systems coevolve dialectically, rearranging but only temporarily resolving the fundamental paradoxes. They coevolve through spontaneously self-organizing processes to produce emergent patterns of behavior. The general conclusions about causality and predictability listed in Figure 3.6 for nonlinear feedback networks must, therefore, apply to human systems. This means that the following general principles apply to organizations when they occupy the space for creativity.

Links Between Specific Action and Long-Term Outcomes Are Lost

Causal links between specific actions and specific organizational outcomes over the long term disappear in the complexity of the interactions among people within an organization and across its borders with other organizations. It must follow that intended specific long-term outcomes cannot be realized by the members of an organization; creative and innovative outcomes can only emerge. Members of an organization, no matter how intelligent and powerful, will be unable to predict the specific long-term outcomes of their actions. They may specify any specific long-term state they wish to or have any dream, fantasy, or vision they like, but they will never be able to determine the sequence of actions required to actualize them. They may have whatever intention they like, but they will never be able to realize it. Only when their organization is operating in the stable zone—when they are conducting ordinary management to reinforce what they already do well—will they be able to realize intended long-term outcomes, and then only if the fitness landscape as determined by others stays stable enough for long enough. The conclusion is clear: we can actualize intended long-term outcomes only by chance.

The long-term outcomes a creative organization will display will unfold through time as a result of the activities within its shadow system and the tension between that shadow system and the legitimate one. The only way to know the outcome is to operate the system and pursue the processes of extraordinary management.

Short-Term Outcomes Are Predictable

Because nonlinear feedback networks are the product of their precise history and because it takes time for small changes to escalate in such systems, their short-term behavior is predictable. The processes of ordinary management within the legitimate system therefore match the short-term needs of current primary task performance.

Control Parameters Can Be Influenced

As with all nonlinear feedback systems, the general dynamic progression of an organization is determined by the state of the control parameters, and at certain critical points those control parameters cause the space for creativity to materialize. We can identify the conditions required for an organization to occupy the space for creativity and in principle we can predict whether or not it will. The most important of the control parameters for human systems are, first, the level of anxiety that can be contained and, second, the degree of power difference and the manner in which that difference is used. The more an organization is designed to assist members in containing rather than avoiding high levels of anxiety, the more power differences will be exercised to assist members in engaging in rather than avoiding self-reflection and the more it will be possible to work creatively despite high rates of information flow, large differences between schemas, and rich connectivity between people.

This implies that the emphasis on managing long-term specific outcomes is completely misplaced. They cannot be managed, but it is possible to influence the control parameters, namely, the containment of anxiety, the use of power, the flow of information, the degrees of difference that are tolerable, and the extent of the connections across organizational networks. Although it is impossible for managers to realize intentions and plan long-term creative outcomes, they may be able to realize an intention to occupy the space for creativity by influencing the control parameters outlined above. From this perspective, managers still need strategic plans; however, they relate not to outcomes and actions to achieve them, but to methods of affecting anxiety, power, difference, and connectivity.

Archetypal Patterns Are Predictable

The simulations of adaptive nonlinear feedback networks showed how we can predict general, qualitative archetypes even though we are not able to predict specific actualizations of them. Thus, the schema rules used in the Boids simulation produce an emergent form of behavior in which the Boids flock and learn to part around obstacles and then re-form as a flock. It is not possible to predict from the rules each Boid follows that it will behave in this way: the behavior is emergent. However, once we have run the system, we can safely predict that if we run that set of rules again, we will observe the emergence of flocking behavior. The rules contain flocking behavior and iteration causes it to emerge. Even once we know about the flocking pattern, we can predict, not the specific flocking pattern that any run of the simulation will display, but simply the fact that flocking will take place. In other words, we are predicting the archetype, but the actualization, depending as it does upon precise experience, is unpredictable.

This also is the kind of predictability that is possible for human systems. We can usually predict that certain individuals will become angry in certain conditions, but we normally cannot predict just how that anger will unfold. We can predict that in certain conditions a group of people will display highly dependent behavior, but we normally cannot predict just what form it will take. We can predict that under certain pressures an organization will decentralize its operation, but we normally cannot predict just how this will unfold. This suggests that we might experience more success in predicting the behavior of organizations if we focus on what kinds of archetypal behavior tend to be produced by a general kind of schema, rather than trying to forecast the specific outcomes of specific actions.

How the Human Factor
Enters into the Comparison

In this chapter I have argued that it not only is possible to map the space for novelty onto organizations, but it is also quite clear that organizations display stability and instability for the same reasons as all other adaptive nonlinear feedback networks and coevolve in the same dialectical manner. I have also suggested that the same principles of causality and predictability apply to organizations that apply to other nonlinear feedback systems. The principal conclusion is that when an organization occupies the space for creativity, its specific long-term future emerges from the complex interactions within and between its shadow and legitimate systems and with other organizations; this emergent specific future is inherently unpredictable. This has immediate consequences of a profound nature for much of the thinking about, and prescribing of, management behavior, which Chapter Ten will highlight. Nevertheless, much is still predictable. We can identify causal links between control parameters and organizational dynamics. In principle, we can design creative organizations and then rely on them to produce emergent futures. And we can predict the archetypal patterns that will be actualized in such emergent futures. What this means for management and organization theory will also be touched on in Chapter Ten.

At this point, however, we should return to the procedure adopted in the three previous chapters and ask whether anything about the specific nature of human beings and human systems invalidates the mapping of the science of complexity onto organizations. By now this is becoming, I hope, a rather superfluous procedure. The discussion in this chapter, as in the last three, has been framed very much in terms of peculiarly human dynamics. But the nagging question may still remain: is there nothing in humans' intelligence, self-awareness, ability to think systemically, strength of will, and determination that allows us to take a different view of how creative organizations develop? Once we have gotten used to the idea that humans are ultimately in control, it is difficult to accept that no one can control the specific long-term outcomes of creative processes, that we are agents in systems that are coevolving into an open-ended evolutionary space.

It seems to me that we have no realistic alternative but to accept that we cannot be in control of the kind of complex coevolutionary process that drives all nonlinear feedback networks but can only participate in producing emergent patterns. No amount of human intelligence, self-awareness, and determination can alter the fundamental dynamics of nonlinear feedback. In the end, creativity is inevitably destructive. Our recognition of this is attested to by ancient myths in which the god of creation is also the god of destruction, and in which it is necessary to lose one's life in order to gain it. This paradox will always make us anxious; it is a force that lies at the bottom of the dynamics of human systems, their irremovable nonlinearity, and their radical unpredictability.

Conclusion

The conclusion I have reached is that the human mind is a complex adaptive system with all the general properties of such systems. This does not add anything to psychoanalytic theory; it is simply another way of describing it. No new understandings or prescriptions seem to come from seeing the individual human mind or the human group as complex adaptive systems. However, when we reach the levels of the organization, the society, and the economy, the science of complexity provides a coherent framework for the construction of theories of how organizations, economies, and societies develop that are rather different from those that now dominate thinking and practice. These different theories can be constructed using notions that have long been discussed in the literature, but the science of complexity brings a coherent overall framework within which to place them. The result is a dialectical theory of organizational processes in which creativity is driven by play in a shadow system that operates in tension with and is subversive of the legitimate system.

This is certainly not a widely accepted view of how organizations develop, and its policy implications are not part of the thinking of most managers today. However, before exploring the implications of this view for research and practice, we need to consider whether any real-life experiences exist that illustrate the kind of system I am suggesting. This is the purpose of the next chapter.

8

Avoiding and Occupying the Space for Creativity in Practice

The purpose of this book is to explain what the science of complexity is and to demonstrate how it applies to human systems. The science of complexity tells us that all nonlinear feedback networks may operate in a stable zone where they repeat past patterns of behavior and ossify, in an unstable zone where they disintegrate, or in a phase transition between stability and instability, at the edge of system disintegration, where behavioral patterns of great variety emerge through processes of spontaneous self-organization. My contention is that all human systems are nonlinear feedback networks and that these three zones of operation apply to them too.

As we have seen, the phase transition is the only state in which any nonlinear feedback system is capable of surprise and novelty. No matter what the system, the phase transition is a state of tension between stability and instability, and this basic paradox is played out in many different forms from one kind of system to another. One important manifestation of this paradox, which

220

seems to be present in all adaptive systems, is the tension between dominant and recessive symbol systems. You will recall that the dominant symbol system is expressed as a dominant schema that drives current engagement with reality, that is, implementation of current survival strategy. The recessive symbol system is expressed in recessive schemas that drive playful activity. The tension between the two arises because it is the purpose of the dominant system to ensure efficient performance of current strategy, whereas the purpose of the recessive system is to replace the dominant system through creative play in the interest of greater effectiveness and thus higher chances of long-term survival.

Chapters Four through Seven have established the existence of a phase transition for the human mind, the human group, and organizations. At all levels, it is a state of paradox and is also manifested as a tension between dominant and recessive symbol systems: the dominant system seeks to sustain the status quo and the recessive system employs creative play to change it. At the level of an organization, dominant schemas are embodied in the structures and routines of a legitimate system; recessive schemas consist of the mental contents of an organization's members that are used not to engage current reality but to engage in playful activities in a shadow system. An organization is in the stable zone when its shadow system colludes with the legitimate system to sustain it. It disintegrates when its shadow system is dominated by basic assumption behavior and psychotic fantasy that its legitimate system is not strong enough to contain. And it occupies the phase transition and becomes potentially capable of creativity when its shadow system operates in tension with the legitimate system, seeking to undermine and replace at least parts of it. Without tension between subsystems, an organization can at best only perform simple single-loop learning. If it is to perform the complex double-loop learning needed for creativity, tension is required between the two subsystems.

The zone in which any nonlinear feedback network operates is determined by the state of a number of control parameters. The control parameters that seem to be common to all nonlinear feedback networks are the rate at which information or energy flows through a system and the degree of connectivity between the agents in the system. All adaptive systems appear to have an additional parameter—the degree of diversity in the schemas that are driving behavior—and human systems seem to have still further control parameters—power differences and the manner in which they are expressed and the level of anxiety that can be held and contained. It is only when the control parameters reach a critical point that systems operate in the phase transition at the edge of disintegration, and it is only then that they occupy the space for creativity. If the control parameters are below the critical point, organizations will be stuck in the stable zone; if they are pushed above the critical point, the system will disintegrate.

I have argued that the level of anxiety that can be held and contained in human systems is the most important of these parameters: creativity requires that we be able to hold, rather than avoid, high levels of anxiety, because only then can we perform complex learning. But human beings have a powerful tendency to avoid the space for creativity. Our experience causes us to dislike complex learning, and we often seek to kill our own learning. We do this in a number of ways. The most important of the strategies for avoiding the space for creativity are (1) a tendency to unconsciously fabricate and then occupy comforting fantasies connected with early family life and (2) a propensity to employ rather rigid defense mechanisms. When this happens, no matter how large and intensive the change management program, the system will simply keep reproducing the same patterns.

So much for the theory of creativity in human systems that can be derived from the science of complexity. Now can we identify its operation in real human organizations? I hope to show in this chapter that we can, and to do so I am going to describe two organizations I have worked with. Their names and some of the background details have been concealed for obvious reasons, but in all other respects the stories are presented as I understand them. The first case study illustrates how members of an organization unconsciously blocked all attempts to change it. They employed defenses against engaging in complex learning that are rather difficult to understand. Members of this organization resolutely avoided occupying the space for creativity, primarily because the society they operated in did not provide them with a good enough holding environment. Instead, it was positively persecutory, making it essential for members of the organization to create their own fantasy holding environment to avoid anxiety. I will suggest that this created so powerful a block to change that little short of a major crisis could shift the organization from the stable zone to the area where it might become changeable. The great danger, however, lay in the very real possibility of tipping it into the unstable zone, where it could disintegrate, with serious consequences for the community.

Avoiding the Space for Creativity: Enigma Chemicals

Enigma Chemicals (Stacey, 1993, 1995a) is a large company in the United Kingdom that produces a limited range of chemical products from a number of sites. Two features of this company's operations are of particular importance for the purposes of the present discussion.

First, the chemicals Enigma produces are of a hazardous, environmentally threatening nature. Although the company's policies and monitoring systems place tremendous importance on environmental protection and safety matters, a few incidents have occurred over the years, some of a dramatic although not disastrous nature, and this made Enigma a target for environmental pressure groups. As a consequence, the company is frequently attacked by the media.

Second, Enigma occupies an almost monopolistic position in its principal markets through various patent arrangements. These patents, however, are due to expire in ten years, after which Enigma can expect fierce competition to cause a dramatic decline in its sales. The long recession of the early 1990s had already caused a significant decline in sales, and for the first time in its thirty-year history Enigma was forced to reduce its work force through early retirement and voluntary redundancy.

As part of the strategy for coping with the new commercial realities, Enigma's management-reporting structure had recently been reorganized from a centralized functional structure to a more decentralized divisional structure. Also, the role of the central planning function had been changed: in the past it had prepared five- and ten-year plans with little involvement of managers at the operational level, but now it was to act more as an adviser to members of divisional management who were charged with preparing plans for the approval of the main board.

The chief executive had spent his entire career at Enigma and knew from previous attempts to change strategic direction that simply reorganizing and pushing strategic responsibility further down the hierarchy would not be enough. He therefore appointed a team of consultants.

The Presenting Problem

In presenting their problem to the consultants, managers said that they had already agreed upon a strategy to counter the prospective decline in their business; this consisted of improving performance and cutting costs in existing businesses, diversifying and developing new businesses, retaining high employee commitment, and securing the backing of the public. The managers knew what was required to implement their strategy, namely, that everyone must become much more cost-conscious and commercially aggressive, as well as more innovative and entrepreneurial: strategy implementation would only occur if the organization became "creative." Creativity would occur, they thought, when structures and systems were flexible, decision making was participative, and people were empowered to develop new ideas and take new opportunities. They believed that their organization was not creative because it was bureaucratic (for example, it had highly centralized and cumbersome procedures for appraising, rewarding, appointing, transferring, and promoting staff), was dominated by powerful trade unions, and was characterized by the "wrong" values and beliefs (for example, managers were unwilling to discipline staff for nonperformance, people were unwilling to take much initiative, and few felt a strong need to change when they knew that Enigma's patents would last for only the next ten years). The task to be carried out by the consultants, therefore, was to identify, in specific terms, what aspects of the existing bureaucracy and culture should be removed, what specific participative and empowering systems and attitudes they should be replaced with, and how this was to be done.

Is This Really the Problem?

I joined the consulting team that was supposed to deal with this presenting problem. The dominant view was that we should conduct an analysis of the structures, procedures, and cultures and then mount a comprehensive change program to install new structures, procedures, and cultures. We were expected to realize top management's intention of changing this organization from a bureaucracy to an entrepreneurial firm, and the implicit way that managers and consultants alike were thinking about this process was in terms of a move from one equilibrium state to another, more desirable, one.

However, for some considerable time an explicit and rather widespread consensus had existed among Enigma's managers and staff on this formulation of the problem and on what needed to be changed. They all agreed that they wanted to be an entrepreneurial firm. Furthermore, numerous consulting interventions had addressed these problems and much of what had been recommended with regard to changes in structures, systems, and cultures had indeed been implemented. Five years previously, I had been a member of a large consulting team that was faced with exactly the same problem in the dominant division of this organization, and now I found that very little had changed. Despite all that was agreed upon, all that was said and done, the organization had remained stubbornly the same.

Why was this group of managers unable to realize their intentions? Why were the consulting interventions not working? What guarantee was there that another consultancy project of the same kind as before would fare any better? These are the questions that needed to be addressed before embarking on yet another change management program; they indicated that the presenting problem was not a helpful formulation of the real difficulties.

If we think in the terms developed in this book, it is quite clear that this organization was operating primarily in the stable zone and its members all knew this. They were now saying that they wished to move to a state in which their organization would be creative and could develop new businesses to replace those that were dying. Despite repeated and rather expensive attempts to do this, nothing happened. Using the complex system theory of organizations, we would expect to find that the control parameters of the system were below critical levels and that managers and other members of this organization were operating in a shadow system that colluded to sustain the legitimate system in the state it had always been in. We would expect to find that members of this organization were using some defensive device to avoid holding the anxiety of being creative, which made it impossible for them to engage in complex double-loop learning. We would expect them to have been tightly caught up in ordinary management processes, with little evidence of any extraordinary management. The real problem, according to the complex system perspective, was that this organization had no creative tension between the legitimate and shadow systems and, until something was done about that, no amount of change management would produce any change. Let us see if any evidence exists for these assertions in this case.

Were Control Parameters Below Critical Levels?

Information flows were rather slow. Enigma was something of a monopoly and so faced a rather stable, slow-moving environment. Connectivity was not particularly rich; people tended to have roles limited to the hierarchy and not much movement took place between production sites, resulting in relatively few opportunities to make new links in the network. Members of Enigma consti-tuted something of a closed society with a high degree of confor-mity in behavior: the schemas driving behavior tended to be rather uniform. Power differentials were large and were used in benignly authoritarian ways. Finally, the anxiety that was actually experienced was low because of elaborate fantasies and defensive routines that were employed to avoid it. These will be explored in the next two sections. The result was an organization that was strenuously avoiding the creative space; perhaps the main way this was being accomplished, and certainly the most difficult to under-stand, had to do with the fantasies and defense routines played out in the shadow system.

Was the Shadow System Being
Unconsciously Used to Avoid Anxiety?

The main anxieties of working in this organization arose from the nature of the rather dangerous production processes and, even more, the hostile persecutory environment. The first evidence for this assertion came from interviews using semistructured questionnaires with some 250 managers, spread across all of Enigma's sites, at the middle and supervisory levels. These managers showed a quite remarkable disinclination to talk about the prospects facing the company as its monopoly hold on its chief product weakened, but they all mentioned the unreasonable way in which pressure groups and the media pilloried them for what they felt were imaginary environmental dangers. Further evidence came from rather unstructured interviews with top-level managers, who emotionally and vehemently denied that the process contained any danger or that a hostile environment was much of a problem. They talked about "those outside not understanding" and about the steps that were being taken to "explain things to them." However, these same managers would then tell stories about how wives or children had been stigmatized because their husband or father worked for Enigma.

Clearly, then, the environment of this organization provided no containment of anxiety; rather, it generated the major part of it. What, therefore, were members doing with this anxiety? The complex system theory of organizations would lead us to expect them to be using their shadow system primarily as a psychodynamic system to hold at bay the anxieties they faced (Menzies Lyth, 1975, 1988; Jacques, 1955). It seems to me that Enigma's psychodynamic system took the form of a fantasy about early family life; Bion's basic assumption dependency behavior was very much in evidence. The most frequent image used by people at Enigma was that of a family. The organization was seen as a caring mother, but also an irritating one who imposed many restrictive rules; parts of the organization other than one's own were experienced as siblings who aroused envy and provoked rivalry, making it vital for "authority to be seen to be fair." The other image frequently used was that of clubs and secret societies, which also aroused envy that had to be contained by publicly fair practices.

In almost all the interviews, managers and supervisors stated their support for the company, which they viewed as a good employer that provided them with job security. However, having stated how good the organization was to them, many then suggested that things would be a lot better if, for example, they were provided with a gym, a crèche, free private health insurance, or a day off every month. They were also critical of more senior managers who, they said, avoided tough decisions. Despite all the efforts to promote participation, most saw it as a sort of front: they believed that decisions were really made in rather autocratic ways.

Most complained about communication with higher levels. They had to rely on the grapevine, despite large numbers of meetings, because feedback after each meeting was so poor. They called for more detailed and precise information on the company's objectives and strategies, and when the consultant pointed out that they had been sent a summary copy of the ten-year plan, some said that they could not remember what was in it, others that it was in a drawer somewhere, and yet others that it was not detailed and precise enough. They claimed that top managers had no sense of direction and that they, at the middle- and lower-management levels, needed to be told what the direction was before they could function properly. Most interviewees talked about the good teamwork within departments, but a number also spoke about departmental and divisional rivalries: "them and us" attitudes and "sibling rivalry."

Similar points came up in unstructured interviews with twenty-five top managers. For example, one of the divisional directors described how twenty years ago the organization had been extremely bureaucratic and status-conscious: a sharp division existed between the shop-floor workers, on the one hand, and the staff, on the other; the staff, in turn, were divided into administrative and scientific streams. People entered the company as either administrators or technicians and tended to remain in the stream they had joined, moving regularly up a strictly graded structure.

The system had changed when the distinction between administrative and scientific grades was abolished. All new entrants came into a unified stream and the terms and conditions of employment were set out in a staff handbook with a brown cover. They then progressed up the grade structure according to experience, encountering two important break points. At the first of these points, entry into the ranks of middle management, those who were promoted were given significantly better terms and conditions that were set out in a green staff handbook. Then, when a person reached senior management status, the terms and conditions changed once more, this time set out in a blue staff handbook. Managers, therefore, came to be classified into clear-cut groups known as Greens and Blues. Everyone knew to which group a manager belonged and every year separate management conferences were held for Greens and Blues. It was everyone's ambition to reach Blue status, which was thought of as a kind of club, or secret society, by those who were not members. To move from one status to another, an employee had to attend a Promotions Committee, so that moves could "be seen to be fair."

At all levels, therefore, those who were interviewed were using imagery that seemed to be saying, "We want to be treated like children and told exactly what to do and exactly where we are going and we want to be punished when we are bad, but in fact this does not happen. So although we are well looked after and 'held' by this organization, that security is not as satisfactory as it could be. We want even more security. Furthermore, we demand that we be treated fairly and that means that even-handed choices between people should be seen to be carried out. Fear that we might not be treated fairly leads to sibling rivalry. And if this rivalry gets out of hand, it will attract the attention of, and leave us exposed to, a hostile environment." The in-use unconscious theory may be that Enigma existed not to supply product in a way that sustained the support of the environment, but to be depended upon and to provide people with lifelong employment and protection against a hostile environment. To do this, it was necessary for bureaucratic procedures to be preserved essentially unchanged, because although they were irritating, they provided day-to-day predictability and thus safety in a world that was very hostile.

It was also necessary for top managers to provide people with comfort by magically telling them what the future would hold, that is, telling them the direction the company was going in and planning the future for them. In fact, however, people did not really want to know because it was too depressing, and so they ignored market trends, forgot what the objectives were, put any copies of plans distributed to them into drawers, and participated in workshops and committees that hardly ever seemed to produce anything concrete. Anxiety was also held at bay by the lack of differentiation between people on the basis of performance. Any differentiation had to be safely contained in visible "clubs," and promotions were given according to impersonal procedures that were "seen to be" fair. Poor performance was not to be punished and unions were not to be antagonized because that might attract the attention of the hostile environment.

So behavior at Enigma was driven by a very powerful, self-reinforcing, and self-perpetuating psychodynamic system that had been unconsciously created to protect people against the anxiety of their work, consisting of the danger of the processes they used and, particularly, the hostility of the community they operated within and for. In a sense they were being cast into the role of scapegoats by a community that wanted their products as cheaply as possible but feared the possible destructiveness of the production processes. This psychodynamic system allowed the image of change to be presented at a surface level but prevented changes from occurring below that; thus, one set of clubs, the administra-tive and scientific, could be removed but it was replaced by another, the Blues and Greens. As long as this psychodynamic sys-tem remained intact, the chief executive would continue to com-plain that everything he tried to do "gets lost a fog" and the many interventions by consultants would continue to effect surface change only.

Not surprisingly, the comprehensive change management project in which I participated as a consultant failed to effect any significant change, as had the one five years before it. This was not its real purpose. Its real purpose, I suggest, was an unconscious one. Managers needed to create the impression that change was afoot, but unconsciously this was never a serious intention. The shadow system had been spontaneously organized by all of the members themselves in a largely unconscious response to threats posed by their environment. It had come about through a process of spontaneous self-organization as people interacted together over the years in their work and social environment.

But how did this spontaneously self-organized shadow system make Enigma so unchangeable, so lacking in creativity? The answer seems to be that it worked with and supported the formal bureaucracy and hierarchy. Because both systems worked together, the whole organization was maintained in a state of stable equi-librium in which it was impossible to make any significant changes. Only when the shadow system works against the legitimate system will an organization be changeable. Enigma will not change unless the psychodynamic system that holds it stable is somehow destroyed. However, attempts to change such defensive systems are notoriously difficult, and destroying defenses can have disastrous consequences. If this defense against anxiety is destroyed in the absence of a good enough holding environment, will people con-tinue to operate the production processes as safely as they currently do? The evidence from other organizations that have been put under such pressure is that they will not (Schwartz, 1990). It follows that creativity in this particular organization may not be worth the price to be paid.

The second case study is about a completely different situation that prevailed in an international aid agency (Stacey, 1995b).

Occupying the Space for Creativity: The Aid Agency

In 1975 a European Technology Transfer Committee (ETTC), consisting of governmental representatives, was set up to allocate aid funds to technology projects. It was supported by the Technology Division of the European Commission, which in fact did all the work and had the real decision-making authority, with the Committee exercising a legitimizing function. In the mid 1980s José Fonseca became the executive secretary of the ETTC and head of the Technology Division. He was concerned about the way in which technology projects were prioritized for funding, the way they were implemented, and their ultimate benefits. He wanted to introduce more team effort and greater quality controls into the whole technology development process in developing countries, and this meant addressing the dominant position of the Technology Division. He therefore set up a review group of formally nominated ETTC members, headed by someone brought in from outside the organization, in order to find out what the developing countries were really looking for with regard to technology and to review how effectively the ETTC and the Technology Division were meeting those needs. Another purpose of this review group was to identify priority areas for future technological efforts.

The report of the review group came out in late 1984. At its meeting in 1986, the ETTC was still arguing about the recommendations. Fonseca's contract was not renewed at the end of 1986, and in early 1987 another head was appointed who had a different set of priorities that did not include the reform program. At a 1988 ETTC meeting, the argument about reform continued as it did in 1989 and 1990. All attempts at implementing a comprehensive formal program of change for the ETTC and the Division, as well as the attempt to form a rational plan for prioritizing and allocating technical assistance, failed to materialize.

Making Sense of the Experience

From a complex system perspective, nothing is surprising about this; legitimate systems exist to sustain the status quo and they therefore resist change in a perfectly open, overt political manner. This is what seems to be happening in this case. From a complex system perspective we would look for the origins of any change in the shadow system, and, as will be shown, this seems to have happened here.

Although the formal debate about changes in the legitimate system dragged on over the years, some small steps were taken, largely in the shadow system, by people who had no foresight at all about what they were touching off.

Developments in the Shadow System

At around the time of the report, Fonseca initiated a workshop in Mauritius to explore the problem of managing technological projects. He hired a temporary aide, who had worked with him previously in a multinational commercial organization, to organize the workshop. The aide, Peter Johnson, had not been trained in running Commission-style conferences, so instead of organizing the presentation of official papers, he arranged for participants to work on an expert system he had developed called VALTEC (short for technology evaluation). This expert system incorporated a number of principles, suitably weighted according to expert opinion, that had to do with prioritizing research. The system made it possible for policy makers to ask a number of questions about a specific set of research projects presented to them and to be guided by the system in making priority judgments. Participants were to use their own research programs to consult VALTEC and to then discuss with each other the problems that were raised.

About fifty scientists and civil servants attended the Mauritian workshop. Their response to the interactive event was to form themselves into teams, first to understand what an expert system was, and then to work with the system on common sets of problems. In doing so, the apparently fixed divide between developing and developed countries seemed to melt, and delegates began to realize that they could work out their own science and technology priorities themselves without hiring consultants. The effect of working on the expert system was to make clear to delegates that no rational set of techniques for determining priorities existed; instead they saw each set of circumstances as unique and as requiring the exercise of expert judgment, which might be assisted by using broad principles extracted from judgments that had previously been made in analogous situations.

The workshop was particularly important to members from a number of small African countries. Each of these countries had been pursuing its own attempts to manage its science and technology programs in isolation from the others. At the workshop, however, they spontaneously formed a team to work jointly on VALTEC. In doing this they discovered how similar their problems were, and after the workshop they asked Johnson for further help in using the expert system. In his personal capacity, he applied to the Hatfield Fund, a private research foundation, for a grant to conduct research on prioritizing projects. It happened that the Hatfield Fund managers were themselves facing this problem, and Johnson was given a substantial personal research grant, while he continued to get short-term renewals of his employment contract with the Technology Division.

Johnson then assembled about twenty senior managers of research institutions and departments in small African countries. They each came with their own problems and the aim of developing generic methods for evaluating projects in small countries. It was their intention to apply such methods over the three years of the research grant and to observe how effective they were, using the classic observer-participant approach of action science (Argyris, Putnam, and Smith, 1985). Through working on this project, they established a network among themselves that still exists.

These developments had to be reported to the ETTC and the Division and the response was largely critical: the others could not see what useful purpose was served by informally getting together to discuss the principles of prioritizing projects. To deal with this criticism, Johnson approached individual members of the ETTC and invited them to attend meetings of the African VALTEC network. When a very junior and temporary member of the Division personally approached senior civil servants without using the proper channels, the civil servants in the Division objected to this breaking of protocol. However, the VALTEC project attracted a trickle of important visitors despite the opposition.

Then, having heard about VALTEC, the government's scientific adviser in Canada invited Johnson and his colleagues to attend a conference he was organizing in Vancouver. One delegate to this conference was an Indonesian permanent secretary who asked Johnson to return home via Djakarta to discuss the problems his department faced in selecting and prioritizing research projects, for which they had been allocated a large budget. If they could not rapidly come up with a sensible priority that was likely to attract political agreement, the Treasury might well remove their budget. On arrival in Djakarta, Johnson was taken to see the scientific adviser to the prime minister. It was easy for this to happen because Johnson had no official standing and therefore no official channels had to be followed to arrange for his visit.

This discussion was followed by a second one, when the scientific adviser was on a visit to Brussels, Belgium, in early 1987. On that occasion they sat down with the country's five-year plan and within two days had come up with prioritization principles that could be defended to the Treasury and other departments. Johnson described the African network to the Indonesian scientific adviser and indicated how a similar network of leaders of research institutions in Indonesia could be used to apply the prioritization principles to identify a set of projects on which they could all agree to spend the research budget. Shortly thereafter, Johnson was invited once more to Djakarta, this time to assist in setting up an African-style network. During this week he helped to set up Prioritizing Applied Technology (PAT), which consisted of an informal network of selected individuals from the Treasury, the Economic Planning Ministry, and forty research institutes and universities. This network was centered around the scientific adviser and it still functions today. By June 1987, this network had completed the budget exercise, which was shown to be a success: the rather informal network had indeed produced an agreed-upon set of priorities and the budget had been approved.

In the meantime, Johnson brought network members from Canada, Africa, and Mauritius to PAT meetings in Indonesia. What was developing was a system in which people in one network could call on people in another geographic area to provide consulting services, drawing on their experience of similar problems. The prioritization project had started with attempts to set up a system but had evolved into a judgmental procedure for applying some very general principles within a mutually cooperative setting. The scientific establishments in other countries also began to take up this mutual self-help idea.

The Commission back in Brussels, however, did not approve. Johnson was told that he was working outside his brief. He was contacting very senior people without going through the proper hierarchical channels, and he was engaged in personal consulting work rather than in developing the training programs he had been hired for. His explanation that he was training people to act as consultants to each other and that he was facilitating the establishment of links between people was not accepted as satisfactory. The notes telling him that he should not be talking to the senior people he was in touch with continued. He was able to continue with his way of working, however, because he had Fonseca's support within the Division and influential support outside of it. He also had money from his own research contract and various overseas supporters were paying for air tickets. He therefore did not have to apply for resources for every activity through formal Commission channels.

By early 1987 about eighty individuals were actively participating in a worldwide network of technology policy makers, assisting each other on issues of mutual concern. The network operated on a system of bartering favors. However, the problems with the official structures of the ETTC and the Commission were multiplying. Johnson was now a full-time employee of the Technology Division and the members of the network were members of, or associated in some way with, the ETTC. But although the network was related to the formal ETTC and divisional structures in many ways, it was also clearly in opposition to it in many others.

The dilemma was as follows. On the one hand, the relationship with Commission institutions was important to members of the network because it provided something they could identify with and provided some visible structure, some way of demonstrating accountability and legitimacy. On the other hand, in order to continue to assist each other in practical, flexible ways, they had, in a sense, to flout the rules of the ETTC and the Commission. For example, the official view was that ETTC and Division work should focus on technology itself rather than on multidisciplinary policy matters. Network members, however, were working in a multidisciplinary way across governmental departments trying to integrate technology development budgets into national plans. Also, within the Commission, Johnson's work cut across divisions.

So in mid 1988, the eighty or so members of the informal network, together with the head of the Technology Division, established a body they called Technology Management Network (TMNET) to formalize to some extent the consulting assistance they were providing each other in relation to the management of science and technology. TMNET elected a chair and an advisory group and appointed Johnson to provide a central communication node. It was hoped that this formalization would meet the objections to the work of the network within the Commission, but this was not to be the case. The visibility of the network created by this formalization did, however, increase interest in it, and ETTC members now seemed more interested in it than in the ETTC itself.

During the course of 1991, some structure and routine were installed in TMNET. For example, when members wanted consulting assistance on some issue, they made a formal application to the unit, which would then pass it on to the TMNET members who were judged likely to be able to assist; in this way an informal project would be set up. Some 230 projects of this kind were carried out between 1991 and 1994, which must be seen in relation to the TMNET's budget of under $300,000 per year. The network was to grow to over four hundred members and it is still operating, generating tension and new initiatives.

Making Sense of the Experience

What the legitimate system failed to do was accomplished in the shadow system as it worked, sometimes subversively and always in tension with the legitimate system. It is striking that the control parameters were in completely different states than those of Enigma Chemicals.

First, members of the aid agency worked in an international environment in which they were exposed to rapid change and a large number of factors that they had to take into account. In other words, information flows were rapid. The operations involved a large number of people from many different countries, races, religions, and professions. The schemas driving behavior in the system these people constituted was, therefore, very diverse. The people involved occupied many diverse roles and traveled a great deal, and most worked actively at developing their own personal networks. Connectivity across this organization was therefore very rich. Power differentials were large: some members were close to the center of power in their countries and others held rather low positions in their legitimate system. However, these differences were normally used in a manner that encouraged true dialogue. Finally, the people involved displayed a clear ability to hold, rather than avoid, high levels of anxiety. The consequence is that the space for creativity was occupied, the people concerned spontaneously self-organized, and novel strategies emerged. It is striking how in this case the legitimate system was under pressure from its shadow and in fact was being subverted by that shadow.

PART FOUR

IMPLICATIONS OF
COMPLEXITY THEORY
FOR ORGANIZATIONS

Parts One and Three presented what are, I suggest, highly convincing arguments for concluding that human systems are complex adaptive feedback networks with the same general dynamic properties as all other such systems. Those properties were outlined in Part Two. Part Four shows that when we adopt the complexity perspective, we come to understand organizational life in a way that is completely different from today's dominant frame of reference. When we accept that we cannot foresee creative outcomes and therefore cannot be in control of their realization, we immediately undermine the basis of all the dominant prescriptions for organizational success that receive majority attention these days. Consequently we need a new management and organizational research agenda, and we have to think about management practice and organizational design in rather different ways. The following chapters indicate what lines this rethinking might take, and Map G depicts the journey we will have completed by the time we come to the end of them.

Map G. An Explanation That Resonates with Experience.

4
A complex adaptive system framework thus resonates with our experience and now enables us to see that we can accept lack of foresight and control because self-organizing processes inherent in all complex adaptive systems come into play at the edge of chaos. In human systems this occurs when we are able to hold anxiety but do not become suffused by it. The key to avoiding anarchy lies in containing anxiety.

3
Anxiety is thus inevitable, and since avoiding it destroys creative, complex learning, the key management task becomes enabling people to hold the anxiety of learning.

2
A complex adaptive system framework for making sense of life in organizations explains why no single agent—or group of them—can possibly design or intend creative outcomes for distant time frames or distant geographic spaces. Such outcomes can only emerge from complex, anxiety-provoking learning processes that require self-reflection. The difficulty is compounded by the need to practice intentional planning over short time frames—a completely different mindset to complex learning. But both mindsets are essential for survival.

1
We need to develop a new framework to make sense of life in organizations.

1a
Organizations are networks consisting of large numbers of agents—people—who interact with each other according to a set of behavioral rules we can call a schema. A dominant part of this schema drives current survival strategies, the primary task carried out by an organization's legitimate system. But there is also a recessive part that drives playful and destructive behavior in a shadow system that may or may not support the legitimate (see Figure 1.1). Schemas change in organizations; that is, organizations are systems that learn in complex ways. We can describe groups, minds, and even brains in similar ways.

PART ONE

5
The management research agenda should thus focus on identifying and understanding the nature of emergence and self-organization, on models of learning that incorporate the role of anxiety and its containment. The importance of self-reflection, anxiety containment, and the manner in which power is used become focal points for management practice.

PART FOUR

HOW CAN WE MAKE SENSE OF OUR EXPERIENCE OF LIFE IN ORGANIZATIONS?

1d
Organizations are complex adaptive systems and they, too, are creative and innovative when they occupy a space for novelty at the edge of chaos or disintegration. This is a state in which people play in an organization's shadow system with concepts and actions that in the end undermine their legitimate system in the sense of changing it. Organizations transform themselves through tension between the legitimate system and its shadow; this is the essence of organizational learning or extraordinary management (see Figure 7.3). Such real-time learning, or self-reflection, is a self-organizing process that produces radically unpredictable, emergent outcomes. It operates in tension with the intentional processes of the legitimate system—ordinary management (see Figures 7.1 and 7.2).

PART THREE, cont.

1b
The science of complexity explores the nature of deterministic (see Figure 2.1) and adaptive (see Figures 3.1 and 3.2) networks. The latter—complex adaptive systems—are networks of large numbers of agents who interact according to schemas that contain both dominant and recessive parts. The key discovery complexity scientists have made about complex adaptive systems is that they are creative only when they operate in what might be called a space for novelty. This is a phase transition at the edge of chaos, that is, at the edge of system disintegration. The state is a paradoxical one that is both stable and unstable at the same time, driven by contradictory dynamics of both competition and cooperation, both amplification and constraint, both exposure to creative tension and protection from it. Such systems evolve dialectically with radically unpredictable outcomes. The coevolving process is that of self-organizing creative destruction and reconstruction in which a recessive schema undermines a dominant one to produce emergent outcomes (see Figures 2.3, 3.4, and 3.5). These are systems that learn in complex ways and they are ubiquitous in nature.

PART TWO

1c
For about half a century now, psychoanalysts have very clearly understood that individual minds are creative (a) when they occupy the depressive position, that is, when they can hold paradox in the mind; and (b) when they can use transitional objects to play (see Figure 4.1). These mental states are intermediate between neurotic defenses and psychotic fantasy—genius is literally at the edge of madness. It has also been understood for a long time that groups of people, both small and large, can perform creative work only when they occupy a psychic state between heavily defensive behavior and psychotic, basic assumption behavior (see Figure 5.1). Since organizations are collections of groups, the same points apply to them (see Figure 6.1). We can map the properties of complex adaptive systems in general onto human systems (see Figure 6.2) and it is clear that human consciousness, determination, and intention cannot alter these fundamental dynamics.

PART THREE

7
Because we are learning in complex ways, we need no longer depend upon "savior" recipes.

And so we escape the vicious circle.

6
The new framework enables us to abandon the fantasy that we can know the future and be "in control." It leads us instead to self-reflection and learning from experience at all levels in human systems and gives greater insight into what we actually do in organizations, rather than what we say we do or what we believe we are supposed to do.

9

Implications of the Complexity Paradigm for Research into Management and Organizations

The international community of researchers in management and organization, like all other communities of researchers, is a human system and, as with other human systems, it constitutes a complex adaptive system. This system has its legitimate component: those who are employed in universities, business schools, and research institutes, who belong to learned societies and publish in their recognized journals. Like the agents of other nonlinear feedback networks, members of this legitimate system share a dominant schema, which determines their research agenda. Work that is part of this agenda is financed by the official research funding bodies and the results are published in prestigious journals. A shadow system also exists in which some members of the legitimate system and others may play with various notions outside the dominant schema—that is, in the recessive parts of the research community's schema. These notions, however, are normally not accepted by the legitimate research establishment as more than

243

interesting or entertaining sidelines, and they do not easily find their way into prestigious journals.

The complexity paradigm is still in the shadow system; it does not govern the current research agenda. If it did, how would the resulting agenda differ from the one that currently dominates research? What would the new research agenda focus on?

Perhaps these questions can be answered in an illuminating way by starting off with a discussion of the current dominant schema of the research community and the agenda it determines. The part of the study of management called strategic management is a good place to focus this discussion because strategic management is concerned with the future evolution of an organization, what role its managers play in that evolution, what kinds of patterns changing organizations exhibit, and what determines those patterns. There is a very clear exposition of the dominant schema, or paradigm, that drives the agenda in this area of research. I claim that this is also the dominant schema in other areas of research into management and organization.

Fundamental Research Questions Posed by the Dominant Paradigm

Ironically, the existence of a paradigm for strategic management is denied by the very writers who have summarized most succinctly the dominant schema of the research community and its consequent research agenda. In his introduction to the Summer 1994 Special Issue of the *Strategic Management Journal*, whose topic was new paradigms, Dan Schendel describes how he and a group of colleagues came together in 1977 and articulated a paradigm for the field in which they saw "six major tasks for the strategic manager: (1) goal formation; (2) environmental analysis; (3) strategy formulation; (4) strategy evaluation; (5) strategy implementation; and (6) strategic control" (Schendel, 1994).

This articulation has become widely shared by both re-searchers and practitioners since then—it provides the structure for almost all textbooks on strategic management—but now Schendel and his coauthors (Rumelt, Schendel, and Teece, 1994) argue that sophisticated scholars of management no longer see the management process as quite so rational. There is no agreement on a paradigm and they believe that there probably never will be. The reason for this, it is argued, is that strategic management is "an interdisciplinary subject, a field of practice and application, whose perspective will shift and whose research approaches will be incommensurable, rendering it unlikely that a single paradigm will ever govern the field" (Schendel, 1994). Instead of a paradigm, these authors propose that research in the field should be governed by articulation of the fundamental issues underlying the field and by focusing on a small number of fundamental research questions.

However, every articulation and every formulation of funda-mental questions that commands widespread agreement is itself proof of some dominant schema, some paradigm, that determines the articulation and the questions posed. In spite of the lack of widespread agreement on a specific paradigm for the field of strate-gic management research, such agreement does exist on what the fundamental questions are and on the mental framework that leads researchers to pose these questions rather than others. Rumelt, Schendel, and Teece (1994) give an authoritative sum-mary of that mental framework or paradigm. It consists of the fol-lowing set of assumptions.

Equilibrium

In dynamic terms, it is assumed that successful organizations are drawn to operate in the stable zone, where the dynamics are deter-mined by the forces of equilibrium. The following quotes demon-strate how clearly this assumption is made:

The challenge is to retain the power of equilibrium thinking [Rumelt, Schendel, and Teece, 1994, p. 43].

Equilibrium assumptions are the cornerstone of most economic thinking. Researchers who eschew equilibrium assumptions risk gross errors in the causal interpretation of data. On the other hand, the risk in adopting an equilibrium assumption is that it may be unwarranted. . . . Which risk is undertaken is not just a matter of preference. . . . The general approach to making the judgement is to rule in favor of equilibrium when the underlying assets or positions are frequently traded, or contested, when the level of aggregation and the type of data is familiar to actors in an industry, when the data are widely available and frequently reviewed, and when the connections between the data and profits are widely understood.

While equilibrium assumptions often drive out consideration of innovation, change, and heterogeneity, this is not invariably the case. . . . More sophisticated views now permit more sophisticated equilibria [Rumelt, Schendel, and Teece, 1994, p. 537].

So the limitations of assuming equilibrium are recognized, but it is argued that the assumption must not be dropped because of them.

Causality and Predictability

The assumptions about causality and predictability follow from the focus on equilibrium. In the last quote the authors point to the danger of making errors in the causal interpretation of data. The implication is that research is about detecting links between a specific cause and a specific effect; if it is assumed that systems are moving toward equilibrium, it follows that such links can be detected, in principle at least. The authors' point is, however, that the possibility of sophisticated, multiple equilibriums rules out

links between cause and effect at a very general level, in many situations: "There can be no general rules for generating wealth. . . .
Opportunities worth undertaking must be rooted in the particu-
lars of the situation. . . . Acceptance of this level of economic
equilibrium . . . suggests a framework for where to look for opportunities and, once identified, a basis for judging relative merits"
(Rumelt, Schendel, and Teece, 1994, p. 538). This quote clearly
assumes the presence of identifiable links between specific actions
and specific successful opportunity realizations, although they may
not be present at a more general qualitative level. Furthermore,
when the authors consider whether predictable patterns can be
seen in the evolution of industries (p. 532), they dismiss the questioning of this predictability as an "also-ran" question that does
not compel further inquiry.

Internal Consistency

Rumelt, Schendel, and Teece also consider the question of whether
there are "internally consistent antecedent decisions and actions
that create functional policies aimed at competing in a certain
way or targeted at a particular product-market goal" (p. 531).
They point to the literature, which claims that such carefully
thought out strategies are rare and that instead strategy formation
and implementation are a process of "muddling through" (Lindblom, 1959), "logical incrementalism" (Quinn, 1980), "emergent
strategies" (Mintzberg and Waters, 1985), and "garbage can
choice" (Cohen, March, and Olsen, 1972). Then, without further discussion, they draw the following conclusion about questioning the existence of coherent antecedent decisions and
actions: "Nevertheless, this question was thought too skeptical in
tone and content, almost insulting. In the end we did not use this
question because there did not appear to be enough systematic
empirical research on the subject to generate any light" (Rumelt,
Schendel, and Teece, 1994, p. 531).

Choice and Intention

The above discussion also makes it clear that Rumelt, Schendel, and Teece are assuming the presence of antecedent patterns of choice that are then realized in organizations; they say, "Strategy is about the choice of direction for the firm" (p. 42). The assumption that coherent patterns in organizational actions are put there by antecedent choice and intention follows quite naturally from assumptions that organizations are systems tending to equilibrium, and that, in principle, identifiable links exist between specific actions and their long-term outcomes.

The Dominant Schema of the Research Community

The dominant schema of the research community, therefore, quite clearly consists of a metaparadigm through which the world of organizations is seen as an equilibrating system in which members are able to intend and choose coherent, orderly outcomes, to a large extent because they can jointly link their next specific actions to specific long-term outcomes. This is not a paradoxical world, but one that is ultimately regular and uniform. Rumelt, Schendel, and Teece propose what they see as the fundamental research questions and reject others, all in a manner that is perfectly consistent with this metaparadigm.

The science of complexity, however, presents us with a completely different metaparadigm. Through this lens, the world of organizations is seen as a system held far from equilibrium, at the edge of chaos, by the paradoxical dynamic of competition and self-organizing cooperation. In this fundamentally paradoxical world, the links between actions and their long-term outcomes are lost in the complex interactions between various components of the system. Predictability of specific outcomes is also lost, and what remains predictable is the system dynamic and the archetypal behavior it produces: predictability is possible at the general level but not the specific, the opposite of the conclusion reached with the aid of the dominant schema. Coherent, orderly patterns exist, but that coherence takes the form of irregular, fractal patterns and it comes about, not through some kind of comprehensive shared antecedent intention and choice, but through many individual real-time choices embedded in a self-organizing process. The coherence emerges, without prior system-wide, shared intentions, out of the local interactions of the agents in the system. This is a world of creative destruction in which irregularity, disorder, and difference play a major part and in which equilibrium is death rather than success.

What fundamental research questions will be posed if we adopt this complexity paradigm? Surely not the same ones as those posed from the perspective of the dominant stable equilibrium paradigm.

The Fundamental Research Questions

The fundamental questions settled upon by Rumelt, Schendel, and Teece are summarized below and then are commented upon from the perspective of the complexity paradigm.

How do firms behave?

This is a question about whether or not choices are made in a rational way and, if they are, what kind of rationality is used. However, the question to be researched is not as open-ended as it sounds, because later on the authors reject from the fundamental list the question: how does policy process matter? In their discussion of why this is not a fundamental research question, the authors cite a number of empirical studies (Mintzberg, Theoret, and Raisinghani, 1976; Lindblom, 1959; Quinn, 1980; March and Olsen, 1976) that show how messy and disorderly the strategy process can be in practice. They then conclude that this research does not cut "to the heart of the fundamental issue in strategy—the link between the policy process and the quality of decision, defined in competitive terms" (p. 531).

The observed presence of messy processes is thus dismissed from interest because the observers have not provided theoretical or empirical evidence that links the observed mess to some kind of successful outcome in survival terms. The authors expound on this further: "We fully understand the criticism that the 'policy' decision literature sees decisions as mandated by the top, whereas process researchers increasingly see significant innovations as flowing from the coordinated insights and actions of many actors, each possessing specialized information and competences. Nevertheless, . . . there are times when firms (or nations states) do face critical choices and their leaderships also face choices about how to choose. . . . Might not the 'garbage can' mode of policy making in most organizations simply reflect the lack of a superior proven alternative?" (p. 532). The authors quote Irving Janis (1989) as calling for a theory linking procedures for arriving at policy decisions with good and poor outcomes so that prescriptions for improving governance can be derived. They also recall Frederick Taylor's insight that naturally emergent practices can be improved through careful analysis.

So from the dominant paradigm, a fundamental question is posed as to whether strategy is a consequence of rational intention or some emergent process. The discussion of the question makes it quite clear, however, that researchers should be looking for rational processes. Any evidence to the contrary will be treated with skepticism because it is not backed by theory about, or observation of, a link between process and favorable outcome.

Governed by a complexity paradigm, however, we have a completely different kind of discussion. A theory explains why researchers observe the messy processes they do and what the connections are between these processes and competitive success. That theory tells us that creative organizations operate at the edge of chaos where the links between action and long-term outcome get lost, making it impossible for their members to use rational, intentional processes. Instead they have no option but to rely on spontaneous self-organization to produce emergent outcomes, and in this essentially messy process, disorder prevents the organization from becoming trapped on a local fitness peak. These processes produce the creative new strategies that the force of competition compels organizations to develop if they are to survive in the complex suprasystem of which they are a part.

We can see a direct causal link between being at the edge of chaos, engaging in the messy self-organizing processes of creative destruction, and competitive survival. What cannot be postulated, however, is a link between a particular kind of overall decision-making process and a successful outcome, because such links get lost. All we can say is that when a system operates at the edge, it is capable of creative and innovative behavior. We cannot say exactly what processes this requires, nor can we claim that being at the edge guarantees success, because it all depends on what the other systems the organization is interacting with are doing.

From a complexity perspective, then, the question about how process matters is retained and the one about how firms behave is seen to be simply another way of wording this question. The fundamental research questions from a complexity perspective are: How does the process of spontaneous self-organization actually operate in organizations to produce emergent strategies? What is the process of creative destruction that does this? What part do the mess and disorder we observe in organizational processes play in creative outcomes? And what does an organization do to influence the parameters that determine whether or not it occupies the creative space?

Why are firms different?

If one approaches the study of organizations and management from the direction of neo-classical economics, firmly built as it is on the stable equilibrium paradigm, then an important and puzzling question relates to why firms are different. If the shape of an organization is determined by the forces of the environment acting upon it, so that it tends toward a state of equilibrium adaptation to that environment, then it is a puzzle that firms in the same marketplace differ so much. Competition should remove these differences. Rumelt, Schendel, and Teece admit that if one does not accept equilibrium, heterogeneity is not a puzzle. The complexity paradigm sees successful systems as those that operate far from equilibrium, with the current state of each being the consequence of its precise history. Therefore, as many explanations exist for difference as there are organizations. The question is a trivial one and drops from consideration. Perhaps the only difference of interest relates to the dynamic zone in which a system operates. Is an organization in the stable zone heading for death? Or is it managing to hold itself at the edge of chaos, where it might be creative?

What is the function, the value added, of the headquarters unit of a diversified firm?

Rumelt, Schendel, and Teece argue that large, diversified corporations will continue as a dominant form of organization, and that further research is therefore required into how the headquarters unit adds value by formulating strategy and allocating resources, on the one hand, and by monitoring operations and thus minimizing errors on the other. As subsidiary questions, they propose that research should focus on whether strategy or structure is primary, whether the entrepreneurial or administrative roles of headquarters units are primary, and whether the amalgamation of businesses into one organization has limits.

From a complexity perspective, members of headquarters units are important agents in the total system, but they cannot strategically control it or direct it in the way that the formulation of the above research question presupposes. However, leadership at headquarters levels plays a major part in influencing the dynamic of the whole system. The style of leadership and the way power is used are among the control parameters that help to determine whether an organization is in the stable zone or at the edge of chaos. Headquarters units may also act as containers for the anxiety of members of other units, and this anxiety containment is a crucial control variable when it comes to positioning an organization dynamically.

This question, therefore, remains important from a complexity perspective, but the focus changes: it becomes much more a question of leadership and what this means in conditions that are far from equilibrium. In addition, the either-or posing of questions changes to both-and, because we are dealing with paradoxical systems.

What determines success or failure in international competition?

This question concerns the dynamic of the competitive process that leads to success and failure, and thus it is also a central question from a complexity perspective. Rumelt, Schendel, and Teece state that the above four questions are fundamental to understanding how groups are formed, how they succeed, how they are managed, and ultimately how they adapt and survive. They reject the question about process in the list of fundamental questions and they also drop questions that have to do with whether strategies actually exist and, if so, what their nature is, how industries evolve and whether predictable patterns can be found in this evolution, and how organizational competence is generated. As we shall see below, these questions, somewhat reformulated, survive in the list of questions we would regard as fundamental from a complexity perspective.

Finally, the authors discuss a question they missed, namely, why organizations find it so hard to change. To pose much the same question in other ways, we might ask: Why do organizations differ so much in the quality of their management processes, and what causes organizational inertia? As we shall see below, these missed questions are central to a complexity-driven research agenda.

Fundamental Research Questions
Posed by the Complexity Paradigm

The management research community's current dominant schema, its metaparadigm, reflects the origins of that schema in neoclassical economics, an attempt to understand the organizational world at a level that ruthlessly abstracts from human behavior. This frame of reference determines both the fundamental questions that are judged to be the legitimate foundation of research and the methods used to conduct that research.

The research questions have to do with how firms behave as opposed to people; why firms are different in terms of what causes them to do what they do rather than why groups of people are different and how they utilize those differences; what is the function of headquarters units in firms rather than what is the nature and impact of the leadership-followership; and what determines the success of firms in international competition rather than what makes groups of people creative. The research methods used to explore these questions focus on formulating falsifiable hypotheses and gathering evidence to disconfirm those hypotheses. Evidence is gathered primarily from cross-sectional surveys, questionnaires, and structured interviews. Although longitudinal studies using ethnographic methods and action research are increasingly used, researchers, especially doctoral students, are nervous about how acceptable the findings from these sources will be. Interviews are therefore painstakingly recorded and analyzed using content analysis, various cognitive mapping procedures, and so on. The notion that researchers need to get as close as possible to the dispassionate, repeatable experiment of the natural sciences is still strong.

This book has demonstrated that it is possible to approach an understanding of organizational life from a completely different perspective that is at least as intellectually comprehensive as the one that now dominates thinking, and that is also much closer to the observable and felt realities of individual mental and shared group life. This new approach originates in two different areas: the science of complexity and the field of psychoanalysis. In this approach, the human agent is understood in terms of the feedback network system that human agents constitute when they interact, leading to a far deeper insight into the dynamics of human systems. The result is a metaparadigm that is the complete opposite of the currently dominant paradigm. This has major implications both for fundamental research questions and for research methods.

The basic purpose of the management field of study remains the same: we are trying to determine what it is possible to say about the link between methods of organizing, managing, decision making, and control, on the one hand, and the long-term survival of the organizational systems we form, which are engaged in a paradoxically competitive and cooperative struggle, on the other. Our interest in doing this lies, ultimately, in the belief that we will be able to design organizations with improved chances of survival. It might be asked why we want organizations to last a long time. Why not let them die and be replaced by others? In this way, they could be stable during their lifetime. Those asking this question seem to be looking for a way to save stability. However, this simply displaces instability one level up to the level of the industry or economy. We would still have to explain creativity and the process of birth, death, and rebirth at that level. The inevitable instability will simply reappear one level higher.

I suggest that when we approach the task of designing either creative organizations or creative collections of them from a complexity perspective, the fundamental research questions may be posed along the following lines.

How do groups of people form and behave in the shadow system of legitimate organizations?

The central proposition of a complex adaptive system theory of organizations is that a specific space for creativity exists at the edge of system disintegration that can be defined in two ways. First, it is a particular psychological state that prevails in the shadow system that people spontaneously form in a self-organizing manner as soon as they become members of an organization's legitimate system. The psychological state in question is one in which at least some people, individually and in groups, are able to hold enough of the anxiety generated by the ambiguity of organizational life and the destructive nature of creativity to enable them to play without being tipped into psychotic fantasy, on the one hand, or rigidly defensive reliance on the legitimate system, on the other. Play here means the ability to engage in dialogue and exploration without having a clear purpose: it is engaged in for its own sake, at least initially. The result is that some people in an organization are manipulating the organization's recessive symbol system and are actively utilizing the differences and disagreements between people.

Second, the space for creativity is a state of tension between an organization's dominant schema, which is embodied in its legitimate system, and its recessive schema, which is embodied in its shadow system. At the edge of system disintegration, the shadow system, in effect, is seeking to destroy the current legitimate system in the interest of creativity and thus better long-term prospects of survival.

Some research around the above proposition has been done. The psychoanalytic perspective on organizations (for example, Hirschhorn, 1990) and the studies of emergent strategies (for example, Mintzberg and Waters, 1985) are relevant here. However, what is now needed is a much more systematic study of people who are engaged in what appears to be creative behavior in organizations, in order to indicate whether this framework allows us to make more sense of what is happening.

The above general question suggests a number of subsidiary questions:

Is there consistent evidence that organizations are creative when they are at the edge of system disintegration in the sense defined in this book?

What causes an organization to occupy the space for creativity?

Does evidence exist that occupation of the space for creativity is caused by the following parameters reaching critical points: information flow, degree of difference among agents, level of network connectivity, power use, and anxiety levels and their containment?

Are there other control parameters?

Can we measure the control parameters? What other ways of observing them are there?

How can the space for creativity be identified empirically? How does an organization determine whether it is in the space for creativity?

How can the control parameters be influenced?

In particular, how can power use be managed?

Even more important, how can anxiety be managed?

What does self-organization and emergence mean in organizational terms? How do we identify and observe them?

What other contextual factors are relevant to an understanding of the space for creativity? For example, what is the relevance of personality and personality differences? How does the spiritual dimension come in?

What causes self-organization?

What causes emergence?

What are the dynamics of the clash between the legitimate system of an organization and its shadow system?

A complexity approach to understanding the dynamics of human systems focuses clearly on the inevitable clash between the legitimate system of an organization and its shadow system, where creative developments originate. Actual change and innovation can therefore take place only if this clash ends up with replacement of at least some aspects of the legitimate system, but without the whole organization tipping over into the unstable zone, where it disintegrates. The kinds of questions this poses are as follows:

What examples are there of this clash leading to system disintegration?

What examples are there of attempted creative changes being aborted so that the legitimate system continues unchanged?

What examples are there of what amounts to a successful revolution in organizational life?

What do members of an organization, leaders, and those in control of the legitimate system do that makes a successful revolution possible?

What are the characteristics of the leader-follower dynamic in the space for creativity?

When organizations occupy the space for creativity, behavior is controlled by the process of self-organization itself and no one is in control. In this space no one can determine the future direction an organization will take. This poses the following research questions:

> How is controlled behavior maintained?
>
> What is the role of leaders in this space?
>
> If their role is to nurture and articulate, manage anxiety and facilitate, how do they successfully do this?
>
> How does leadership shift about during the play that is an essential aspect of creativity?
>
> What other roles do people take up and what is the contribution of the mature follower role?
>
> What are the consequences of occupation of the space for creativity by specialization and participation between leader and followers?
>
> What are the causes and consequences of neurotic and psychotic forms of leadership and followership?

What link can be identified between processes in organizations and successful competitive capability?

Because the link between action and long-term outcome is lost when an organization occupies the space for creativity, it follows that it is impossible to identify a link between specific managing, organizing, decision-making, and control processes, on the one hand, and successful organizational competitiveness on the other. However, it is possible to link occupation of the space for creativity, not with the certainty of survival, but with its possibility.

Avoiding this space ensures that an organization will not survive, but it could take a very long time dying. This leads to the following questions:

What cause an organization to lock in to particular strategies?

What determines how long such locked-in organizations survive?

Do organizations that occupy the space for creativity in fact show higher survival rates?

Is the link between occupation of the space for creativity and survival detectable at the individual, group, organizational, or system-wide levels?

Does it matter whether particular individuals, groups, and organizations survive, or is it only important for the system as a whole to survive?

What is the role of redundancy and slack resources in practice?

What kinds of schemas produce specific types of archetypal behavior?

Is it more effective for a few to occupy the space for creativity on behalf of the many, or is a wider participative occupation of the space for creativity more likely to lead to survival?

How does thinking differently alter behavior in organizations?

What kinds of management and consulting interventions make sense in the space for creativity?

Because creative organizations produce emergent strategies through processes of self-organization, the perception of the role of the consultant has to change. This role can no longer be to design and implement comprehensive programs of total system change. Instead, the following questions seem more relevant in relation to consultant and, for that matter, top-management interventions:

How might groups of people in an organization, and even whole organizations, self-reflect?

How can consultants intervene in organizations in an unstructured way so as to provoke self-organization?

How can people be assisted to become more aware of, to hold, and to work with the paradoxes of organizational life?

How can people be trained and encouraged to engage in dialectical types of analysis?

Research Methods

It is not only the content of the research agenda that is fundamentally altered by the move from the stable equilibrium paradigm to the complex system paradigm. The methods for answering the one set of questions become inappropriate for answering the other set. Any residual notion that a researcher is some kind of independent, objective observer has to be abandoned. Intervening in an organization always affects it. The emphasis then shifts to the role of the participant observer; this means that research projects may well produce more interesting results if they utilize people who are actually engaged in the work and management of an organization. The academic researcher's role becomes more that of a supervisor and counselor to the front-line researchers who are engaged in an organization's activities but who are practicing the skills of self-reflection, using their feelings and adopting what some have called the consultancy stance (Carr and Shapiro, 1995).

Ethnographic methods, action science, and the consultancy stance become the more appropriate methods of research, with other methods open to much suspicion, the reverse of the present situation. Let us consider why this is so. The complex system paradigm leads us to expect that at any one time, a population of organizations will include some organizations that are occupying the space for creativity. However, much larger numbers of organizations are likely to have become sucked into the stable zone, with unchallenged legitimate systems locked in to what were successful strategies in a previous period. Observation suggests that locked-in organizations can last for considerable periods of time, the length of the period depending upon just how aggressive their competitors are. Also, a number of organizations will be in the process of disintegration. If a researcher takes a cross-section of this population and relates current states of variables to current performance, he or she will get totally misleading results, because for the majority of organizations in the population, states of the variables that are long past are accounting for the current apparent success. Where long lags exist, cross-sectional analysis, which does not take account of the dynamics, is worthless. In the kind of organizational population suggested, it is possible to find evidence through cross-sectional analysis for just about any hypothesis one wishes to suggest. This applies whether questionnaires or interviews are used.

The research problem is compounded by the fact that people in organizations say one thing when they are doing another (Argyris and Schön, 1978, call this espoused and in-use theories), and they often do not know why they are doing what they are and often not even what they are doing—this is called tacit knowledge (Nonaka, 1991). Simple questionnaires, surveys, and interviews will then not reveal what is really going on. In these circumstances the clinical methods of the psychoanalyst or the consultancy stance are more appropriate. The sensitive participant observer can use his or her feelings in the situation to hypothesize what is actually happening. This means that we have to give up the notion that we can understand the system by formulating falsifiable hypotheses and then seeking to disconfirm them. Instead, we may have to reformulate what we are doing as trying to make more sense of our own and others' experience of organizational life.

The methods used by those who are applying complexity science to the natural sciences also indicate how it might be used for human systems. Researchers might observe agents in a human system, infer the rules that make up the schemas, and then run simulations on computers. This is already being done by Robert Axelrod (1984) and others working with prisoners' dilemma type of games. Perhaps there is a great deal more scope for this kind of attempt to understand the dynamics of human systems and make more sense of our experience of organizational life.

What the Complex Systems Approach Adds

The distinctive contribution that the science of complexity could make to our understanding of organizational life can be brought into focus by considering what it adds to similar notions to be found in the literature.

First, the science of complexity studies nonlinear feedback network systems. Substantial literature exists on systems theories of organizations: organizations as open systems that are paradoxically pulled in different directions by the opposing forces of differentiation and integration (Lawrence and Lorsch, 1967; von Bertalanffy, 1968); organizations as interconnected technical and social systems (Miller and Rice, 1967); organizations as formal and informal system that are often in conflict with each other (Trist and Branforth, 1951); and organizations as nonlinear, dynamic systems where connections between cause and effect are distant in time and place (Forrester, 1958, 1961; Senge, 1990). A literature is also growing on organizations as formal and informal networks; it explores the nature of the links in human networks and what flows through those networks, and the part those networks play in organizational development (Nohria and Eccles, 1992).

The common thread running through all of this literature is that the research it reflects is conducted within the stable equilibrium paradigm; in addition, the studies of networks are primarily reductionist. An unquestioned assumption exists in most of this literature that the point of the theory and the research is to identify how the system might be controlled, how it might be intentionally redesigned so that it operates more efficiently or more effectively. For example, Senge (1990) presents a model in which the complex nonlinear system is directed by the vision of some charismatic leader and is controlled by identifying leverage points that can be operated on to produce intentional outcomes. The implicit theory of causality is that the system is driven by laws in which the causal links between specific action and specific outcome can be identified to some useful degree.

What the science of complexity adds is a different theory of causality, one in which creative systems are subject to radical unpredictability, to the loss of the connection between action and long-term outcome. The purpose of the theory and the research is then to indicate how conditions might be established within which spontaneous self-organization might occur to produce emergent outcomes. This is a radically different focus on the system dynamics that has major implications for the practice of management and the design of organizations. One of these implications is the tremendous importance of the shadow system as the generator of the mess and disorder that are vital if a learning, evolving system is not to be trapped on a local fitness peak. This and the notion of the space for creativity as the edge of organizational disintegration is a radically new notion, with major practical implications.

The literature does also contain a substantial amount of model building and descriptive research having to do with disorder in the process of organizations and the existence of emergent strategies, which has already been referred to. However, this literature lacks a coherent theoretical framework, a lack that enables those who espouse the dominant schema of the research community to dismiss it in the manner we saw above. The science of complexity adds a coherent theoretical framework within which researchers can understand self-organization and emergence and conduct appropriate research. The key notion here is that of a space for creativity at the organizational level, which consists of a psychological state in the shadow system that puts it in tension with the legitimate system.

A raft of models and notions come from sociology (Hyman, 1987; Giddens, 1979) and Austrian evolutionary economics (Schumpeter, 1934; Hayek, 1948) that do utilize the dialectical evolution, the paradoxical nature of organizations (Hampden-Turner, 1990), to model what happens. The psychoanalytic literature on organizational life has already been referred to. What previous chapters have shown is that a complexity approach enables us to integrate all of this into a coherent theoretical framework.

Perhaps the science of complexity adds most value because it provides new analogies and metaphors for those in the research community who are inclined to play in that community's recessive schema, in tension with the dominant schema, to produce creative change in our understanding of organizations.

10

Implications of the Science of Complexity for Management Practice

It is immediately evident that the theory of organizational dynamics derived in previous chapters from the science of complexity and the discipline of psychoanalysis has major implications for the practice of management. These implications are often experienced as anxiety-provoking because they challenge so many deeply held beliefs about what management ought to be, even if it is clear that it has not yet reached that ideal state. The following are typical concerns:

- Because we cannot identify what the long-term outcome of our actions is going to be, we have no basis for a rational choice, and so we may as well pack up and go home.
- Spontaneous self-organization cannot be the basis of strategy in human systems because if we have to rely on people doing whatever they want to, we will simply have anarchy.

- If no one can be in control of an organization's long-term direction because strategies emerge from bottom-up, spontaneously self-organizing processes, top managers have no role in a corporation.
- If organizations really do self-organize to produce creative, emergent strategies, what are the prescriptions for success? What new management behaviors and leadership styles must we adopt? What are the practical things we must do? What are the tools for operating with this new method?
- How do we know this is going to work? Where are the examples of best practice, the benchmarks, in which organizations use this new model and succeed?

These responses and the questions they give rise to display how tightly the managers concerned are thinking within the same dominant schema as the one that is employed by the research community. Success is held to be a stable, predictable state that can be secured by comprehensive, prior, shared intention. Those who propose that instability and mess are essential are simply saying that coherent behavior is impossible and, therefore, what they are saying must be wrong. Consider, however, how one might respond to each of the concerns raised above from the complex system perspective, which indicates that not only coherent but also creative behavior is possible, and that it is possible precisely because the system is messy.

Criteria for Designing Actions in Conditions Far from Certainty

Members of an organization, whether they are in the role of manager or managed, all face much the same fundamental issue. They must take action and respond in the here and now to the consequences that the actions of others have just created for them. If individuals are to act coherently as a group, each of them has to answer a key question: What criteria are to be used in choosing the next action?

The dominant schema immediately points to one major criterion for selecting the next action, namely, the extent to which long-term outcomes of that action achieve some objective determined in advance of acting. The design of an action requires that people first identify the potential consequences of each action option open to them individually and as a group, then select the one that is reasonably likely to achieve the objectives of their organization. However, as soon as they try to do this, they are confronted with a problem: as they look into the future, trying to identify potential consequences, they find it harder and harder to do so the further they try to look into the future. At some point, and nowadays that point is not all that far in the future, they have to admit that they do know what the consequences of their actions might be, and the future becomes open-ended.

The dominant schema then prompts them to make assumptions about what they do not know so that the rational design of actions may proceed. This schema leads people to believe that the open-endedness they face is the result of their ignorance: they have not done enough research into the laws of causation and have not gathered enough data to work out the future consequences of their actions. Or the data and the analysis are available but others are either too incompetent or too badly behaved to use them properly. The immediate conclusion drawn is that ignorance can be overcome by greater investment in gathering information, funneling it to some central point where it can be analyzed, and then feeding it back to the actors. The dominant schema therefore leads people to believe that ignorance can be overcome by research into organizational excellence, incompetence can be overcome by training and developing managers, and systems can be used to prevent bad behavior. All of this is expected to enable members of an organization to be clear enough about the consequences of their actions, at least in a probabilistic sense or in terms of assumptions, so that these consequences may provide the necessary criteria for choosing their actions. The future is not unknowable; it merely is currently unknown.

From the complexity perspective, however, we reach the opposite conclusion, namely, that the future is truly unknowable. Creative futures emerge unpredictably from self-organizing interactions between members; therefore, they clearly cannot use some forecast of long-term outcomes to decide between one action and another. Furthermore, the complexity perspective would lead us to believe that because the identification of long-term outcomes is impossible, successful practitioners will use other criteria while, perhaps, pretending that they are not doing so.

For example, during a consultation to one organization, I attended a meeting of the senior management group, who were discussing whether or not to invest many millions in a new plant. They had before them a paper setting out twelve different scenarios for the next twenty-five years, together with the cash flows associated with investment in each of the twelve scenarios and the rates of return on their investment that these implied. In doing this they were, of course, following standard best-practice investment appraisal procedures. Soon into the discussion of the paper, however, confusion arose as to just what the differences were between one scenario and another; even the experts had forgotten how the huge number of assumptions made in each scenario differed from those made in the others. The confusion began to turn to anger, so the chief executive relieved the pressure by laughingly saying, "The one thing we know for sure is that none of these scenarios contain what will happen. We all know from past experience that reality will turn out to be completely different."

These intelligent and competent managers were using a procedure that is widely held to be rational and entirely appropriate in the circumstances. The very act of doing this, however, was completely irrational. Rationality requires that each individual expose, for joint scrutiny, his or her reasons for undertaking a joint action. In this way the reasons for acting jointly in a particular manner can be discussed and tested by the knowledge and experience of other players. When I asked the senior executives at this particular meeting whether they had already decided to back the proposed investment, most said that they had, and that they had reached their conclusion before they saw the paper on scenarios and rates of return. When they were asked if they had disclosed and discussed their reasons to each other, they replied that they had done so in casual conversations in twos and threes up and down the corridors. But now, in their formal, public meeting, they were acting as if they were seriously considering a decision based on the figures before them, and they had no intention of publicly discussing the real reasons.

Why not? Because those reasons had nothing to do with the long-term outcome and the profitability of the investment, and yet this is the basis upon which rational managers are supposed to make their decisions. The real reasons had to do with staying in the marketplace even though no one knew how it would develop, and with preventing competitors from building too strong a position. In fact, then, the real reasons for deciding to undertake the investment related to the here-and-now characteristics of the action itself—the means, rather than the ends.

When asked why they were pretending to make the decision in one way when they had already effectively made it in another way, they indicated that they were not aware of doing this and then said that the real reasons were so general and experience-based—gut feeling is the pejorative for this—that they could not hope to persuade the nonexecutive members of their board and the financiers that the investment should go ahead. However, close questioning of nonexecutive board members and financiers revealed that they did not believe the forecasts any more than the managers making them did. The apparently rational method, however, protected them if the investment subsequently failed. The real criterion for making the finance available was the track record of the management team and the financiers' gut feeling.

In this case and, I suggest, in all other cases in which discounted cash flow analysis is used, managers are acting out an apparently rational process, claiming that they are using a rational technique, when in fact, if they were really doing this, they would be behaving entirely unreasonably, because they would be making major decisions on the basis of information that they clearly knew to be worthless. However, they are being reasonable, because they are using the apparently rational as a cover behind which they are doing something quite real. The purpose of the cover is to reduce the anxiety levels that arise from dealing with the unknowable.

So instead of concerning themselves with the ends, which they cannot determine in advance, managers are compelled to judge what it is appropriate to do entirely on the basis of the means. The criteria for quality actions become, not ends, but ethical considerations and criteria having to do with maintaining positions, keeping options open, retaining flexibility, and revealing errors as fast as possible. The quality action is not one with a predetermined outcome, because that effectively excludes all creative actions, but the action that is morally good in itself, the action that keeps options open by allowing an organization to stay in the game and not yield to competitors, the action that allows managers to detect their errors as soon as possible.

Consider the revolution that this last criterion implies. At present it is common to hear top executives saying to their subordinates, "Make sure that I do not have to deal with surprises." This instruction quite naturally leads subordinates to cover up their errors until it is too late, a procedure that is disastrous in conditions that are far from certainty (Schwartz, 1990). If, instead, senior executives say, "Make sure that you surprise me as early and as frequently as possible," they change the criteria for a quality action to include one that allows the rapid uncovering of errors (Collingridge, 1980). For such a change to occur, managers will have to develop a tolerance for errors.

Note how the complexity perspective facilitates awareness of the distinction between espoused and in-use management theories of action and assists in understanding why managers do what they actually do instead of what the management literature suggests that they should. The complexity perspective indicates that many of the messy processes that managers employ behind the cover of technical rationality are entirely appropriate. In that sense, the complexity theory of organizations does not present anything new, anything that is not happening or has not happened. What it does present is a more comprehensive and more useful way of making sense of what managers actually do. In other words, it is a useful framework for organizational self-reflection. It is an approach that assists managers in reflecting upon automatic behaviors that are driven by rules lying beneath the level of awareness. Such reflection is the essence of double-loop learning, without which no new knowledge is created.

Freedom and Control in the Space for Creativity

The dominant schema encourages managers to assume the following:

- Quality actions are based on some knowledge of their outcomes.
- Such knowledge is best obtained from some centralized point to which data has been funneled and where it is then analyzed before being fed back to those who must act.
- At least the objectives, if not the actions themselves, need to represent either the intention of a small number of the

most powerful or the democratic intention of the whole group.

The result of thinking in this way is that most members of an organization are left with very little individual freedom. It is the role of the majority of the members to implement the actions that are likely to achieve the outcomes intended by the most powerful or by the majority.

From this perspective, legitimate authority flows from the roles occupied by the powerful, who may or may not be democratically elected. That authority will, of course, be diminished if the members of an organization take their own authority; it is believed that disorder would ensue if large numbers of individuals acted according to their own local rules of behavior in the absence of some blueprint. Thus, the notion that all members must act only to achieve some predefined outcome not only obstructs creativity and encourages us to avoid actions with long-term outcomes; it is also an enormous constraint on individual freedom in an organization.

However, the science of complexity shows that complex adaptive systems produce order for nothing, that is, without any blueprint, plan, or set of instructions being fed to them. In organizational terms, this means that we do not need to fear that when individual members take their own authority for their actions it will automatically lead to anarchy. Taking our own authority does not mean doing anything we feel like. Authority is the legitimate use of power, so we need to look for the source of legitimacy when we take our own authority. That source lies in two locations: in the task itself and in our own humanity. Taking our own authority means taking the steps necessary to accomplish the task, as dictated by that task rather than by some figure in an authority role, within the internal constraints we set ourselves for ethical behavior. The constraints lie in what we believe to be right and in the need we all have to sustain the support of those we interact with.

Mature members of an organization who take their own authority for performing the tasks of the organization, that is, who self-organize, will not produce anarchy but may well produce creative new strategic directions.

There are, then, two diametrically opposed ways of answering some of the most basic questions to be posed about organizational life. One way is based on the belief that order is put into organizational behavior by prior shared intention, by either the most powerful or the majority. This leads to ways of managing and organizing that greatly constrain individual freedom—the few do the thinking and the creating while the many do as they are told. The opposite view is based on the notion that a creative new order emerges unpredictably from spontaneous self-organization. This leads to ways of managing and organizing in which individuals are free to take their own authority, constrained only by the nature of the task, the need to sustain support, and the imperative to behave ethically. The new science of complexity offers a hopeful justification for freedom in organizational life.

Leading in the Space for Creativity

The dominant schema that currently drives the thinking of both the research community and practicing managers leads to the belief that organizational joint actions must be selected according to how likely they are to achieve desirable outcomes. The desirability of an outcome is to be determined by those who occupy authority roles. Such views lead to particular notions of leadership: leaders determine and articulate the direction in which a group or organization is to develop and then employ a number of motivational methods, ranging from force to inspiration, encouragement, and facilitation, to persuade others to move in that direction.

A complex adaptive system theory of organizations does not reject such notions of leadership; rather, it puts them into a context that enables us to see that they are limited, special-case notions. They are the concepts of leadership that apply to ordinary management through the medium of the legitimate system, which is confined to single-loop learning and to making more efficient what an organization already does well. When it comes to articulating where an organization has come from and then sharpening our understanding of how it may continue in much the same direction, the notions of leadership set out above are entirely appropriate.

However, far from certainty and equilibrium, leadership has a rather different meaning. In these circumstances the leaders of the legitimate system cannot know, any more than anyone else can, where their organization is going. It is extraordinary management, the self-organizing process of double-loop learning pursued in the shadow system, that determines creative new directions. The leaders of the legitimate system are simply participants in the functioning of the shadow system, albeit rather important and influential participants. They are particularly important and influential because other members of the shadow system project leadership and authority into them. The manner in which they cope with these projections has a profound effect upon the degree to which the anxieties of creative learning are contained rather than avoided.

Leaders, then, do not determine direction when they take up their roles in the shadow system. Instead, they become important participants whose primary function has to do with the containment of anxiety. They need to be involved in the group processes of the shadow system, but from a position on the boundary, where they can understand the processes but not get sucked into them (Miller and Rice, 1967). As people operate in the shadow system, leadership roles emerge spontaneously from the interaction. When the creative space is participatively occupied, then, the role of leadership shifts around the system according to which people have a contribution to make and how effectively they are able to attract the attention of others to that contribution.

The other possibility is that a leader will emerge who occupies the creative space on behalf of others. Such a leader contains the anxiety of the others and articulates and initiates potentially creative thought, discoveries, and behaviors. Such a leader still cannot be in control of the outcome of this creative behavior—the dynamics of the system make this impossible. However, as part of the anxiety-containing function, the leader may subsequently present what has happened as intentional and this myth will be gratefully accepted by the followers. When they are caught up in this kind of dependent specialization in occupying the space for creativity, followers will be furious with, and dismissive of, leaders who admit that they do not know what the future direction is, and the leaders will be quite fearful of making any such admission. Together they will collude to make meaningful empowerment impossible.

Leadership from an extraordinary management perspective is thus very different from leadership from an ordinary management perspective. The leadership required in extraordinary management includes the capacity to contain anxiety for others, on the one hand, and the ability to provoke and contribute to the double-loop learning process on the other. Anxiety-containing capacity is a function of the behavior of the leader that has to do with the manner in which power is used and with compassion for the feelings and fears of others in a group. Leaders contain anxiety when they are able to empathize with others and articulate or interpret what they are experiencing (Carr and Shapiro, 1995). Provoking double-loop learning requires the capacity to play with metaphor and images and pose stretching challenges for others and the ability to listen and hold oneself open to changing one's mind.

A complexity theory of organizational development therefore ascribes very important and very difficult roles to management in addition to the currently dominant notions that also continue to be important from an ordinary management perspective. Complexity theories of management lead to a very rich, paradoxical theory of leadership in which leaders have to be both the conventional directors of others and the far more subtle containers of their anxiety and provokers of their double-loop learning capacity. These different attributes of leadership do not blend harmoniously with each other. Instead, they conflict with each other; directing and intentionally not directing are diametrically opposed ways of behaving and both are required of an effective leader in a complex adaptive system.

Self-Reflecting, Changing Mindsets, Designing the Use of Power, and Managing Anxiety

We come now to the requests managers make for the prescriptions for success that a complexity theory of organizational life leads to and the proof that it does indeed lead to success. The way in which this request is normally phrased indicates that it is posed from the stable equilibrium perspective that so dominates current thinking. The complex adaptive system theory outlined in this book is seen as a "new way of managing," and people want to know how they should go about implementing this new way, just as previously they were advised how to implement, say, Total Quality Management or Business Process Reengineering.

The first point to make is that I am not talking about a new way of managing. All the building blocks used to construct a view of organizational life based on complex adaptive systems are already reasonably well known and are also used in practice. In that sense nothing is new here. I am not, therefore, suggesting a new set of prescriptions, a new system along the lines of Business Process Reengineering. What I am saying is that a new overall framework is now available with which to think about and try to make sense of what people in organizations are already doing. Thus, extraordinary management is not a new process; it is what people in organizations are already doing in an automatic way without much awareness or reflection. What is new is a coherent overall framework for people to use in reflecting upon what they are doing so that they may make more useful sense of it. I have argued that on a very widespread scale, people say that they are using one kind of management approach as a cover behind which they are actually doing something else. Rarely do any of us reflect in a consistent and public way on what that something else is.

The prescription, then, is to use the insights of complexity science as a framework for individual, group, and organization-wide self-reflection, that is, an examination of, and dialogue about, the processes of extraordinary management. What is the point of this? It is that self-reflection is the way to improve the kinds of messy processes required for extraordinary management rather than continuing to believe in the fiction of stable equilibrium. The prescription is for people to think about complexity and what it means and to develop their own responses to it. People who begin to think differently will almost certainly begin to act differently, and they will then almost certainly affect someone else who will begin to behave differently.

I am firmly convinced that attempts to provide rather precise sets of general prescriptions are simply an invitation for people to stop thinking. Sometimes this might be a good thing to do in the interest of action. However, when it comes to creativity in organizations, it is more important to present ideas and then leave it to the actors to make what they will of them in their own situations. Let me quote from the recollection of one articulate manager after he had been exposed to the kind of thinking that the science of complexity suggests:

> As I have read about complexity theory I feel like I have become aware of a new world around me. . . . I discovered ethnography and more importantly action learning and reflection-in-action techniques. . . . Almost

straight away my behavior changed. I began openly asking people for their thoughts and assumptions behind
statements when they came up in discussion and when
I disagreed with them. Almost immediately I felt much
more satisfied with my inputs and with the responses I
was getting from people, particularly with the factory
manager I am working with. . . . We have a time set
aside to reflect now—it kind of happens though—not
in a planned way. This line of thinking opened the box
though. . . . Time after time we are now exploring the
motivation and potential assumptions behind behaviors we see and attempting to modify ours to continue
to develop support and momentum for change. . . . We
have also begun to identify patterns of behavior among
our work force. . . . Something we have identified is
that there seems to be an underlying fear of failure and
an expectation of coming second.

What this manager is describing is a process of individual self-
reflection being amplified to his closest colleagues. This process is
changing mindsets and getting people to examine how they are
using their power and what impact it is having on others, particularly what it has to do with the anxieties and fears of others
and how they might be addressed. This call for self-reflection and
the consideration of how anxiety is to be managed is perhaps the
most important prescription of a complex adaptive system view
of organizational life. Strategic plans cannot be about creative outcomes, but they could be about installing appropriate psychological and emotional conditions to encourage the spontaneous
self-organization that might produce creative outcomes.

Redundancy, Slack Resources, and Play

Extraordinary management is a process that is practiced in a spontaneously self-organizing shadow system that is strongly akin to

play. It is true dialogue in which people engage with each other, not to be in control, but to provoke and be provoked, to learn and contribute to the learning of others, to change their own minds as well as the minds of others. This process is like play in that it invites operation in the transitional zone of the mind, where reality and fantasy come together in the form of metaphors, analogies, and images. Experience-based intuition, rather than sequential, logical analysis, leads to the creative insight.

Play, however, takes up time, and much of it has no visibly beneficial outcome. A great deal of it will turn out to be futile, but some probably will not. Without it, however, an organization cannot innovate. Creativity and innovation, therefore, require slack in an organization's resource utilization. Creativity and efficiency are enemies: the first requires slack resources and the second requires that there be none. They are enemies in another way, too. Efficiency requires that there be no redundancy, no repetition of the same tasks in different parts of an organization or at different times. Creativity, however, requires redundancy. First, it allows for the repetition of different ideas and experiments in slightly different ways, and small differences can have large outcomes. It also means that the organization will be more resilient in the face of inevitable failures in the innovative experiments going on.

There Are No Guarantees

Many managers, on first being exposed to the kind of theory outlined in this book, ask for evidence of organizations that have used it to lead to success. Using it means engaging in self-reflection, which sometimes leads to successful changes in behavior and sometimes does not—the space for creativity has no guarantees. Furthermore, a period of success in any organization's life will have so many and such complex causes that trying to identify thinking along any particular lines as the cause of success would be to fall into the trap that the dominant paradigm is currently caught in.

The fact is that no one knows what causes success until he or she has tried it and seen if it does. A complex adaptive system approach to understanding organizations offers, not a guarantee of success—there is no such thing—but a more useful framework for making sense of experience, reflecting, and thus potentially designing more effective actions.

Keep It Boiling

Finally, a complex adaptive system approach to understanding organizational life contains a warning against complacency. The forces that operate to lock an organization into a successful strategy, to suck it into the stable zone, seem to be extremely powerful. The antidote is continually to seek to keep the shadow system on the boil, to keep coming up with novel ways of doing this and then containing the anxiety that is raised.

Conclusion

This book has attempted to draw the attention of researchers, consultants, and managers, those concerned with life in organizations, to new efforts being undertaken to understand life in nature. I suggest that these new efforts, making up the science of complexity, provide an overall framework for pulling together many existing building blocks in the literature on management and organization into a new way of approaching organizational life. I believe that this new way, which is built firmly on a psychodynamic approach, provides a more useful way of making sense of life in organizations than the stable equilibrium paradigm that currently dominates attempts to understand the problems of managing in organizations. I am not suggesting that the science of complexity provides us with a new set of comprehensive prescriptions for managing and organizing. I am suggesting that it provides a framework for making more sense of what we have been doing all along. The novelty of what I am proposing lies in the suggestion that we reflect in public on what we are doing, using the science of complexity to inform that self-reflection. Why should we be concerned about such self-reflection at this point in our history? The answer, I believe, is that the speed of change is faster than ever before and the level of complexity we all must deal with is greater than ever before. If we are to contain the anxiety of creative activity in the midst of such complexity, we must find a way of making sense of our experience of life in organizations that resonates more with that experience and the way we feel about it. I suggest that the science of complexity provides us with just such a framework.

Glossary

Antichaos: This term is used interchangeably with *self-organization*.

Archetype: An archetype is a potential behavior that preexists experience and awaits specific experience to be actualized or realized. Although the archetype exists in a recognizable general form, its specific actualization is always unique and depends upon the specific experience. An archetype is therefore a similar concept to an immanent, implicate, or enfolded order as used by Bohm (1980) and by Aristotle. It is also similar to Plato's concept of an ideal form.

Attractor: This is a state of behavior into which a system settles if left undisturbed. Equilibrium states are attractors of the single point and periodic oscillation, or cycle, types. *Strange attractor* is another term used for low-dimensional chaos or fractal behavior.

Bounded instability: Bounded instability is used in this book as a general term to include all forms of behavior found in a phase transition between the stable and unstable zones of behavior for a system. It therefore includes low-dimensional chaos, but not high-dimensional chaos. It includes fractal behavior and behavior at the edge of chaos.

Chaos: Low-dimensional chaos has a precise mathematical meaning: behavior that has global structure but is specifically unpredictable over the long term. Its presence is indicated by a positive Liapunov coefficient and it is generated by a few simple mathematical rules. High-dimensional chaos is generated by a set of many rules and it displays very little structure; it is close to randomness and thus closer in meaning to the normal usage of the term *chaos*.

Collapse of chaos: This term means the same thing as *self-organization*.

Complex adaptive system: A complex adaptive system consists of a number of agents interacting with each other according to schemas, that is, rules of behavior, that require them to inspect each other's behavior and adjust their own in the light of the behavior of others. In other words, complex adaptive systems learn and evolve, and they usually interact with other complex adaptive systems. They survive because they learn or evolve in an adaptive way: they compute information in order to extract regularities, building them into schemas that are continually changed in the light of experience.

Complexity: When information about behavior is so irregular that its description cannot be compressed, then the algorithmic information complexity is maximal. Information cannot be summarized, only reproduced in full; that is, only a short computer program (schema) is required to describe the extremely few regularities that do exist. Effective complexity is defined as the length of the schema, so it is low when the environment is random, although the algorithmic information complexity is very high. For example, the schema might be a mean and a standard deviation that would allow the boundaries around the environment's behavior to be established, but nothing more. This obviously has a very limited usefulness in terms of guiding behavior. A system trying to adapt or learn in these circumstances will not be able to extract much in the way of regularities, nor will it be able to predict much in specific terms. Randomness equals high information complexity but low computational or effective complexity. Furthermore, when information is highly orderly, it is easy to compress, or summarize it. A short computer program, or schema, will be able to reproduce such information. Here, the algorithmic information content, or algorithmic complexity, is very low and the effective complexity, the length of the schema that captures the regularity, is also very low. In this situation, nothing much happens, nothing much changes, and there is no need for much learning or adapting.

A complex adaptive system will therefore only function in the sense of adapting when effective complexity is sizable, that is, in conditions that are intermediate between order and disorder. Effective complexity is defined in terms of the length of the adapting system's schema and, as such, it is an internal property of the system just as much as it is a feature of the environment. However, it has to be supplemented by the notion of potential complexity. This is the potential that complex adaptive systems have for creating a great deal of new effective complexity from only a modest change in their schema. An example of this is provided by humans, whose genome (biological schema) varies only slightly from that of apes, but who have much greater effective complexity in terms of their behavioral schema. Potential and effective complexity together amount to a form of bounded instability. Systems in this state operate in an intermediate phase between stability and instability.

Control: This book distinguishes between behavior that is controlled and people who are "in control." For people to be in control they must be able to specify desired outcomes and identify actions that are likely to produce those outcomes, and then be able to employ negative feedback to keep actual outcomes close to desired ones. People can therefore only be in control in rather limited circumstances. However, even when no one can be in control, the behavior of groups of people can display the characteristics of control—coherent pattern, connection, and constraint—through the process of spontaneous self-organization.

Creativity: Creativity is defined in this book as some alteration in the recessive schema of an individual, a group, or an organization that leads to a change in the dominant schema that then turns out to improve fitness. A change can only be judged to be creative, therefore, after the event.

Dissipative structures: Dissipative structures have stable, recognizable forms that are continually being dissipated and renewed, as when the cells in a human body are replaced.

Dominant schema: The dominant schema of an agent or a system is the set of rules or symbol system that models an agent's or system's perception of the current primary task and thus drives the performance of the currently perceived primary task.

Double-loop learning: Double-loop learning occurs when a system adapts its behavior to the stimuli presented to it in a beneficial way as a result of changing its schema. This is sometimes called complex or deutero learning and is to be contrasted with single-loop learning. Double-loop learning is therefore the change of a dominant schema and this requires a change in recessive schemas. Double-loop learning results in innovation and creativity.

Edge of chaos: This is a form of bounded instability found in the phase transition between the order and disorder zones of operation for a complex adaptive system.

Emergence: Emergence is the production of global patterns of behavior by agents in a complex system interacting according to their own local rules of behavior, without intending the global patterns of behavior that come about. In emergence, global patterns cannot be predicted from the local rules of behavior that produce them. To put it in another way, global patterns cannot be reduced to individual behavior.

Feedback: This refers to the process in which information about the outcomes of an action is fed back into the decision-making, or regulation, process to affect the next action. Feedback is negative when the information about a gap between expectation and outcome is fed back to dampen deviations from the expectation. Positive feedback does the opposite, feeding back information to amplify the gap between expectation and outcome.

Fitness landscape: This is a conceptual ram for thinking about the evolutionary journey of a system. Strategies that make the system fitter for survival represent movement up a hill, whereas disadvantageous strategies represent movement down into a valley. Each system's landscape is determined by the strategies of the other systems it interacts with. Evolution is therefore a journey across a heaving landscape. Smooth landscapes represent the ordered zone of operation and very rugged landscapes represent the disordered zone of operation. Landscapes that are rugged but not too rugged are optimal for evolution and constitute the edge of chaos.

Fractal: This refers to behavior that "fractures" so as to produce self-similar copies of itself. It is found in the phase transition between the stable and unstable zones of operation of a system and is a form of bounded instability. It is very close to low-dimensional chaos.

Implicate, immanent order: This is a pattern of behavior that exists as a potential because of the properties of some set of rules. Such order is enfolded and is then unfolded by the running of the rules, the experience of the system. See also *Archetype*.

Innovation: Innovation can be potential or actual. Potential innovation occurs when an agent or system alters its dominant schema. This is the same as saying that it alters its perception or model of current primary tasks or their manner of performance. Actual innovation occurs if this alteration is beneficial to the agent or system in the sense of increasing its fitness, and that happens when the change in behavior delivers what those agents and systems being interacted with demand or accept as the price for further interaction.

Legitimate system: This refers to the hierarchy, bureaucracy, and shared ideology that members of an organization recognize as having the authority to sanction actions and allocate resources.

Nonlinearity: A system is nonlinear when actions can have more than one outcome and when actions generate nonproportional outcomes, in other words, when the system is more than the sum of its parts.

Power law: This refers to a typical pattern of distribution of many small events and few large events that is typically found at the edge of chaos.

Primary task: The primary tasks of an agent or a system are the tasks that must be performed if the agent or system is to survive. Primary tasks produce what the other agents and systems being interacted with demand as the price for further interaction. The test of whether or not an activity is actually a primary task is whether it produces what those being interacted with demand in return for continued interaction. Performance of primary tasks is driven by the dominant part of an agent's or system's schema and that dominant schema models what the primary tasks are as far as the performing agent or system itself is concerned. This may or may not coincide with the actual primary task; survival follows only when the dominant schema models the actual primary task as determined by other agents and systems.

Recessive schema: This refers to the part of a system's symbol system that is not being utilized to form the rules driving the system's performance of the current primary task. It is therefore the symbol system that can be employed in play.

Schema: A schema models regularities in the stimuli experienced by a system. A schema consists of a set of rules that reflects regularities in experience and enables a system to determine the nature of further experience and make sense of it. A schema also contains rules indicating how the system should respond to its experience, which may include extending, modifying, or changing the rules comprising the schema. The rules in a schema are coded in the form of symbols, such as changes in electrical currents, chemical interactions, mental images, and numbers, that stand for some aspect of real experience. A schema is thus a symbol system.

Self-organization: This is the process by which agents in a system interact with each other according to their own local rules of behavior without any overall blueprint telling them what they are to accomplish or how they are to do it. The concept includes but does not coincide with double-loop learning, because deterministic systems, which do not learn, also display spontaneous self-organization.

Shadow system: This is the set of interactions among members of a legitimate organizational system that fall outside that legitimate system. It comprises all social and political interactions that are outside the rules strictly prescribed by the legitimate system. It is the arena in which members of an organization pursue their own gain, but also the arena in which they play, create, and prepare innovations.

Single-loop learning: Single-loop (sometimes called simple) learning, or conditioning, occurs when a system employs its schema without change, adapting its behavior to the stimuli being presented to it so that its behavior becomes more beneficial to it. This is to be contrasted with double-loop learning.

References

Ackley, D. H., and Littman, M. (1992). Interactions between learning and evolution. In C. G. Langton, C. Taylor, J. Doyne Farmer, and S. Rasmussen (Eds.), *Artificial life II* (Santa Fe Institute Studies in the Sciences of Complexity, Vol. 10) (pp. 501–502). Reading, MA: Addison-Wesley.

Ansoff, I., and McDonnell, E. (1990). *Implanting strategic management.* Englewood Cliffs, NJ: Prentice-Hall.

Argyris, C. (1990). *Overcoming organizational defenses: Facilitating organizational learning.* Needham Heights, MA: Allyn & Bacon.

Argyris, C., Putnam, R., and Smith, D. M. (1985). *Action science: Concepts, methods, and skills for research and intervention.* San Francisco: Jossey-Bass.

Argyris, C., and Schön, D. (1978). *Organizational learning: A theory of action perspective.* Reading, MA: Addison-Wesley.

Arthur, W. B. (1988). Self-reinforcing mechanisms in economics. In P. W. Anderson, K. J. Arrow, and D. Pines (Eds.), *The economy as an evolving complex system.* Reading, MA: Addison-Wesley.

Axelrod, R. (1984). *The evolution of cooperation.* New York: Basic Books.

Baddeley, A. (1990). *Human memory: Theory and practice.* Hove, Sussex, England: Lawrence Erlbaum.

Bateson, G. (1972). *Steps to an ecology of the mind*. New York: Ballantine Books.

Baumol, W. J., and Benhabib, J. (1989, Winter). Chaos: Significance, mechanism and economic applications. *Journal of Economic Perspectives, 3* (1), 77–105.

Beer, M., Eisenstat, R. A., and Spector, B. (1990). *The critical path to corporate renewal*. Boston: Harvard Business School Press.

Berne, E. (1964). *Games people play*. New York: Grove Press.

Bion, W. R. (1961). *Experiences in groups and other papers*. London: Tavistock.

Blauner, R. (1964). *Alienation and freedom*. Chicago: University of Chicago Press.

Bohm, D. (1980). *Wholeness and implicate order*. London: Routledge & Kegan Paul.

Briggs, J., and Peat, F. (1989). *The turbulent mirror*. New York: Harper-Collins.

Brunsson, N. (1985). *The irrational organisation*. Chichester, England: Wiley.

Brunsson, N. (1987). *The organisation of hypocracy*. Chichester, England: Wiley.

Burks, A. W. (1970). *Essays on cellular automata*. Urbana: University of Illinois Press.

Carr, W. A., and Shapiro, E. R. (1995). *Lost in familiar places*. New Haven, CT: Yale University Press.

Casti, J. (1994). *Complexification: Explaining a paradoxical world through the science of surprise*. London: HarperCollins.

Chakravarty, B. S., and Doz, Y. (1992). Strategy process research: Focusing on corporate self-renewal. *Strategic Management Journal, 13*, 5–14.

Charan, R. (1991, Sept.–Oct.). How networks reshape organizations—for results. *Harvard Business Review, 12*, 479–494.

Cohen, J., and Stewart, I. (1994). *The collapse of chaos: Discovering simplicity in a complex world*. New York: Viking.

Cohen, M. D., March, J. G., and Olsen, J. P. (1972). A garbage can model of organizational choice. *Administrative Science Quarterly, 17*, 1–25.

Collingridge, D. (1980). *The social control of technology*. Milton Keynes, England: Open University Press.

Colman, A. D., and Bexton, W. H. (1975). *Group relations reader I*. Washington, DC: A. K. Rice Institute.

Colman, A. D., and Geller, M. H. (1985). *Group relations reader II*. Washington, DC: A. K. Rice Institute.

Damassio, A. R. (1994). *Descartes' error: Emotion, reason and the human brain*. New York: Grosset/Putnam Books.

Doyne Farmer, J., and Sidorowich, J. J. (1988). Can new approaches to nonlinear modelling improve economic forecasts? In P. W. Anderson, K. J. Arrow, and D. Pines (Eds.), *The economy as an evolving complex system*. Reading, MA: Addison-Wesley.

Duguid, P., and Brown, J. S. (1991). Organizational learning and communities of practice: Toward a unified view of working, learning and innovation. *Organisational Science, 2* (1), 40–57.

Festinger, L., Schachter, S., and Back, K. (1950). *Social pressures in informal groups: A study of a housing project*. New York: HarperCollins.

Forrester, J. (1958). Industrial dynamics: A major breakthrough for decision-making. *Harvard Business Review, 36* (4), 37–66.

Forrester, J. (1961). *Industrial dynamics*. Cambridge, MA: MIT Press.

Gell-Mann, M. (1994). *The quark and the jaguar*. New York: W. H. Freeman.

Gemmell, G., and Smith, C. (1985). A dissipative structure model of organizational transformation. *Human Relations, 36* (8), 50–74.

Gibbard, G. S., Hartman, J. J., and Mann, R. D. (Eds.). (1974). *Analysis of groups: Contributions to theory, research, and practice*. San Francisco: Jossey-Bass.

Giddens, A. (1979). *Central problems in social theory*. London: Macmillan.

Gleick, J. (1988). *Chaos: The making of a new science*. London: Heinemann.

Goldberg, D. (1990). *Genetic algorithms in search, optimization and machine learning*. Reading, MA: Addison-Wesley.

Goldstein, J. (1994). *The unshackled organization: Facing the challenge of unpredictability through spontaneous reorganization*. Portland, OR: Productivity Press.

Goodwin, B. (1994). *How the leopard changed its spots*. London: Weidenfeld and Nicolson.

Gordon, R. (1993). *Bridges: Metaphor for psychic processes*. London: Karnac Books.

Gould, S. J. (1989). *Wonderful life: The Burgess Shale and the nature of history*. New York and London: W. W. Norton.

Gouldner, A. (1964). *Patterns of industrial bureaucracy*. New York: Free Press.

Granovetter, M. S. (1973). The strength of weak ties. *American Journal of Sociology, 78*, 1360–1380.

Greiner, L. E., and Schein, V. E. (1988). *Power and organization development: Mobilizing power to implement change*. Reading, MA: Addison-Wesley.

Hamel, G., and Prahalad, C. K. (1994). *Competing for the future*. Cambridge, MA: Harvard University Press.

Hampden-Turner, C. (1990). *Charting the corporate mind*. New York: Free Press.

Harth, E. (1993). *The creative loop: How the brain makes a mind*. Reading, MA: Addison-Wesley.

Hayek, F. A. (1948). *Individualism and economic order*. Chicago: University of Chicago Press.

Hayek, F. A. (1982). *Law, legislation and liberty*. London: Routledge & Kegan Paul.

Hillis, W. D. (1992). Co-evolving parasites improve simulated evolution as an optimization procedure. In G. C. Langton, C. Taylor, J. Doyne Farmer, and S. Rasmussen (Eds.), *Artificial life II* (Santa Fe Institute Studies in the Sciences of Complexity, Vol. 10). Reading, MA: Addison-Wesley.

Hirschhorn, L. (1990). *The workplace within: Psychodynamics of organizational life*. Cambridge, MA: MIT Press.

Holland, J. (1975). *Adaptation in natural and artificial systems*. Ann Arbor: University of Michigan Press.

Hsieh, D. (1989). Testing for nonlinear dependence in daily foreign exchange returns. *Journal of Business, 62* (3), 85–99.

Huff, A. S. (1988). Politics and argument as a means of coping with ambiguity and change. In L. R. Pondy, J. R. Boland, and H. Thomas (Eds.), *Managing ambiguity and change*. New York: Wiley.

Huff, A. S. (1990). *Mapping strategic thought*. New York: Wiley.

Hyman, R. (1987). Strategy or structure? Capital, labour and control. *Work, Employment and Society, 1* (1), 25–55.

Jacques, E. (1955). Social systems as a defence against persecutory and defensive anxiety. In M. Klein, P. Heimann, and P. Money-Kyrle (Eds.), *New directions in psychoanalysis*. London: Tavistock. (Also published in G. S. Gibbard, J. J. Hartman, and R. D. Mann (Eds.) (1974), *Analysis of groups: Contributions to theory, research, and practice*. San Francisco: Jossey-Bass.)

Janis, I. (1989). *Crucial decisions: Leadership in policymaking and crisis management*. New York: Free Press.

Jefferson, D., Colins, R., Cooper, C., Dyer, M., Flowers, M., Korf, R., Taylor, C., and Wang, A. (1992). Evolution as a theme in artificial life: The Genysis/Tracker system. In G. C. Langton, C. Taylor, J. Doyne Farmer, and S. Rasmussen (Eds.), *Artificial life II* (Santa Fe Institute Studies in the Sciences of Complexity, Vol. 10). Reading, MA: Addison-Wesley.

Kauffman, S. A. (1991, Aug.). Antichaos and adaptation. *Scientific American*, pp. 78–84.

Kauffman, S. A. (1993). *Origins of order: Self organization and selection in evolution*. Oxford, England: Oxford University Press.

Kauffman, S. A. (1995). *At home in the universe*. New York: Oxford University Press.

Kellert, S. H. (1993). *In the wake of chaos*. Chicago: University of Chicago Press.

Kets de Vries, M.F.R. (1980). *Organizational paradoxes: Clinical approaches to management*. London: Tavistock.

Kets de Vries, M.F.R. (1989). *Prisoners of leadership*. New York: Wiley.

Kets de Vries, M.F.R., and Miller, D. (1984). *The neurotic organization: Diagnosing and changing counterproductive styles of management*. San Francisco: Jossey-Bass.

Kets de Vries, M.F.R., and Associates. (1991). *Organizations on the couch: Clinical perspectives on organizational behavior and change*. San Francisco: Jossey-Bass.

Klein, M. (1975a). *Envy and gratitude*. London: Hogarth Press.

Klein, M. (1975b). *The psycho-analysis of children*. London: Hogarth Press.

Klein, M. (1975c). *The writings of Melanie Klein*. London: Hogarth Press.

Krackhardt, D. (1992). The strength of strong ties: The importance of philos in organizations. In N. Nohria and R. G. Eccles, *Networks and organisations*. Cambridge, MA: Harvard University Press.

Kuhn, T. S. (1970). *The structure of scientific revolutions*. Chicago: University of Chicago Press.

Langton, G. C. (1984). Self reproduction in cellular automata. *Physica, 10D*, 135–144.

Langton, G. C. (1986). Studying artificial life with cellular automata. *Physica, 22D*, 120–149.

Langton, G. C. (Ed.). (1989). *Artificial life I* (Santa Fe Institute Studies in the Sciences of Complexity, Vol. 6). Reading, MA: Addison-Wesley.

Langton, G. C. (1990). Computation to the edge of chaos: Phase transitions and emergent computation. *Physica, 42D*, 12–37.

Langton, G. C. (1992). Life at the edge of chaos. In G. C. Langton, C. Taylor, J. Doyne Farmer, and S. Rasmussen (Eds.), *Artificial life II* (Santa Fe Institute Studies in the Sciences of Complexity, Vol. 10). Reading, MA: Addison-Wesley.

Langton, G. C. (1994). *Artificial life III* (Santa Fe Institute Studies in the Sciences of Complexity, Vol. 17). Reading, MA: Addison-Wesley.

Langton, G. C., Taylor, C., Doyne Farmer, J., and Rasmussen, S. (1992). *Artificial life II* (Santa Fe Institute Studies in the Sciences of Complexity, Vol. 10). Reading, MA: Addison-Wesley.

Lawrence, P. R., and Lorsch, J. W. (1967). *Organization and environment*. Cambridge, MA: Harvard University Press.

Levy, S. (1992). *Artificial life*. New York: First Vintage Books.

Lindblom, L. (1959). The science of muddling through. *Public Administration Review, 19*, 79–88.

Lorenz, C. (1963). Deterministic nonperiodic flow. *Journal of the Atmospheric Sciences, 20*, 130–141.

Lovelock, J. (1988). *The ages of Gaia: A biography of our living earth*. New York: W. W. Norton.

March, J. G., and Olsen, J. P. (1976). *Ambiguity and choice in organizations*. Bergen, Norway: Universitetsforlaget.

May, R. M. (1976). Simple mathematical models with very complicated dynamics. *Nature, 26*, 459–467.

Menzies Lyth, I. (1975). A case study in the functioning of social systems as a defence against anxiety. In A. Coleman and W. H. Bexton (Eds.), *Group relations reader*. Sausalito, CA: GREX.

Menzies Lyth, I. (1988). *Containing anxiety in institutions*. London: Free Association Books.

Miller, D. (1990). *The Icarus paradox: How excellent organizations can bring about their own downfall*. New York: Harper Business.

Miller, E. J. (1983). *Work and creativity* (Occasional Papers). London: Tavistock.

Miller, E. J. (1989). *The Leicester Conference* (Occasional Papers). London: Tavistock.

Miller, E. J., and Rice, A. K. (1967). *Systems of organization: The control of task and sentient boundaries*. London: Tavistock.

Minsky, M. (1968). *Semantic information processing*. Cambridge, MA: MIT Press.

Mintzberg, H., Theoret, A., and Raisinghani. (1976). The structure of the unstructured decision-making process. *Administrative Science Quarterly, 21*, 246–275.

Mintzberg, H., and Waters, J. A. (1985). Of strategies deliberate and emergent. *Strategic Management Journal, 6*, 257–272.

Mueller, R. K. (1986). *Corporate networking: Building channels for information and influence*. New York: Free Press.

Nelson, R., and Winter, S. (1982). *An evolutionary theory of economic change*. Cambridge, MA: Harvard University Press.

Nicolis, G., and Prigogine, I. (1989). *Exploring complexity: An introduction*. New York: W. H. Freeman.

Nohria, N., and Eccles, R. G. (1992). *Networks and organisations*. Cambridge, MA: Harvard University Press.

Nonaka, I. (1988, Spring). Creating organizational order out of chaos: Self renewal in Japanese firms. *California Management Review*, pp. 57–73.

Nonaka, I. (1991, Nov.–Dec.). The knowledge-creating company. *Harvard Business Review*, pp. 96–104.

Oberholzer, A., and Roberts, V. Z. (1995). *The unconscious at work: Individual and organizational stress in the human services*. London: Routledge & Kegan Paul.

Parker, D., and Stacey, R. (1994). *Chaos, management and economics: The implications of nonlinear thinking* (Hobart Papers 125). London: Institute of Economic Affairs.

Parker, D., and Stead, R. (1991). *Profit and enterprise: The political economy of profit*. London: Harvester Wheatsheaf; New York: St. Martins Press.

Pascale, R. (1990). *Managing on the edge: How successful companies use conflict to stay ahead*. London: Viking Penguin.

Pascale, R. T., and Athos, A. (1981). *The art of Japanese management*. New York: Simon & Schuster.

Perrow, C. (1972). *Complex organizations*. Glenview, IL: Scott, Foresman.

Perrow, C. (1984). *Normal accidents: Living with high risk technologies*. New York: Basic Books.

Peters, E. E. (1991). *Chaos and order in the capital markets: A new view of cycles, prices and market volatility*. New York: Wiley.

Piaget, J. (1953). *The origins of intelligence in the child*. London: Routledge & Kegan Paul.

Porter, M. (1990). *The competitive advantage of nations*. London: Macmillan.

Prigogine, I., and Stengers, I. (1984). *Order out of chaos: Man's new dialogue with nature*. New York: Bantam Books.

Quinn, J. B. (1980). *Strategic change: Logical incrementalism*. Homewood, IL: Richard D. Irwin.

Quinn, R. E., and Cameron, K. S. (1988). *Paradox and transformation*. New York: Ballinger/HarperCollins.

Rasmussen, S., Knudsen, C., Feldberg, R., and Hindsholm, M. (1990). The core-world: Emergence and evolution of cooperative structures in a computational chemistry. *Physica, 42D*, 111–134.

Ray, T. S. (1992). An approach to the synthesis of life. In G. C. Langton, C. Taylor, J. Doyne Farmer, and S. Rasmussen (Eds.), *Artificial life II* (Santa Fe Institute Studies in the Sciences of Complexity, Vol. 10). Reading, MA: Addison-Wesley.

Reynolds, C. (1987, July). Flocks, herds and schools: A distributed behavioural model. *Computer Graphics, 21*, 25–36.

Richardson, G. P. (1991). *Feedback thought in the social sciences and systems theory*. Philadelphia: University of Pennsylvania Press.

Ruelle, D. (1991). *Chance and chaos*. Princeton, NJ: Princeton University Press.

Rumelt, R. P., Schendel, D. E., and Teece, D. J. (1994). *Fundamental issues in strategy: A research agenda*. Boston: Harvard Business School Press.

Schein, E. H. (1985). *Organizational culture and leadership*. San Francisco: Jossey-Bass.

Schendel, D. (1994, Summer). Introduction to Special Issue: Strategy: Search for new paradigms. *Strategic Management Journal, 15*, 1–5.

Schenkman, L., and Le Baron, B. (1989). Nonlinear dynamics and stock returns. *Journal of Business, 62* (3), 67–80.

Schön, D. A. (1987). *Educating the reflective practitioner: Toward a new design for teaching and learning in the professions*. San Francisco: Jossey-Bass.

Schumpeter, J. A. (1934). *The theory of economic development*. Cambridge, MA: Harvard University Press.

Schwartz, H. S. (1990). *Narcissistic process and organizational decay: The theory of the organization ideal*. New York: New York University Press.

Senge, P. M. (1990). *The fifth discipline: The art and practice of the learning organization*. New York: Doubleday Currency.

Stacey, R. (1990). *Dynamic strategic management for the 1990s*. London: Kogan Page.

Stacey, R. (1991). *The chaos frontier: Creative strategic control for business*. Oxford, England: Butterworth-Heinemann.

Stacey, R. (1992). *Managing the unknowable: Strategic boundaries between order and chaos in organizations*. San Francisco: Jossey-Bass. (Also published in the United Kingdom as *Managing Chaos*. London: Kogan Page.)

Stacey, R. (1993). *Strategic management and organisational dynamics*. London: Pitman.

Stacey, R. (1995a). Creative organisations: The relevance of chaos and psychodynamics systems. In A. Montuori and R. E. Purser (Eds.), *Social creativity*. Rochester, NJ: Hampton Press.

Stacey, R. (1995b). The role of chaos and self organisation in creative organisations. In A. Albert (Ed.), *Chaos and society: Frontiers in artificial intelligence and applications*. Amsterdam: IOS Press.

Stacey, R. (1995c, Aug.). The science of complexity: An alternative perspective for strategic change processes. *Strategic Management Journal, 16* (6), 477–495.

Stapley, L. F. (1994). *The personality of the organisation: A psychodynamic explanation of culture change*. Unpublished thesis, Sheffield Hallam University.

Stewart, I. (1989). *Does God play dice? The mathematics of chaos*. Oxford, England: Blackwell.

Tarnas, R. (1991). *The passion of the Western mind: Understanding the ideas that shaped our world*. New York: Ballantine Books.

Trist, E. L., and Branforth, K. W. (1951). Some social and psychological consequences of the long-wall method of coal getting. *Human Relations, 5,* 6–24.

Turquet, P. (1974). Leadership, the individual and the group. In G. S. Gibbard, J. J. Hartman, and R. D. Mann (Eds.), *Analysis of groups: Contributions to theory, research, and practice*. San Francisco: Jossey-Bass.

von Bertalanffy, L. (1968). *General systems theory, foundations, development and application*. New York: George Braziller.

Von Neumann, J. (1963). *Collected works* (A. H. Taub, Ed.). Elmsford, NY: Pergamon.

Waldorp, M. M. (1992). *Complexity: The emerging science at the edge of chaos*. New York: Simon & Schuster.

Weick, K. (1979). *The social psychology of organizing*. Reading, MA: Addison-Wesley. (Original work published 1969)

Wheatley, M. J. (1992). *Leadership and the new science: Learning about organisation from an orderly universe*. San Francisco: Berrett-Koehler.

Winnicott, D. W. (1965). *The maturational process and the facilitating environment*. London: Hogarth Press. (Reprinted 1990 by Karnac Books, London)

Winnicott, D. W. (1971). *Playing and reality*. London: Tavistock. (Reprinted 1993 by London Routledge)

Wolfram, S. (1984). Cellular automata as models of complexity. *Physica, 10D,* 1–35.

Wolfram, S. (1986, Sept.). Computer software in science and mathematics. *Scientific American*.

Zimmerman, B. J. (1992). The inherent drive towards chaos. In P. Lorange, B. Chakravarty, A. Van de Ven, and J. Roos (Eds.), *Implementing strategic processes: Change, learning and cooperation*. London: Blackwell.

Index

D

The Author

Ralph Stacey is professor of management and director of the Complexity and Management Centre at the Business School of the University of Hertfordshire in the United Kingdom. He is also a consultant to managers at all levels across a wide range of organizations in many countries and the author of a number of books and articles that have been translated into other languages: these include *Managing the Unknowable* (published by Jossey-Bass, and in the United Kingdom by Kogan Page as *Managing Chaos*) and *Strategic Management and Organizational Dynamics* (published by Pitman).

For the past several years Stacey has been developing a way of understanding life in organizations from the perspectives of complexity science and various psychological approaches to group behavior. This approach is essentially holistic in that it seeks to avoid splits between formulation and implementation of organizational action and between theory and practice; instead, it searches for ways in which members of organizations can jointly engage in dialogue and reflection upon their experience while they act. The Complexity and Management Centre invites individuals who are intervening in organizational life (managers, consultants, and other members of organizations) to bring their experience to the Centre to reflect upon it with others while they engage in it, all in the interest of greater understanding. This reflection-in-action produces the research that the Centre was set up to promote and stands in contrast to more traditional research centers that formulate projects, raise money to fund them, and then observe organizational life in a way that separates the researcher from the practitioner. The intellectual framework for the kind of intertwined management-consulting-research approach Stacey and his colleagues are developing is set out in this book.

Stacey started his career as a lecturer in economics at the University of the Witwatersrand in South Africa after acquiring a doctorate at the London School of Economics. Stung by his inability to reply to students who questioned the usefulness of economics to practitioners, he left for a spell in industry. He joined the British Steel Corporation and then moved to an international construction company, John Laing, where he eventually became the corporate planning manager and a senior executive. The "spell" seemed to have turned into a lifetime career. However, a midlife drive to restore his youth sent him, after a short and somewhat bewildering sojourn in a stockbroking and investment house, back to academia. The search for his lost youth seems not to have ended: he is now a student again, training as a group therapist at the Institute of Group Analysis in London.

It was his diverse background, and chance, that led to his passion for the new science of complexity. Struck by the difference between what he taught managers working on MBA's at the university on a Monday and the way he worked, often with the same people, in their offices on a Tuesday, he started vaguely and somewhat unconsciously searching for some more meaningful way of making sense of life in organizations. It was in this frame of mind that he wandered through a bookstore looking for a novel to read on the lawn on a sunny July day. He chanced upon Gleick's *Chaos* and read that instead, and life has never been the same since.